RETIRE EARLY WITH REAL ESTATE

RETIRE
EARLY
with
REAL ESTATE

how SMART INVESTING *can*
help you ESCAPE THE 9-TO-5 GRIND *and*
DO WHAT MATTERS MORE

CHAD CARSON

BiggerPockets®
PUBLISHING

Retire Early with Real Estate
Chad Carson

Published by BiggerPockets Publishing LLC, Denver, CO
Copyright © 2018 by Chad Carson.
All Rights Reserved.

Publisher's Cataloging-in-Publication data

Names: Carson, Chad, author.

Title: Retire early with real estate : how smart investing can help you escape the 9-to-5 grind and do more of what matters / by Chad Carson.

Description: Includes bibliographical references. | Denver, CO: BiggerPockets Publishing, LLC, 2018

Identifiers: ISBN 978-1-947200-03-6 (pbk.) | 978-1-947200-02-9 (ebook) | LCCN 2018944519

Subjects: LCSH Real estate investment--United States. | Finance, personal. | Retirement. | BISAC BUSINESS & ECONOMICS / Real Estate / Buying and Selling Houses

Classification: LCC HD1382.5 .C364 2018 | DDC 332.63/24

Published in the United States of America
10 9 8 7 6 5 4 3 2 1

Dedication

For Kari, Serena, and Ali.
Our incredible life journey together is the inspiration for this book.

TABLE OF CONTENTS

How to Access Retirement Funds Early (If Necessary)
Profile of a Real Estate Early Retiree: Lucas Hall

Expense Backup Plans
Income Backup Plans
Profile of a Real Estate Early Retiree: Matt B.

Invest in Your Greatest Asset (You!)
Be Flexible in Early Retirement
A Life Without Absolute Security
Profile of a Real Estate Early Retiree: Doug and Traci Burke

How to Get Started with Real Estate Early Retirement

Line Up Your Dominos
Step #1: Get Clear on Your Why (What Matters?)
Step #2: Calculate Your Financial Independence Number and Wealth Goals
Step #3: Determine Your Wealth Stage
Step #4: Pick Your Real Estate Wealth-Building or Retirement Income Plan
Step #5: Get Started!
Strategy, Tactics, and Additional Resources
Profile of a Real Estate Early Retiree: Douglas Orr

The Sting of Regret and the Joy of Freedom
Remember the Purpose of Plans
Commit to the Process
Acknowledgements

INTRODUCTION

If you have built castles in the air, your work need not be lost; that is where they should be. Now put the foundations under them.

—HENRY DAVID THOREAU

Beginnings

Welcome to the Book on Real Estate Early Retirement! The primary purpose of this book is to help you retire earlier and more confidently by using the fantastic tool of real estate investing. Look at this as your step-by-step guide to climb the mountain of an early retirement (aka achieve financial independence) using real estate.

The "early" in the title of the book could mean 30 years old, 45 years old, or 55 years old. Or it could just mean sooner and more comfortably than you would have otherwise. And the "retirement" in the title could mean a point where you stop working. Or just as likely, it could mean a point where you no longer *need* to work for money, yet you continue with a job, a business, or projects that you love. That second idea of early retirement has been my own personal preference.

Whatever "early retirement" means to you will work just fine with the content of this book. But before we get into the nuts and bolts of a real estate early retirement, I want to share with you my bigger reason for writing this book. The book is about more than real estate investing and money. It's actually about life.

My Motivation to Retire Early Using Real Estate

I chose to begin investing in real estate as a full-time entrepreneur at 22 years old right after college. Looking back, I now realize why I made that choice. I was afraid of giving away my independence, my flexibility, and my ability to create a life that mattered to me.

It wasn't that I was afraid to work. I actually love working on interesting and meaningful projects. The issue was freedom. My particular career options—working for a big company or going to medical school—basically gave control of my life to those particular career paths for a *very* long time.

Have you discovered the same lack of freedom in your career? Do you feel like the need to work for money really controls your life? Even with a job you enjoy, wouldn't it be better if you had the wealth to work on a schedule and on terms that *you* choose?

Because of that initial motivation, I began investing in real estate as a career. And over the last fifteen years, I've used it to pay my bills, build wealth, and eventually create passive income streams that replaced my need to trade time for dollars. Real estate investing and the wealth it built have given me control over my life.

And that's exactly what I want to help you do with this book. Real estate investing is the vehicle. And taking control of money and your life is the destination.

Put Money in Its Place

So, my goal with the book is to help you put money back in its place. And its place is not at the center of all your decisions. Instead, I would love your values, your friends and family, your personal goals, and your life aspirations to guide all your decisions.

Instead of working eight- to ten-hour days just for money, I want to help you spend eight- to ten-hour days on projects that fire you up in the morning. If these projects still pay you money, fine. But if they pay you little or no money, that's fine, too.

The projects could be about contributing, like spending more time raising your kids or helping those in need. They could also be about doing things purely for enjoyment and growth, like traveling or learning something new. Or they could mean continuing to pursue a career or business you love.

The difference will be, as Warren Buffett says, that you'll "tap dance to work every day" because you're doing it for love and not for a paycheck. And if someone or some company changes the rules of work in a way you don't like, you'll be free to walk away.

I hope all of that sounds good to you. But I realize that the grind and hectic schedule of a career may have made it difficult to think about life after mandatory work. What would you even do with your life if you didn't have to get up every day and trade your time for money?

To help spark some ideas, I wrote the Money-Life Manifesto, which is about how to stop selling out for money. I originally published it on my personal website, but I felt it was important to include it here.

The Money-Life Manifesto: Do What Matters

Ancient Greek philosopher Aristotle once coined the term "The Golden Mean." It suggests that any virtue can become a vice when there's too much or too little of it. For example, courage is a virtue. But too much courage makes you rash and foolhardy, and too little courage makes you a coward. This manifesto is about the magical middle ground of money. You could call it the Golden Mean of Money. Here is how I see it:

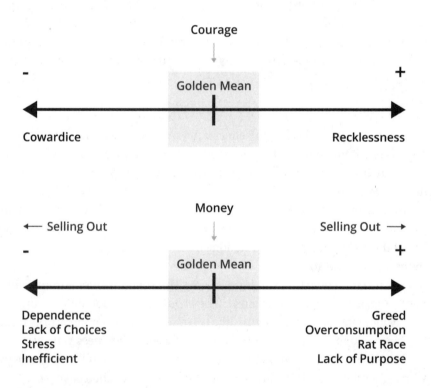

The Golden Mean of Money is a place where you don't emphasize money too much or too little. It's about winning with money, and then using the resulting freedom to do what matters in life.

The True Cost of Living

Here's a life-changing question to ponder:

> *If money were no obstacle ... if you had all the money in the world, what would you do differently in your life?*

In other words, is money keeping you from something? Is money an obstacle to something important? After thinking about it, some of you will say, "*Absolutely!* Money is a *huge* obstacle." Still, some of you will have to dig deeper. You might be comfortable with your life. At the moment, nothing seems wrong that money can satisfy.

Some of you might also point out that amazing world changers in the past like Mother Teresa, Gandhi, Martin Luther King Jr., and others didn't worry too much about money. It wasn't an obstacle for them. Or was it? Did their famous causes require money and other resources? Of course, they did! And while it's true none of them were rich or were obsessed with money, they certainly knew enough to use resources, including money, to further their true missions in life. Money was a tool.

So I respectfully ask you to get uncomfortable and think. Step out of your normal life, and step into your imagination. What would your life look like if you could create it from scratch? What would your ideal life look like if money were not a primary concern? I suggest you actually do the exercise of taking out a pen and paper and answering those questions for yourself. This is one of those exercises that can change your life.

A Life That Matters (My Definition)

Another way of asking this is: *What does it mean to live a life that matters?* I have asked this question a lot. I have asked myself, and I have asked others. The answers I received may sound familiar to you ...

> *Sleep more. Relax in the morning. Sit on a rocking chair.*
> *Learn something new. Be impractical. Explore.*
> *Visit amazing places. Go on adventures. Hike trails. Ride a bike again.*

Unplug from the matrix. Do work you love. Buck the system. Say "shove it" to the man.
Raise your own kids. Play silly games. Help with homework. Spoil your grandchildren.
Plant a garden. Grow your own food. Eat healthy. Exercise.
Slow Down.
BREATHE.
Pursue your passions. Volunteer. Listen to people. Make an impact.
Advance your cause. Create your art. Write your story.
Get OFF the 9-to-5 treadmill.
STOP selling out!
DO what matters!

Do any of these resonate or excite you? If so, you already know the recipe for a life that matters. The real question is what is keeping you from doing it right now? Is it because you're too busy working? Do you have too little money in the bank? Are you stuck making monthly payments? Do you need more security? Is it because you're afraid?

For most of us, money seems to be directly or indirectly part of the problem. It's not the goal itself, but it is preventing us from achieving the goal. The good news is that you are still in control. Money is a tool. It does not have to control you. You can learn to use and master money. And in case you're wondering, that's the point of the rest of the book!

"Early retirement" is just the term I'll use for taking back control of your money and your life. And real estate investing is one of the best methods to do that. I'll show you how in the chapters that follow. But before we jump into that, I want to tell you a little more about me and why you might find my perspective and advice helpful.

My Story: A Sprint up the Real Estate Mountain

As I said earlier, I graduated from college and decided to jump full-time into real estate investing. This is not a normal path, by the way. Most real estate investors I know began part-time while working another full-time job.

I began my real estate investing with a business partner, and we still actively invest together, fifteen years later. Our business started slowly our first two years, and we made very little money. In fact, I lived in the spare bedroom of my business partner's small house to save money. We ate a lot of inexpensive ramen noodles for a long time (and loved it).

Eventually our original business of flipping houses (i.e., buying and quickly reselling properties) began to succeed. This allowed us to pay our bills and pile up some cash savings. I even moved out of the spare bedroom and got my own property (a four-unit apartment building, which I'll explain more about in Chapter 11 on the House Hacking Plan).

We also started buying a few rentals. Over time, rentals and other income-generating real estate investments became our main strategy. We used these investment properties to generate regular monthly income and build wealth. Eventually these investments also replaced our need to work as hard flipping houses to pay the bills.

But our path was certainly not straight or without challenges. Five years after starting our business, we grew (sprinted) and bought a lot of properties. But this was probably the worst possible time, *right* before the 2008–2010 Great Recession in the United States. Luckily, we had not spent much of the money we had made before that, so we had cash savings to draw on. And we needed it.

In addition to having costly rental turnovers because many of our tenants lost their jobs, we also faced costs from mistakes we made during our sprint. Basically, we bought some properties that we shouldn't have. Some were in bad locations that did not attract ideal tenants. For others, we underestimated up-front repairs and rental expenses. And all of this led to negative cash flow that drew upon our cash reserves.

But we worked hard, adjusted strategies as needed, and lived inexpensively. As a result, we made it through. But the difficulty of overcoming this challenge taught us an important lesson that helped to shape all of the advice you'll get in this book.

Why Massive Real Estate Empires Aren't Always Better

Our growth in real estate investing moved us up the financial mountain to higher altitudes. In the end, we had more properties and more money coming in. But we also had more risk, more hassle, and less time. The mistakes we made caused us to pause and reflect.

We realized that big real estate empires aren't always better. We had modeled ourselves after other real estate investors who had big goals to own a lot of properties. But we hadn't really thought about our own personal life goals.

We hadn't asked important questions like the ones I proposed in the Money-Life Manifesto. We didn't focus on the actual activities and schedule that would make us happy. And we didn't build a real estate investing portfolio that served our personal goals.

We realized that getting bigger and growing faster brings problems, too. I look at it like trying to control Frankenstein's monster. *Frankenstein* is the famous fictional story of a scientist who created a person from scratch in his laboratory. But his creation took on a life of its own and became an angry, uncontrollable monster.

In real estate investing, we also create a new entity—a business. It's possible to build systems, outsource everything, and tame the monster so that you still have a *passive* big business. But it's not easy! And when it doesn't go well, the oversized business monster can gobble up all your free time and your money. In graph form, this business creation and growth cycle looks like this:

Business Life Cycle

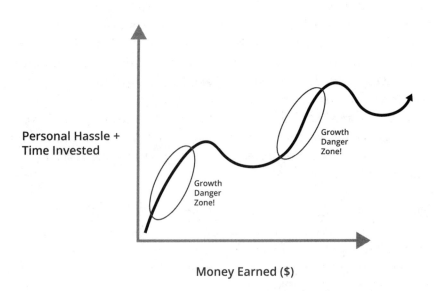

The Danger Zones are where real estate "Frankenstein monsters" attack.

The growth spurts of this graph are the steep inclines. These are the Danger Zones. This is when you, the business owner, are most susceptible to cash crunches, dramatic market crashes (such as the 2008–2010 Great Recession), people problems, and even personal burnout. These Danger Zones are where the Frankenstein monster rears its ugly head. You can win against the monster; just be prepared for a tough battle.

But the point of telling you my story isn't to scare you away from growth. After all, any worthwhile destination involves challenges and risks. My point is to help you decide the *purpose* of your growth before you start. That way you can build a real estate investing portfolio that serves *your* goals instead of serving growth for growth's sake. This process involves finding the sweet spot of your real estate investing business.

Real Estate Investing Sweet Spots

You as an entrepreneur have to decide where on the business life cycle graph you want to end up. You have a virtually endless choice of plateaus that you could aim for. The sky's the limit in our economic system.

But again, your choice will depend on your personal financial goals. And your choice will also depend on your willingness to take on the risks and hassles of the perilous climb up to higher economic ground. The reward at the top better be worth the sacrifice of the climb (and the fights with Frankenstein's monster)! Unfortunately, plenty of people have arrived at the top of gigantic financial mountains only to realize they lost everything they really wanted along the way.

The key is to find your personal business sweet spot. As you'll see in the graph below, I've marked two different sweet spots (although there are an infinite number in reality). One is smaller (fewer assets, fewer employees/team members, less money), and the other is bigger (more assets, more employees/team members, more money).

Business Life Cycle

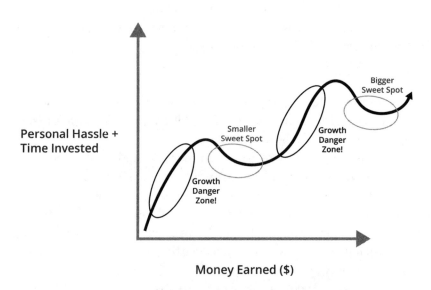

Smaller or bigger business sweet spot? It's your choice.

Both sweet spots are beautiful, level plateaus where you've increased income while also gaining efficiency that frees up your personal time and reduces hassle. The bigger sweet spot has more money earned. But nothing comes without a cost. You must make the choice if bigger is worth it for you. And that choice may come down to the concept of "enough."

A Place Called "Enough"

One of my favorite personal finance books is *Your Money or Your Life* by Vicki Robin and Joe Dominguez. In the book, they share a graph called the "Fulfillment Curve." Here's my drawing of what that looks like:

Fulfillment Curve

Source: *Your Money or Your Life*, Penguin Books, 2008

While the authors shared this as a personal finance concept, it also can apply to a real estate investing business. As you move up the curve, you pass milestones like survival, comfort, and even small luxuries that make life sweeter. But you finally arrive at a place called enough, the peak of the fulfillment curve. In terms of happiness, it doesn't get much better than this.

But as you continue moving past the peak of the curve, each subsequent amount of money you earn and spend has diminishing returns on your personal happiness. This occurs because all of the "extra" above and beyond the peak fulfillment carries clutter, complexity, stress, and hassle with it. Later in "Part 3: Preparations for the Climb," I'll offer some specific ideas and exercises to help you get clearer on what enough means to you. But for now, just know that you don't have to build a massive real estate empire to live an amazing life. Owning two, ten, or even fifty real estate investments could all be appropriate, depending on your goals.

"Success" does not mean getting bigger or earning the most money. Success is when money and your investments support the life you want. And you are the only one who will know what that means.

Following most chapters, you will see a profile of real estate early retirees I interviewed for this book. These will give you an idea of the real numbers and stories of people who've actually used real estate investing to retire early (or who are on the verge of retiring early). There are a variety of different starting points, perspectives, and styles of real estate investing included in these profiles. I hope they'll inspire you for your own journey. And in order to let you know my story a little better, the first profile I'll share is mine!

——————— PROFILE OF A REAL ESTATE EARLY RETIREE ———————

CHAD CARSON (yes, it's me!)
Coach Carson (coachcarson.com)
Location: Clemson, South Carolina
My Favorite Quote:
"Keep life simple. Getting to financial independence by chasing huge expenses is a losing game."

WEALTH-BUILDING STATISTICS
- **Profession/Career:** Real Estate Investor
- **Income During Wealth-Building Phase:** $75,000 to $99,999/year
- **How Big a Role Did Real Estate Play in Wealth-Building?** Primary
- **Primary Real Estate Strategy(ies):** Long-term hold rentals, short-term hold rentals, fix and flips, private lending/notes, self-directed retirement account

FINANCIAL INDEPENDENCE STATISTICS
- **Age at Financial Independence:** 36 to 40
- **Annual Expenses in Retirement:** $30,000 to $50,000
- **Ideal Number of Rentals in Retirement:** 20 to 50
- **Primary Source of Retirement Income:** Rental Properties
- **Secondary Source of Retirement Income:** Interest from private mortgage notes, side hustles/part-time work, private business, Social Security income

- **Ideal Debt Level of Real Estate Portfolio:** Less than 25% loan to value

—————— Q&A ——————

Q: Can you explain in more detail how you built your current wealth?
I began my career flipping houses with a business partner. Sometimes we found deals and quickly resold them for a small markup. Other times we fixed them up and sold at full price to make a bigger profit. We used these deals to pay the bills and save some money for long-term investing. Later we bought rental properties, both short-term holds and long-term holds. We used something like the Buy-3-Sell-2-Keep-1 plan to sell excess properties and pay off some of the remaining ones. We also created our own seller-financing notes and invested in a self-directed IRA (primarily in private notes and tax liens).

Q: What were the biggest obstacles and setbacks during your wealth-building stage? How did you overcome or push through them?
My career and investing were closely tied, and this was probably my biggest challenge (and strength). It was challenging because I was always focused on survival and paying the bills, so I sold some good long-term hold properties that I would like to still have. And the real estate downturn in 2008–2010 was tough. But in the end, my career as an investor gave me many opportunities to also build wealth using real estate as a tool.

Q: What's your No. 1 best tip for those looking to build wealth with real estate investing?
Always focus first on your savings rate. You can't retire early without saving a lot of money. Then invest in simple assets you understand, and do it consistently and persistently. You won't be perfect, but disciplined savings and investing will win in the end.

Q: Can you explain in more detail your post–financial independence income? How do you plan on living off of this income?
We do our investing primarily in a small college town, so small multi-

unit student rentals produce a core part of our cash flow. We also like single-family houses that we rent to families or local professionals. These are very stable long-term income and wealth builders. Additional income comes from interest from loans to investors and a few seller-financing transactions. Finally, my online business with online courses, books, and occasional consulting is another secondary source of income.

Q: What concerns do you have for the future in terms of retirement income? How will you address them?
It's not a great concern, but I don't want to have all my eggs in one basket over the long run. Real estate will always be my core investment, but I want to diversify to different locations, and I also want to own a bigger piece of other non–real estate businesses (in the form of equity stock investing).

Q: Do you plan to start selling your real estate holdings? If so, when and how?
Nothing drastic, but I plan to continually prune my portfolio by selling to get rid of suboptimal properties. I'll then decide where to move that equity so that it performs better.

Q: What's your No. 1 best tip for those looking to live off of investment income after retirement/financial independence?
Keep life simple. Getting to financial independence by chasing huge expenses is a losing game. Even if you achieve it, you have to work long, grueling hours for many years. And for what? A big house? An expensive vacation? Keep your expenses simple, build income streams to pay for them, and then go do what matters.

How to Read This Book

This book is best understood as a step-by-step *strategy* guide. You are the climber of your own personal financial mountain, and the book is your trusty map to help you safely reach the top. But keep in mind, this guide won't tell you the *one* best way to reach the top. Instead, you will get a choice of several reliable routes and combinations that you can choose from.

Just like the benefits of a map, this book's suggestions can give you clarity and overall direction for your real estate investing. But you will still have to do the hard day-to-day work of climbing. And like all climbers of the financial mountain, you'll have to recover from inevitable stormy weather, rockslides, and other perils that no map can predict. But if you are the type of person who pursues early retirement, I have every confidence that you are prepared for (and even excited about) the climb before you. In my case, the climb toward early retirement has been one of the most fun adventures of my life.

Here is how the book is organized:

"Part 1: Why Real Estate Investing?" may be a review for those of you already sold on real estate investing as a retirement strategy. But in this part, I'll show you why real estate is the ideal vehicle to build wealth, produce passive income, and retire early on your timeline.

"Part 2: A Map of the Financial Mountain" will help you define your financial goals. We'll get clear on the destination at the peak by exploring important questions, such as:

- How much money do you need to retire?
- How many real estate properties will be enough?
- Do you need to endlessly sacrifice and put off happiness, or can you also enjoy your life along the way?

"Part 3: Preparations for the Climb" shares the fundamentals of wealth-building (for example, climbing). These foundational principles help you build wealth safer and faster. And the principles apply whether you invest in real estate or not.

"Part 4: The First Steps" is all about the real estate strategies that can help you get started up the wealth-building mountain. If you are a new investor trying to figure out the right first steps, this section is made for you. Strategies like house hacking, live-in-then-rent, live-in-flips, and BRRRR are made for investors with less cash, less experience, or both. If you already own some properties and have momentum, you may choose to skip to the next section.

"Part 5: The Climb" is all about the primary real estate investing strategies you can use to build wealth after getting started. Like routes on a map, these strategies lead you toward the peak of the mountain where you have enough wealth to achieve full financial independence. Some routes up are more conservative and some are more aggressive. You can choose which makes more sense in your situation, and you can even combine strategies. I'll also give you very detailed examples, diagrams, and case studies to make the strategies come alive.

"Part 6: The Peak and Beyond" is about how to optimize your real estate assets so that you have more than enough income in early retirement. This is the stage where you create your own personal pension plan using real estate. I'll explain the different methods of producing cash flow with real estate, and I'll show how retirement accounts like 401(k)s and IRAs fit into the overall strategy. I'll also give you some tips to avoid big risks and remain flexible so that you don't slide back down the financial mountain.

"Part 7: Your Turn to Climb" is where I bring everything together in a straightforward, step-by-step process that you can apply. Have you ever read a book and not done anything with the information in it? Well, I don't want my book to be one of them! I care too much about you and this information impacting your life. This final part will help you apply what you've learned so that you can begin executing your real estate early retirement plan right now.

The Appendix includes perhaps some of the most interesting information in the book. In my preparations for writing, I surveyed and interviewed *hundreds* of real estate investors—both those who had already achieved financial independence and those still pursuing their goal. In the Appendix, I share the results of the survey questions I asked, including questions like these:

- What are your annual personal expenses after retirement?
- What real estate strategies did you use to achieve an early retirement?
- What's the ideal number of properties for you?
- What's the ideal amount of debt for you in your real estate portfolio?

You can compare your own early retirement goals, personal expenses, and preferred strategies to the investors in this survey.

Throughout the book, I also share more in-depth profiles of twenty-five of these real estate early retirees whom I interviewed more closely. You'll learn the details of their stories, how they used real estate to retire early (or get close), and what their investments look like now.

I hope you get excited and have fun with this book. That was my intention. Real estate investing can be like a game if you make it that way. But unlike board games with play money, winning this game can *actually* improve your life dramatically. Let's get started!

PART 1
WHY REAL ESTATE INVESTING?

---

*Real Estate Investing Is
an I.D.E.A.L. Vehicle for
Early Retirement*

CHAPTER 1
WHY REAL ESTATE IS THE
I.D.E.A.L. INVESTMENT

People are always blaming their circumstances for what they are. I don't believe in circumstances. The people who get on in this world are the people who get up and look for the circumstances they want, and, if they can't find them, make them.

—GEORGE BERNARD SHAW

As you probably know, climbing the financial mountain isn't unique to real estate investing. Just like there are multiple paths up a mountain, there are other vehicles to get there that have been used by successful early retirees. For example, you could use dividend stocks, bonds, small businesses, index funds, bank CDs, and more to climb to your goals.

But of all these choices, real estate investing is my favorite. And my guess is you like it too since you've picked up this book! Real estate investing is a perfectly suited vehicle for aspiring early retirees. It gives you an incredible amount of control over the method and the timing of your exit from the rat race. Let me explain why by showing how real estate investing is I.D.E.A.L.

I learned this acronym in the first real estate book I read after college. And I have yet to find a better way to explain the core benefits of real estate

investing. I.D.E.A.L. tells you the primary ways you can profit with investment properties:
- Income
- Depreciation
- Equity
- Appreciation
- Leverage

I'll explain each one in more detail.

Income

Income is the core benefit of real estate investing. Even the worst rentals I have produce more income than equivalent amounts of money in other assets like stocks or bonds. For example, on March 2, 2018, the dividend rate of the S&P 500 (a group of major stocks) was 1.82 percent.[1] And the interest yield of a ten-year United States Treasury bond (the lowest-risk type of bond and is essentially a loan to the government) on the same date was 2.86 percent.[2]

But in the right markets, I often see unleveraged (no debt) income returns of 5 to 10 percent with rental properties, even after paying all expenses, including a property manager. And with safe, long-term leverage (if you choose to do that) you can sometimes see those income returns double to 10 to 20 percent or more.

To put that into perspective, here's a chart comparing actual yearly income (pretax) for an S&P 500 index fund, a ten-year U.S. Treasury bond, and an unleveraged rental property with a 7 percent income yield.

ASSET TYPE	INCOME YIELD	INCOME/YEAR FOR $100,000 INVESTMENT
S&P 500 Index Fund	1.82%	$1,820
10-Year U.S. Treasury Bond	2.86%	$2,860
Unleveraged Rental Property	7%	$7,000

1 "S&P 500 Dividend Yield Statistics." Last modified March 2, 2018. www.multpl.com/s-p-500-dividend-yield/.

2 "10-Year U.S. Treasury Bond Statistics." Last modified March 2, 2018. www.multpl.com/10-year-treasury-rate.

That's an *enormous* difference! A $1 million portfolio invested 100% in real estate at those numbers would receive $70,000 per year before tax. While the same amount in stocks would produce $18,200, and in U.S. Treasury bonds would produce $28,600. As an early retiree living off of your assets, which would you prefer? More income or less?

And the income from an unleveraged portfolio of quality rentals is very flexible. Prices and rents of quality real estate tend to keep up with inflation. And unleveraged properties, as in this example, can possibly survive deflationary environments if rents go down. But most of all, consistent, steady income from rentals is the Holy Grail for early retirees. That income allows you to live, explore, and do what matters.

Depreciation

Do you ever get excited about the U.S. Tax Code? Well, me either ... until now! As of this writing, the U.S. government requires real estate investors to spread out most of the cost of real estate purchases over 27.5 years (for residential property).[3] This creates what's called a depreciation expense, which can shelter or protect your income from taxes and reduce your tax bill.

Why does this happen? Unlike other business expenses, depreciation doesn't actually come out of your bank account. It's a paper loss. But this paper expense can still offset taxable income and save money on your tax bill. Here is a basic example.

Scenario #1 (without depreciation expense):
$10,000 taxable rental income x 25% federal income tax rate = $2,500 taxes owed

Scenario #2 (with depreciation expense):
$10,000 rental income – $3,000 depreciation expense = $7,000 taxable rental income
$7,000 x 25% federal income tax rate = $1,750 taxes owed

Tax Savings = $2,500 – $1,750 = $750

The higher your tax rate, the more taxes you would save in this example. Depreciation is not unique to real estate, but real estate investing uniquely

---

3 "Publication 946 (2016), How to Depreciate Property." Last updated September 11, 2017. www.irs.gov/publications/p946#en_US_2013_publink1000107524.

benefits from depreciation. Why? Because the cost of real estate is so large and often purchased with debt. A $250,000 building depreciated over 27.5 years provides a tax shelter of $9,091 per year. If you had three rental properties at that cost, you'd shelter $27,273 of income from taxes and *possibly* save $6,818 on your tax bill (at a 25 percent rate).

I say "possibly," because this is a nuanced part of the tax code. There are several layers of rules that affect real estate tax deductions. That's beyond the scope of this book, so for now I'll just say that a CPA (certified public accountant) who specializes in real estate investing is a must-have on your personal real estate team.

And keep in mind that what the IRS giveth, the IRS taketh away. When you sell a rental property, it's very likely that you'll have to recapture the depreciation and pay taxes on it. The tax rate on this recaptured real estate depreciation is typically 25 percent (as of 2018). This creates a big incentive to keep real estate or to use other tax-savings strategies when selling, like a 1031 exchange. I'll discuss the 1031 exchange later in Chapter 17, "The Trade-Up Plan."

Equity
This benefit is one of my *favorite* parts of real estate investing. If you borrow money to purchase your investment property and have at least break-even cash flow, your tenant essentially pays off your property for you. Explained another way, one part of a typical mortgage payment is principal paydown on your mortgage. So, if you have enough rental income to pay your expenses and your mortgage, the tenant is working hard to increase *your* equity in the property.

Equity Buildup &
Loan Paydown Over Time

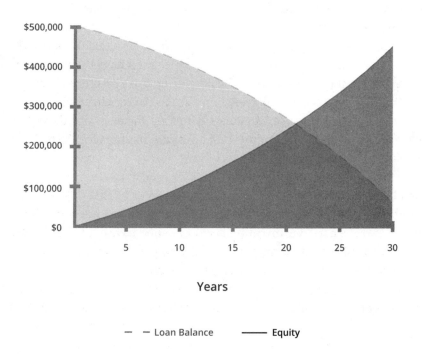

I don't know about you, but I love the idea of other people working hard to build my net worth! And the tenants also get great value in return. They get to live in a nice, clean, well-cared-for rental property, and they get to deal with a fair property owner. It's a clear win-win.

Appreciation

Over many years, real estate tends to appreciate (increase in price) at the same rate as inflation (1–2 percent per year) on average.[4] Of course, real es-

---

4   www.inflation.eu/inflation-rates/united-states/historic-inflation/cpi-inflation-united-states.aspx.

tate is very local, so the actual rate can vary widely from place to place. But when any kind of appreciation is combined with the other benefits already discussed, the total return can be very attractive.

For example, if your unleveraged property produced 7 percent income returns and 3 percent appreciation, your long-term return could average around 10 percent (ignoring tax costs or benefits for the moment). But this passive type of appreciation does not tell the whole story. The *real* power of appreciation in real estate is the type of price increase you can control.

First, appreciation can often be built into a purchase of real estate from the beginning. If you are out looking for properties all the time, you will be able to find bargains purchased below full value. For example, if you buy a property normally worth $200,000 at a 10 percent discount, you've built in appreciation of $20,000 from day one.

Second, there is a concept called forced appreciation. This means that you do something to the property in order to increase its value. This is where the entrepreneur in you can shine and also make a lot of money. For example, let's say you buy an old property in an otherwise attractive neighborhood. The property needs cosmetic upgrades inside and outside the house. You invest $30,000 into carefully chosen upgrades, such as better landscaping, paint, new flooring, a new kitchen, and new bathrooms. The $30,000 investment in repairs may increase the value of the house by $70,000 (this, of course, depends upon the particular situation). The $40,000 difference is the forced appreciation.

Repairs are a typical way to force appreciation, but savvy investors also look for other opportunities. You may be able to increase density (like adding an extra rental unit), improve rental rates, decrease expenses, improve zoning, and more. All of these could potentially force the appreciation of a property.

Leverage

I already mentioned the use of debt (that is, leverage) when discussing equity buildup. But leverage in general can magnify all the other benefits mentioned here. For example, without leverage your $100,000 in savings could only buy one property worth $100,000. But with leverage, using an 80 percent mortgage (say, making a 20 percent down payment), you could instead buy five properties worth $100,000 with $20,000 down on each. All of the income, depreciation, equity, and appreciation benefits above would be magnified because of the leverage.

But keep in mind, leverage works both ways. Just like *benefits* are magnified with leverage, *losses* can also be magnified. I have personally seen more promising real estate investors go out of business because they couldn't make their debt payment than for any other reason. So a smart investor very carefully uses debt, if he or she uses it at all.

You've now learned the core benefits of real estate investing, but in the next chapter, let's look at four more reasons that aspiring early retirees should invest in real estate.

———— PROFILE OF A REAL ESTATE EARLY RETIREE ————

KAT HORN

Cashflow Kat (cashflowkat.com)
Location: Fredericksburg, Virginia
Chad's Favorite Quote from Kat:
"Steel your resolve and just go for it! You can get stuck in a loop of never-ending learning and searching."

WEALTH-BUILDING STATISTICS

- **Profession/Career:** Lawyer, broker, but primarily a stay-at-home mom
- **Income During Wealth-Building Phase:** $150,000 to $199,999/ year
- **How Big a Role Did Real Estate Play in Wealth-Building?** Primary vehicle
- **Primary Real Estate Strategy(ies):** Long-term rentals, live-in flip

FINANCIAL INDEPENDENCE STATISTICS

- **Age at Financial Independence:** 41 to 45
- **Annual Expenses in Retirement:** Between $75,000 to $100,000
- **Ideal Number of Rentals in Retirement:** 6 to 10
- **Primary Source of Retirement Income:** Rental income
- **Secondary Source of Retirement Income:** Periodic sale of stocks, Social Security income, pension
- **Ideal Debt Level of Real Estate Portfolio:** Between 26% to 50% loan to value

Q: Can you explain in more detail how you built your current wealth?
Although I've done two live-in flips, I have primarily focused on long-term buy and holds. I lived in many of the buy and holds prior to converting them to rental properties. Initially my husband and I purchased a home that needed work, and we ended up selling it quickly for a good profit when he was transferred unexpectedly. The flip was unintentional but advantageous. So we used that profit to buy another home that needed work. After remodeling it and living in it for several years, we made the deliberate decision to move out and convert it to a rental property. Once we did that successfully, it was hard to stop! We kept buying homes, living in them, fixing them up, and then turning them into rentals. In addition, however, we purchased two duplexes that we never resided in, because, after a few repairs, they both flowed cash immediately.

Q: What were the biggest obstacles and setbacks during your wealth-building stage? How did you overcome or push through them?
I think the biggest obstacle is always finding the money to do the next deal. Even though *you* know you can meet all of your mortgage obligations with your rents, lenders can be tough with their set debt-to-income requirements. So instead of getting too creative with hard-money loans or partnerships, I just kept building my real estate portfolio slowly. Every couple of years I was able to move forward and make another acquisition through traditional mortgage lending (especially since many of my properties were initially my primary residence). It was great to lock in long-term low-cost financing, and then watch over the years as my rents would continue to climb and my cash flow would continue to grow. That's the beauty of the long-term buy and hold, the numbers just keep getting better.

Q: What's your No. 1 best tip for those looking to build wealth with real estate investing?
Steel your resolve and just go for it! You can get stuck in a loop of never-ending learning and searching while being too intimidated to

just pull the trigger and make a rental property purchase. You have to push through the fear and take a chance. Just remember that you are not alone with your feelings, as most of us started in the same boat with the same fears and uncertainties. Taking action and getting started is the key.

Q: Can you explain in more detail your post–financial independence income? How do you plan on living off of this income?
My husband and I will have more rental income from our long-term buy and hold properties than from any other source in retirement. Happily, this rental income will be enhanced by his government pension (which will be equivalent to about 40 percent of his current salary). Then, for later years, we will be looking to 401(k) and IRA funds. Finally, there is Social Security ... but I can't say I'm counting on it! I'm concerned that by the time I am eligible to draw Social Security, it will be means-tested and I'll no longer have that as an income source. In fact, the lack of stability in Social Security is one huge reason to develop other income streams, like rental real estate.

Q: What concerns do you have for the future related to retirement income? How will you address that?
Honestly, I feel so secure because of my rental property income. Rising rents are a wonderful hedge against inflation. And in my own experience, even during the 2008 Great Recession, I didn't have to lower any of my rents. Also, my properties are located in several different markets that have all seen growth in populations and in their economies. Consequently, I feel as though I've put myself in a great position to weather future storms. As much as I like to gripe about landlord duties some days, I feel tremendously blessed that I began my real estate investing journey in my early thirties.

Q: Do you plan to start selling your real estate holdings? If so, when and how?
I will sell the residential properties once I no longer want to be bothered with the hands-on property management. Instead of hiring managers, I foresee selling most or all of the residential properties and

doing a 1031 exchange into something like a commercial triple-net lease property (or properties). I want to reap the tax advantages of a 1031 exchange and have a stable of properties that require little to no management. I also foresee placing them in a trust so that they will someday be assets for my children.

Q: What's your No. 1 best tip for those looking to live off of investment income after retirement/financial independence?
My tip is to structure your real estate investing to include at least some long-term buy and hold properties. Those are the properties that will provide the income stream and require less effort (hopefully!) as you retire and want to focus on other pursuits. I used to talk to my husband about doing short-term flips in retirement, but it's hard work. And I realized that I don't want to work that hard in retirement.

CHAPTER 2
FOUR REASONS EARLY RETIREES SHOULD INVEST IN REAL ESTATE

The I.D.E.A.L. benefits may be enough for most real estate investors. But for those of us seeking to reach financial independence early, real estate provides even more advantages. In this chapter, I'll share four of these special advantages:

- Control
- Timing
- Tax Benefits
- Simple and Understandable

Control

Real estate gives you the ability to control and affect the outcome of your financial independence plans, whereas many other assets leave control in the hands of others. For example, think about investing in a low-cost index fund in the stock market. I actually think this is a smart way to go over the long run. But how much control do you have over its success in a relatively short period of time like five to ten years? Very little. You simply choose when to buy, how to reinvest dividends, and when to sell. The management teams and employees of the 3,596 companies you own in the Vanguard Total Stock Market Index, for example, control your success.

And if completely hands-off investing is the way you want to go because it's more passive on the front end, then no problem. But if you believe in your own abilities to buy good deals, manage them profitably, and sell at the right time, real estate gives you more opportunities to do that. Why? Because real estate markets are local and imperfect. There are opportunities around every corner for you as an individual to add value and make better returns. You just have to learn the fundamentals and put in the work.

Timing

Related to control, real estate gives you more control over the timing of your climb to an early retirement. Most early retirees have set a target date for their financial independence (FI). After that point they plan to live off of their investment portfolio (or at least be able to if needed). How do they reach that target date on time? By ensuring (or hoping) their investment assets grow sufficiently and on time.

The core growth of many non-real estate investment plans, like index stock investing, depends more heavily on appreciation of prices. While growth of stocks is often steady over the long run, a sudden short-term drop in prices can delay or destroy the target financial independence date of an investor. And as I described earlier in the section on I.D.E.A.L. investments, income from stock dividends and bond interest is much lower as a percentage of asset prices. So, reinvestment of income is less effective with that strategy compared to real estate.

Real estate investing, on the other hand, gives you two very predictable core growth levers:

1. Positive rental income
2. Debt amortization (paydown)

While nothing is guaranteed in the investment world, rental income on quality properties is like a stable dividend. And you can use that dividend to reinvest in new assets, accelerate debt paydown, or improve the value of your current asset.

Even during the 2008–2010 U.S. housing crisis, rents held steady or only slightly decreased in most U.S. markets. And this happened while housing prices themselves plummeted.

Median Asking Rent for Vacant Rental Units

(CURRENT DOLLARS)

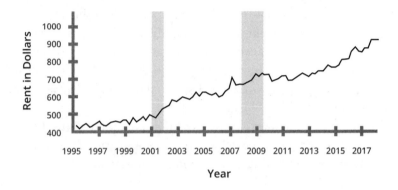

Median Asking Price, Units for Sale: 1995-2017

(CURRENT DOLLARS)

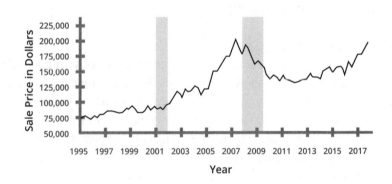

Images courtesy of U.S. Census Bureau[5]

5   "Quarterly Residential Vacancies and Homeownership, Fourth Quarter 2017." U.S. Census Bureau. Last updated January 30, 2018. www.census.gov/housing/hvs/files/currenthvspress.pdf.

These recent rental trends don't mean rental rates won't go down in the future. And the national trend doesn't mean rental rates won't go down in your specific location. Rents are very closely tied to local rates of income and other supply/demand factors, so those will ultimately determine your rates. But the main point is that real estate rental income doesn't always correlate with the prices of assets.

And the second growth lever, debt amortization, is built into your mortgage payment and can be accelerated by reinvesting income to pay down the debt faster. The Rental Debt Snowball Plan, which I'll discuss in detail later in Chapter 15, is a powerful example of this.

Tax Benefits

Politics and changing winds of public opinion can alter tax policy in a heartbeat. For example, in 2017 the U.S. Congress passed a large tax bill that changed many tax rules (although most real estate benefits were left in place). So you can't ever count on any particular tax benefit forever. But I see tax benefits as icing on an already good real estate investing cake. I previously shared one major tax benefit of investing in real estate: depreciation. But here are other tax benefits that give real estate investing an advantage.

Rental Income

Unlike income from your job, rental income is not subject to Social Security or Medicare taxes (aka FICA taxes). In 2018, for example, this could save you between 7.65 percent (employee salary) to 15.3 percent (self-employed earnings). On $100,000, that's $7,650 to $15,300 per year!

No Tax on Appreciation

Because capital gains are paid only when you sell a property, your investment property avoids income taxes on appreciation while you hold it. This reality benefits long-term buy and hold investors who allow their property values to grow and compound over the long-term without the drag of taxes. You can see an example of this in the Buy and Hold Plan in Chapter 16.

Capital Gains

Gains on long-term investments (held over twelve months) are usually taxed at lower rates than comparable earnings from a job. For example, as of 2018 the long-term capital gains rates were between 0 percent and 20 percent, depending on your overall tax bracket. That means if you plan well, you can strategically sell long-term properties to capture gains with lower effective tax rates. You can also see an example of this benefit in action in the Buy and Hold Plan.

Live-In Flips
Living in a fixer-upper house (aka a live-in flip) can be a tremendous tax benefit if you immediately move in after the purchase and live in the house for two years or more. In this situation, tax law in the United States allows from $250,000 (individuals) to $500,000 (couples filing jointly) of tax-free profit when you resell. You'll learn more about this strategy in the Live-In Flip Plan in Chapter 13.

1031 Tax-Free Exchanges
Named after section 1031 of the U.S. tax code, this technique allows you to trade one property for another without paying taxes if you follow the IRS rules. This tax-free sale allows you to grow and compound gains without the drag of taxes. I'll give a detailed example of this strategy in the Trade-Up Plan in Chapter 17.

Installment Sales
This is a technique in which a property owner sells and then receives part of the sales price over time (aka seller financing or seller carry back). The tax benefit is that the seller pays taxes only on the gain in the year it's received. For properties with huge price run-ups over many years, this can avoid a big bump into higher tax brackets in the year of the sale.

Borrowing is Tax-Free
You pay capital gains tax only when you sell a property. Consequently, if you decide to refinance and pull out some of your equity, you can use all the money tax-free. Of course, this increases your property expenses, and you have to pay it back. But this can be a helpful strategy to use the wealth in your properties as you need it. I actually plan to do this with two rentals to help pay for my two kids' college expenses.

Self-Directed Retirement Accounts
You probably know about the tax benefits of 401(k) and IRA plans, but you might not know that you can invest these accounts in real estate and other alternative assets like private mortgage loans. This means any income or

gains you make from the real estate are tax-deferred or tax-free (depending on the retirement account type). Of course, there are many *very* strict rules you must abide by. I'll explain more about this in Chapter 21, The Role of Retirement Accounts for Early Retirees.

Die with Real Estate (Seriously!)

Death itself is not exactly a good strategy. But your dying with real estate can be a big tax advantage for your heirs. Instead of facing capital gains tax and recaptured depreciation tax like you would, your heirs will get what's called a stepped-up basis. This means their basis for taxes is reset when you die. Therefore, if they were to immediately resell, they would pay no tax. Keep in mind, however, that inherited assets are still subject to estate taxes. But there tends to be a large estate tax exemption (in 2018 there is an exemption for anything below a base of $10 million). The actual amount and limit of estate taxes seem to change with every new political administration; certainly keep an eye on it.

As you have seen, tax benefits are a compelling reason to get involved in real estate. But remember that tax benefits are never the sole reason to invest in real estate or anything else. Basic economics and quality of your investments are primary factors to consider when choosing to invest. And one of the most compelling reasons to invest in real estate is its simplicity.

Simple and Understandable

I'm a big fan of Warren Buffett, and I like to study his lessons. One of his primary investment tenets is to buy only assets that are simple and understandable.[6] Of course, what is simple and understandable depends on you. But I choose to invest primarily in residential real estate because for me, it is intuitive and easy to understand. And it's probably the same for you.

Ordinary people live in residential units. They want things like safety, convenience, comfort, affordability, style, and good school districts. When you shop for a residence, you probably look for the same things. Because you are a customer of residential real estate, you intuitively understand the fundamentals that make it valuable (or not valuable).

Real estate is also a "real" asset. It's tangible. In the right locations, its value is buoyed by both construction costs and salaries, which keep getting higher over time. Housing also doesn't easily go out of style or get replaced by

---

6   R. G. Hagstrom. *The Warren Buffett Way*. Hoboken, NJ, USA: John Wiley & Sons, Inc., 2007.

the latest technology. People just remodel instead of abandoning the property. People will still be living in homes long after you and I are gone. And that makes me very comfortable depending on real estate as a safe long-term investment.

Now that I've (hopefully) convinced you that real estate is the ideal vehicle for early retirement, it's time to prepare for the climb up the financial mountain.

─────────── **PROFILE OF A REAL ESTATE EARLY RETIREE** ───────────

SAM DOGEN

Financial Samurai (financialsamurai.com)
Location: San Francisco, California
Chad's Favorite Quote from Sam:
"My No. 1 best tip is to buy utility, rent luxury (BURL). I think this is an absolute no-brainer strategy, given the world has become smaller due to technology."

WEALTH-BUILDING STATISTICS
- **Profession/Career:** Finance
- **Income During Wealth-Building Phase:** $200,000+/year
- **How Big a Role Did Real Estate Play in Wealth-Building?** Equally as important as other investment vehicles
- **Primary Real Estate Strategy(ies):** Long-term buy and hold, apartment syndications, real estate crowdfunding

FINANCIAL INDEPENDENCE STATISTICS
- **Age at Financial Independence:** 31 to 35
- **Annual Expenses in Retirement:** $150,000+
- **Ideal Number of Rentals in Retirement:** 2 to 5
- **Primary Source of Retirement Income:** Rental income
- **Secondary Source of Retirement Income:** Business income
- **Ideal Debt Level of Real Estate Portfolio:** Less than 25% loan to value

Q: Can you explain in more detail how you built your current wealth?
I built my wealth through a combination of:

1. Saving 50 to 80 percent of my after-tax, after-401(k) income each month,
2. Investing all my savings in real estate, stocks, bonds, and private equity for passive income, and
3. Building a lifestyle business online after I negotiated a severance in 2012 that paid for six years of living expenses.

Q: What were the biggest obstacles and setbacks during your wealth-building stage? How did you overcome or push through them?
The biggest obstacle by far was the 2008–2010 financial crisis. My net worth got crushed by 35 percent or so within twelve months after ten years of building it up. But thankfully, I didn't sell anything and just continued to invest. I didn't invest as much as I should have, but at least I did invest. I overcame the downturn by connecting with folks online and starting financialsamurai.com in July 2009. It was the best investment I could have ever made.

Q: What's your No. 1 best tip for those looking to build wealth with real estate investing?
My best tip is to buy the home you actually plan to live in, enjoy life, and then when you have enough money and desire to buy a new home, rent out your existing home. Your mortgage rate will be lower, you'll know all the ins and outs of the home, and it'll provide a lot more meaning to you. Do this three to five times and you'll have a nice real estate mini-empire.

Q: Can you explain in more detail your post–financial independence income? How do you plan on living off of this income?
Originally, I had planned to live off about $200,000 a year in passive income from my various investments. I finally achieved this figure in late 2015. But by then, my lifestyle business income was doing really well, so I decided to just reinvest the entire $200,000 in passive in-

come each year and live off of our online income, while also continuing to save and invest as much as possible.

Q: What concerns do you have for the future related to retirement income? How will you address that?

Honestly, I don't have concerns about retirement because I haven't held a job in six years, and the bull market doubled my net worth after I was already comfortable with the amount that gave me the confidence to retire. My online income is a buffer for my passive income, and we live off less than $200,000 a year gross. Since my wife and I have both maxed out our 401(k)s for fifteen-plus years, we have a seven-figure account balance we can tap into at age 60, and then there's Social Security. And if all else fails, we'll move to our paid-off house in Hawaii and live a simple life! My wife and I are frugal by nature.

Q: Do you plan to start selling your real estate holdings? If so, when and how?

Yes, I finally sold a rental property I bought in March 2005 for $1.52 million for $2.74 million in June 2017. I sold it for around thirty times the annual gross rent and have reinvested the proceeds in heartland and non-coastal city real estate for higher yields. I sold it in an off-market private transaction.

Q: What's your No. 1 best tip for those looking to live off of investment income after retirement/financial independence?

My No. 1 best tip is to buy utility, rent luxury (BURL). I think this is an absolute no-brainer strategy, given the world has become smaller due to technology.

If you want to see my full 2017 passive income details, visit financialsamurai.com.

PART 2

A MAP OF THE FINANCIAL MOUNTAIN

Destination: Early Retirement
(aka Financial Independence)

CHAPTER 3

GETTING CLEAR ON YOUR EARLY RETIREMENT DESTINATION

Alice: *Which way should I go?*

Cat: *That depends on where you are going.*

Alice: *I don't know.*

Cat: *Then it doesn't matter which way you go.*

—LEWIS CARROLL,
ALICE'S ADVENTURES IN WONDERLAND

Welcome to base camp, where you learn how to use real estate investing to climb the mountain called early retirement! In case there is any question, I'm not a *real* mountain climber who tackles big 20,000-foot peaks. The risk of hypothermia, frostbite, and deadly falls into crevasses never appealed to me.

But I am an experienced climber of financial mountains. I've been putting one foot in front of the other, every day, for more than fifteen years as a full-time real estate investor pursuing my early retirement. And I'm excited to help you navigate your own journey.

In Part 2, I'll help you understand the financial destination you'll be climbing toward. In order to know when you've reached your goal, you need to first define what early retirement actually means. Let's start by getting clear on your retirement destination at the peak of the mountain.

As with any climb, you naturally start by looking up to the peak. What does the destination look like? How will you know when you arrive? Pull out your trusty binoculars. Then point your eyes toward the top to get an up close view of retirement. And ... fog! Nothing but clouds. The destination is unclear.

But you might say, "Chad, the title of your book refers to early retirement. That's the destination, right?" Yes, early retirement is the destination. But what does early retirement mean? How do you quantify it? And is your definition the same as everyone else's?

In the past, many employers made the destination of retirement clear with pension plans (aka defined benefit plans). The employer told you how long you had to work, and after that date you received a set amount of money for life. As you probably know, these types of pensions are practically dead for most of us. Except for some military and government worker pension plans, and potential[7] federal Social Security benefits, we're on our own.

For those of us not willing to wait until 67 years of age to free ourselves from the need to work, the destination is even more unclear. And many well-wishers—including your family, coworkers, and friends—will probably tell you that you're crazy for even trying to retire early.

I'll tell you that you are not crazy. Freeing yourself from the tyranny of *having* to work for money is a very worthwhile pursuit. And doing it earlier in life is even more amazing (I can vouch for that). But taking this unconventional path means you have to think and act unconventionally. And you have to dig deep and define your own retirement destination. To begin clearing the clouds and defining your early retirement destination, let's take a quick look at the meaning of the word "retirement."

Is "Retirement" the Right Word?

Part of the challenge I've always had with retirement is the word itself. To retire means to withdraw or go into seclusion. It's even used in the military when you're retreating from the enemy! Your entire life you've been moving *toward* things. Is the ultimate ambition of your financial life now to *withdraw*

---

7 I say "potential" not because I think Social Security benefits won't be around in the future. I do think they'll be around, even though the Social Security fund has long-term solvency issues. But one way to ensure Social Security solvency is to institute means-testing. In other words, those with enough wealth could see their benefits cut or eliminated. For those who are young and who build enough wealth to retire early, it may be wise not to count on Social Security retirement benefits. When you get closer to traditional retirement age and can see the political and fiscal landscape more clearly, you can make a better judgment.

and *retreat*?

And if you're ultra-ambitious, will this withdrawal from life happen in your 20s or 30s? My plans for the years after an early retirement involve a lot of engaging with life, not withdrawing! What about you?

For this reason and others, I prefer to redefine retirement. A more accurate definition for me is the term I've used before, "financial independence," FI for short. Anytime you hear early retirement throughout this book, you're also welcome to think of financial independence (and vice versa).

A Clear View of Financial Independence

My favorite definition of financial independence comes from a fellow real estate early retiree, John, at the blog ESI Money. His definition gets to the essence of the financial mountain peak.

Financial Independence (FI) = having wealth to cover expenses indefinitely

This means that when you arrive at FI, you have enough financial wealth to cover your personal expenses without working. For example, after FI, your expenses might be covered by rental income from properties, stock dividends, interest on CDs, proceeds from selling assets, or a combination of multiple strategies. I'll cover in detail how to fund your early retirement lifestyle using real estate investments in Part 6 of this book.

But for now, know that the tricky part of this FI definition is *indefinitely*. That means the money never runs out! So, how much wealth do you really need to reach this lofty goal? Most advice for those with traditional investments (stocks and bonds) falls in the range of a net worth twenty-five times your annual expenses.[8]

If you need $60,000 per year to cover expenses, you need wealth of $1,500,000 to achieve sustainable financial independence (25 x $60,000 = $1,500,000). But these calculations assume you could only safely withdraw between 3 to 4 percent of your portfolio every year (aka the Four Percent Rule). Why stock and bond investors can only safely withdraw 3 to 4 percent is beyond the scope of this book. But the good news for you is that real estate investments are different.

Quality real estate investments produce much larger *income* returns

---

8 Rob Berger. "The 25x Rule to Early Retirement." Forbes.com. Last updated February 23, 2017. www.forbes.com/sites/robertberger/2017/02/23/the-25x-rule-to-early-retirement/#4b9c5c306faf.

than stocks and bonds, and you never touch the principal of your investment (unless you want to sell). Very importantly, this means you can reach FI with a smaller net worth. Or if you want to build more wealth, you'll just receive a lot more income to support your lifestyle. I'll explain the simple retirement math I use with a concept called the Financial Independence Number.

Your Financial Independence Number

As a real estate investor, financial independence is relatively simple. You need your *stable and secure* income from investments to exceed your personal expenses. A Financial Independence Number can be written as a simple formula:

Investment Income > Personal Expenses

In the end, there are really only two variables in this equation:
1. Your personal expenses
2. Your investment income

When your investment income exceeds your personal expenses, you've reached financial independence. You no longer need to trade hours for dollars to support yourself. Work is optional.

Some call this leaving the rat race, but whatever you call it, this is a clear goal that you can aspire to and measure progress against when you're climbing the financial mountain.

THE CROSSOVER TO
Financial Independence

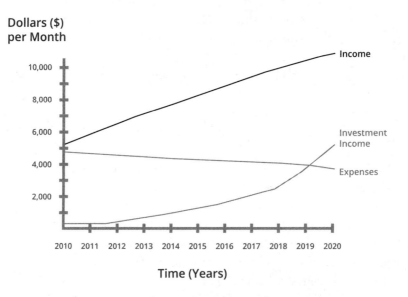

The Crossover Point is a concept from the book
Your Money or Your Life by Vicki Robin and Joe Dominguez[9].

Of course, a simple concept still requires hard work and a solid plan to execute. In Part 6 we'll cover the best ways to safely produce this crossover point income with real estate. But for now, as you prepare to begin climbing, let's estimate the amount of wealth you need to build so that you will have something to climb toward.

---

9 Vicki Robin and Joe Dominguez. *Your Money or Your Life: 9 Steps to Transforming Your Relationship with Money and Achieving Financial Independence*. New York, New York: Penguin Group, 2008.

PROFILE OF A REAL ESTATE EARLY RETIREE

CRAIG AND JANE HORTON

Medford Better Housing (medfordbetterhousing.com)
Location: Medford, Oregon
Chad's Favorite Quote from Craig and Jane:

"Always think about long-term benefits and not short-term problems. Set written goals to move forward on your journey."

WEALTH-BUILDING STATISTICS

- **Profession/Career:** Property manager
- **Income During Wealth-Building Phase:** $50,000 to $74,999/year
- **How Big a Role Did Real Estate Play in Wealth-Building?** Primary role
- **Primary Real Estate Strategy(ies):** Long-term buy and hold

FINANCIAL INDEPENDENCE STATISTICS

- **Age at Financial Independence:** 51 to 60
- **Annual Expenses in Retirement:** < $30,000
- **Ideal Number of Rentals in Retirement:** 11 to 20
- **Primary Source of Retirement Income:** Rental income
- **Secondary Source of Retirement Income:** Social Security
- **Ideal Debt Level of Real Estate Portfolio:** Less than 25% loan to value

Q&A

Q: Can you explain in more detail how you built your current wealth?
We have been in the real estate business since 1975. My strategy is to buy and hold primarily single-family houses. We own twenty houses, with most of them being paid for now. We bought several in 1988 from motivated sellers, including HUD and the Oregon Department of Veterans' Affairs. The current cash flow is more than double what my wife and I receive on Social Security.

Q: What were the biggest obstacles and setbacks during your

wealth-building stage? How did you overcome or push through them?
I was in a partnership to do a condo conversion for thirty-six apartments. We got it done, but I did not make any money and learned a lot. I really do not like partnerships because of this experience. Almost all of the rental properties we own are without partners. We are slow buy and hold investors.

Q: What's your No. 1 best tip for those looking to build wealth with real estate investing?
Always think about long-term benefits and not short-term problems. Set written goals to move forward on your journey.

Q: Can you explain in more detail your post–financial independence income? How do you plan on living off of this income?
We have net positive income from the rental apartments and houses that is more than $5,000 per month, which is net income after all expenses. That income is a supplement to our Social Security income.

Q: What concerns do you have for the future related to retirement income? How will you address them?
My motivation for investing is to never allow my wife to have to stay in a nursing home. We have been married forty-five years and are very close. This goal really drives what I do as a real estate investor. My wife is just the best!

Q: Do you plan to start selling your real estate holdings? If so, when and how?
I never want to sell my holdings, if possible. I will sometimes sell weak properties in a bad area, but that is a rare event.

Q: What's your No. 1 best tip for those looking to live off of investment income after retirement/financial independence?
Set strong written goals and read them on a regular basis. That will help you on your investing journey.

CHAPTER 4

HOW MUCH WEALTH DO YOU NEED TO RETIRE USING REAL ESTATE?

I love real estate investing for many reasons. But one of my favorites is its simplicity. Despite what you may hear from "successful" investors who build empires of hundreds or thousands of units, you can accomplish all your financial independence dreams with a small, simple portfolio of real estate investments. But just how much wealth will *you* need? Let's take a look.

No Real Estate Retirement Calculators Needed

Retirement calculators are helpful in situations where most of your assets are in stocks and bonds. You must balance your future personal expenses against dividends, growth rates, withdrawal rates, withdrawal timing, and more. But luckily, the real estate retirement math is a lot simpler. In fact, it's so simple you could do it on the back of a napkin. It has three variables:

1. Your expenses in early retirement (E)
2. Your wealth invested in real estate (W)
3. The conservative income yield or cash-on-cash return on that equity (r)

The basic formula with these three variables is this:

$$W \times r = E$$
or
$$E \div r = W$$

For example, let's assume you need a minimum of $70,000 a year of on-going investment income to cover your expenses (this is your financial independence number). Let's also assume you can find properties with a 10 percent cash-on-cash yield. This means you need to invest equity of $700,000 into real estate.

$$\$70,000 \div 10\% = W$$
$$\$700,000 = W$$

If that math doesn't work for your situation, you can change each of those three variables as needed. For example, if your financial independence number is $100,000 per year, you may need to invest $1 million instead of $700,000.

$$\$100,000 \div 10\% = W$$
$$\$1,000,000 = W$$

Or if your financial independence number is $100,000, but you want to be more conservative with your cash-on-cash yield, you may need to build more wealth. Let's say, if you only receive a 6 percent yield, you will need to invest $1,666,667.

$$\$100,000 \div 6\% = W$$
$$\$1,666,667 = W$$

Simple math, isn't it? But let's look at an example to translate it to real life. This example assumes our investor owns seven free-and-clear (no debt) rental properties.

Seven Debt-Free Properties and a Comfortable Early Retirement

In this scenario, an investor owns seven rental properties; she uses them to retire early. But every example has assumptions. And you need to understand those assumptions so that you can apply *the principles* and adapt them to your own unique situation. The assumptions for the rental properties in this example are as follows:

RENTAL PROPERTY ASSUMPTIONS	
Property Type	Single-family houses
Market Location	• "Middle America" (i.e., the South, Midwest, and other parts of the U.S. where rent-to-value ratios are reasonable) • A medium-sized city with a growing population and good long-term economic prospects • A median-priced neighborhood (not the lowest, not the highest)
Total Cost of Each Property (Purchase, Closing Costs, Repairs)	$120,000
Total Rental Income	$1,200/month
Operating Expenses	-$500/month
Net Operating Income	$700/month
Mortgage Balance	$0 (all debts have been paid off)
Mortgage Payments	$0

Now, another big assumption is that this is the *end* of a period of wealth-building or growth. The investor did not begin with this portfolio of debt-free, income-producing properties. She had to build it over time. Fortunately, you'll get *many* strategies to help you build toward this kind of financial result in Parts 4 and 5.

Living Beautifully on $58,800 Per Year
Here are the financial results of the investor's real estate portfolio.

RESULTS OF REAL ESTATE RETIREMENT PORTFOLIO

Property	Net Operating Income/Month	Mortgage Payment/ Month	Positive Cash Flow/ Month	Positive Cash Flow/ Year
House 1	$700	$0	$700	$8,400
House 2	$700	$0	$700	$8,400
House 3	$700	$0	$700	$8,400
House 4	$700	$0	$700	$8,400
House 5	$700	$0	$700	$8,400
House 6	$700	$0	$700	$8,400
House 7	$700	$0	$700	$8,400
Total:	**$4,900**	**$0**	**$4,900**	**$58,800**

What has this investor done for herself? She's basically created her own early retirement pension plan. By investing $840,000 over time (seven houses x $120,000), she will receive a consistent stream of rental income indefinitely into the future. And if she bought in the right locations, the rental income will likely keep up with inflation over time so that she can still pay for the same lifestyle.

Of course, there are reasonable questions you might bring up about this situation, like, Are there possible benefits to keeping some debt instead of paying it all off? Won't some people need more income than $58,800 a year? Won't some people need less if they have other assets or pensions producing income? These are all valid questions. And we'll explore each in more depth in Part 6, which is all about creating an unending supply of retirement income.

But the takeaway from the example is the simplicity and the power of a real estate–based early retirement portfolio. Managing seven properties, especially with a property manager, is a *very* part-time project. I personally spend less than an hour a week on many more properties than that. Yet, the $58,800 per year is life-changing. And with solid rentals in quality locations, both the income and the equity in these properties will likely be sustained or go up over time.

So, if one hour per week allows for $58,800/year in income, what will you do with the rest of your time? Could you begin to answer the question

I posed earlier in the Money-Life Manifesto: *If money were no obstacle ... what would you do differently in your life?* It's an exciting question. And the challenge of *living* the answer for yourself can bring you a lifetime of fun and fulfillment.

Speaking of living life, there is big caveat I must tell you before we move on from the topic of your early retirement destination. It has to do with not waiting on happiness.

—— PROFILE OF A REAL ESTATE EARLY RETIREE ——

LISA PHILLIPS
affordablerealestateinvestments.com
Location: Charlottesville, Virginia
Chad's Favorite Quote from Lisa:
"Make sure you pick a strategy that aligns with you and your goals and your pocketbook!"

WEALTH-BUILDING STATISTICS
- **Profession/Career:** IT consultant
- **Income During Wealth-Building Phase:** $150,000 to $199,000/year
- **How Big a Role Did Real Estate Play in Wealth-Building?** Primary vehicle
- **Primary Real Estate Strategy(ies):** Long-term rentals, coaching others in real estate investing, short-term rentals (Airbnb)

FINANCIAL INDEPENDENCE STATISTICS
- **Age at Financial Independence:** 31 to 35
- **Annual Expenses in Retirement:** $30,000 to $50,000
- **Ideal Number of Rentals in Retirement:** 11 to 20
- **Primary Source of Retirement Income:** Business income
- **Secondary Source of Retirement Income:** Rental properties; short-term Airbnb
- **Ideal Debt Level of Real Estate Portfolio:** Less than 25% loan to value

—————— Q&A ——————

Q: Can you explain in more detail how you built your current wealth?

I chose rental properties that had very high cash flow but very low acquisition costs, generally in working-class or lower-income neighborhoods (similar to where I grew up). After that, the strategy started to include property for Airbnb rental, which quadrupled the cash flow ($1,600-plus a month). Up next were vacation rentals. I also leveraged that experience by teaching others how to make their financial dreams possible in neighborhoods like this by being a real estate investing coach. I've helped build and shape more than 500 businesses directly (both locally or investing out of state), and thousands more through my online platform and audiences.

Q: What were the biggest obstacles and setbacks during your wealth-building stage? How did you overcome or push through them?

For me, it was finding someone else with a skill set to navigate rentals. Since I could not find anyone, I definitely learned a lot the hard way and excelled greatly as well.

Q: What's your No. 1 best tip for those looking to build wealth with real estate investing?

Make sure you pick a strategy that aligns with *you* and *your goals* and *your pocketbook*! If a strategy says to buy in an A-class neighborhood and that's too expensive for you, then find a strategy that you're comfortable with in a C- or D-class neighborhood. Just understand that each new strategy and niche has its own set of rules, so don't assume that what works for one will work with another. Learn from someone who has been there.

Q: Can you explain in more detail your post–financial independence income? How do you plan on living off of this income?

Short-term rentals can triple cash flow, and they do not have to be time-intensive if you structure the business properly. That is a great source of monthly income, aside from having a job. And with one to three properties, you're replacing most Americans' income with pure cash flow. Also, you can leverage teaching, mentoring, and coaching others on how they can become financially independent as well. You acquired those skills, so it's beneficial to you and the world at large to help others obtain their own financial independence as well. We're all in this together.

Q: What concerns do you have for the future related to retirement income? How will you address them?
None. At this rate, acquiring properties that pay for themselves is a great way to retire with a lot of assets.

Q: Do you plan to start selling your real estate holdings? If so, when and how?
As needed, if the market is not a good fit (I've done this already in the Baltimore market, as it is not investor-friendly) and when, economically, I may need that capital to invest in a small apartment complex.

Q: What's your No. 1 best tip for those looking to live off of investment income after retirement/financial independence?
Learn how to set your business up so that it's running whether you are there in person or traveling in Aruba.

CHAPTER 5
DON'T WAIT ON HAPPINESS: ENJOY THE PEAK AND THE PLATEAUS

The good life is a process, not a state of being. It is a direction, not a destination.

—CARL ROGERS, TWENTIETH-CENTURY AMERICAN PSYCHOLOGIST

Up to this point, I've emphasized the peak of the mountain, the final destination. So it may be tempting to think that the *good* life will start once you reach the top. *Then* you can be happy, right? Not exactly.

I've realized an important lesson during my climb up the financial mountain. Life can be enjoyed and celebrated at the peak *and* during the climb, at many plateaus along the way. In fact, you may come to love plateaus so much that you see life just as a series of climbs and plateaus.

For example, during my early years of starting a business, I regularly played pick-up basketball and hiked in the middle of the workday. I even took extended multi-month trips (aka mini-retirements) to Spain, Peru, Chile, Argentina, and across the western United States.

Did these experiences matter to me? Absolutely! I would not trade them for any amount of money. Had I arrived at the peak of financial independence before having them? Absolutely not! I still had a goal of climbing higher up the mountain toward the peak. But even a fast climb might take ten to fifteen years. Why not enjoy life along the way?

The idea of financial plateaus (that is, intermediate milestones) has made it possible for me not to wait on the activities that make me most happy. You are welcome to create your own plateaus, but here are five major ones that I recommend you keep in mind during your journey:

1. Self-Sufficiency
2. Mini-Retirement
3. Semi-Retirement
4. Early Retirement
5. Traditional Retirement

Here's what the plateaus look like in picture form. I'll explain each of these in the sections that follow.

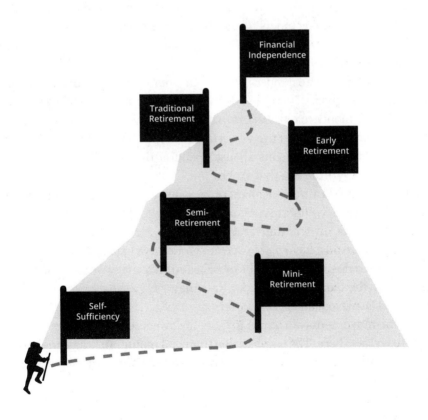

Plateau #1: Self-Sufficiency

It's easy to quickly blow past the milestone of self-sufficiency. But it's important and worth celebrating. Basically, this means your day-to-day finances are not an emergency. Here are a few indicators that you might have reached this milestone:

- Personal debt paid off (for example, student loans, car loans, credit cards)
- Cash emergency fund of three to six months
- In-demand skills at a stable job (or jobs) that pay you well

If you read J.L. Collins's blog at jlcollinsnh.com or read his book *The Simple Path to Wealth*, this is similar to his concept of "F-You Money." I was at this stage when I played basketball and hiked for several hours in the middle of the day as a 25-year-old! Because I was self-sufficient financially, I began to have the courage and leverage to do more of what mattered to me. I didn't have to wait. Financial independence began in small doses early on.

Plateau #2: Mini-Retirement

Mini-retirements are extended breaks from your normal routine of working hard and saving hard. There is no definitive amount of time, but they typically last from a month to more than a year. Many people use mini-retirements to travel, but you can also use yours to do other projects like going back to school, building or remodeling a house, spending time with the kids, planting a garden, or anything else that excites you.

I took my first mini-retirement in 2009, about seven years after I began my real estate investing career (and in the middle of the Great Recession!). For four months, my wife and I traveled to Spain, Peru, Chile, and Argentina. During our travels, I learned to speak Spanish, we explored new cultures, and we hiked through some of the most beautiful scenery we'd ever seen. But more than the specific experiences, the time away gave me a new center and source of energy when I got back.

Mini-retirements allow you to taste the sweetness of early retirement before you get there. The climb up the financial mountain is long and arduous. Mini-retirements are reprieves that remind you why you're climbing in the first place.

Plateau #3: Semi-Retirement

You don't have to be completely financially independent to gain more flexibility and freedom. Even if you are part of the way to your financial independence number, you can enter a phase called semi-retirement. With semi-retirement, you don't stop working. You just work less or on a schedule that's more attractive to you.

For example, let's say your current job situation is not ideal. Your family expenses are $60,000 per year. Your real estate investments produce $30,000 a year in net positive cash flow. And your current job that you don't like pays you $80,000. The $30,000 a year from your rentals doesn't pay all your expenses, but it is enough to give you leverage with your current job. You could choose to:

- Ask to work 50 percent of the time for less pay
- Ask to transfer to a different role that's more fun, even if it's a lower salary
- Quit and find a completely different job that you like, even if the pay is less
- Quit and become an entrepreneur (I recommend building the business before you quit)

The point is that even partial financial independence can lead to more options, flexibility, and enjoyment of life. There is no reason to trudge along miserably in the name of *someday* achieving financial independence. Life is too short. And you just might find that semi-retirement is all the freedom you need for a long time. If so, enjoy the plateau and pick up the intense financial growth again later on, if needed.

Plateau #4: Early Retirement
This milestone is the official topic of the book. You don't have to wait until traditional retirement ages to enjoy the freedom and flexibility normally reserved for retirement. You can do it in your 50s, 40s, or even your 30s.

One of the most famous early retirees is Pete Adeney, the blogger behind Mr. Money Mustache. He and his wife retired at 30 from their engineering jobs to have a kid and spend more time raising him. Inspiring stories from Pete and others have started an entire movement called FIRE (financial independence, retire early). People are shunning long careers, retiring early, and engaging in activities that are more personally fulfilling (often other kinds of work).

There are, of course, challenges to retiring early. One of the biggest is the unknown pattern of future expenses. For example, U.S. health care and college education costs have inflation rates that, as of now, seem out of control.

But early retirement is more about flexibility and self-reliance than it is just living off your assets mindlessly. If hard times come for early retirees, part-time work is always an option. And many early retirees move to new locations—both within their home country or outside of it—in order to reduce expenses while still enjoying life. For example, as I write this book, I'm living a wonderful life for less than $3,000 a month in Cuenca, Ecuador, with my family.

The main point of early retirement goes back to the beginning of this book. When you free yourself from the need to work *for money* at an early age, you become rich in more than money. You gain freedom, flexibility, and the autonomy to spend your time doing what matters. And time is the most rare, priceless treasure of them all.

Plateau #5: Traditional Retirement

This is the milestone most people think of when it comes to retirement. It has to do both with age and with wealth accumulation. In the United States, most retirement account withdrawals begin without penalty at age 59.5. Government Social Security income benefits begin between the ages of 62 and 67 (for those born after 1960).[10] And the Medicare health insurance program begins for most people at 65.[11] For a lucky few, there may even be a pension from a previous job at this age.

If you're in your 20s, 30s, or 40s, you're not counting on these benefits anytime soon. But they do provide a comforting financial floor when you reach the ages mentioned above. And particularly with health insurance, which in the U.S. is a source of anxiety and uncertainty for early retirees, these financial certainties are welcome.

But the gap between these benefits and your desired lifestyle must still be filled by your wealth accumulation. If you have a sufficient amount of wealth and real estate income, filling this gap will be easy and comfortable. But for many others with smaller nest eggs, filling the gap will be a challenge. This is one of the reasons Part 6 will go in depth about how to use real estate to maximize your retirement income. This will help whether you have a small or a large net worth.

---

10 "Full Retirement Age: If You Were Born in 1960 or Later." U.S. Social Security Administration. Last accessed on March 6, 2018. www.ssa.gov/planners/retire/1960.html.

11 "When Will My Coverage Start?" U.S. Centers for Medicare & Medicaid Services. Last accessed March 6, 2018. www.medicare.gov/sign-up-change-plans/get-parts-a-and-b/when-coverage-starts/when-coverage-starts.html.

Ready to Climb?

Part 2 of this book helped you get clear on the destination of early retirement or financial independence. I've also shared some plateaus or milestones that you can use to track your progress during the journey up. But at some point, it's time to stop gazing up and begin the work of climbing, building wealth, and moving toward your goals.

Are you ready to keep going? In Part 3, you'll learn the fundamentals of the climb to build wealth, which are the same whether you invest in real estate or other assets. Then in Parts 4 and 5, you'll learn the specific routes (real estate investing strategies) you can use to build wealth and climb the mountain.

————— **PROFILE OF A REAL ESTATE EARLY RETIREE** —————

MAURICIO RUBIO
Location: New York, New York
Chad's Favorite Quote from Mauricio:
"One day of doing is worth more than 100 days of planning."

WEALTH-BUILDING STATISTICS
- **Profession/Career:** Investment banker; digital marketing/ecommerce; wife is psychiatrist
- **Income During Wealth-Building Phase:** $150,000 to $199,000/year
- **How Big a Role Did Real Estate Play in Wealth-Building?** Primary vehicle
- **Primary Real Estate Strategy(ies):** Long-term hold rentals; 1031 tax-free exchange; short-term vacation rentals

FINANCIAL INDEPENDENCE STATISTICS
- **Age at Financial Independence:** 41 to 45
- **Annual Expenses in Retirement:** $100,000 to $150,000
- **Ideal Number of Rentals in Retirement:** 6 to 10
- **Primary Source of Retirement Income:** Rental income
- **Secondary Source of Retirement Income:** Period sale of stocks; side hustles or part-time work

- **Ideal Debt Level of Real Estate Portfolio:** 26% to 50% loan to value

——————— Q&A ———————

Q: Can you explain in more detail how you built your current wealth?
I didn't realize it back then, but we have been employing wealth-building strategies all of our adult lives. Main lesson: Don't accumulate debt (except for real estate). Start investing in the financial markets and learning how to invest as early as possible. When investing in real estate, don't shop for your dream home. Shop for the best asset in your budget; consider its future rentability and appeal to a wider market.

With these principles in mind, we invested in a couple of condos on the fringe of the Upper West Side of Manhattan in New York. With a growing family, we could have opted for much more space farther away, but we always viewed our condo as an investment instead of a home.

Throughout, we have also kept investing in the stock market and were fortunate enough to save and generate enough gains to finish paying off the mortgages on our condos, and generate the down payment for a third condo in Philadelphia.

We did this all without ever considering ourselves real estate investors. We both had full-time jobs in the city and were raising three kids. Our investment in Philadelphia was simply trying to repeat our success in New York.

And then my professional career hit a wall. The company I worked for was not doing well, and I dreaded the idea of having to look for another job. It occurred to me that, after a few years at that new job, I would likely have to look for another one, and that thought was frightening. My business partner once told me: "Your soul has been sucked dry." That may have been the wake-up moment.

This led to a one-year family sabbatical in South America. It was an opportunity to leave the bubble of NYC and contemplate the rest of my life. With lots of "free" time on my hands, I noticed that I was voluntarily researching local and foreign real estate markets, and traveling throughout South America, mostly using Airbnb.

Upon my return to NYC, I jumped off the cliff and committed to working for myself in some capacity. I just turned my side hustles of real estate investing and financial management investing into my full-time job. It occurred to me that, since most of our wealth was made through our financial and real estate investments, we should be devoting more time and resources to those efforts. Many people take the indirect path to wealth—in other words, they hope their employer or chosen career will lead to wealth. I've now switched to a more direct path.

Since becoming full-time real estate investors, we have pivoted away from condos to short-term vacation rentals. We did this because the ROI (return on investment) on short-term vacation rentals is higher than condos. We think we have stumbled onto a niche that is growing and also provides the lifestyle I have been looking for.

Q: What were the biggest obstacles and setbacks during your wealth-building stage? How did you overcome or push through them?
This is a tough question. Past obstacles are rarely looked back on as obstacles—they were challenges that became lessons. In my experience, the biggest challenge is getting started! And the way to overcome that is to start. I didn't want to buy our first apartment. I didn't really want to buy our second apartment, either, but our family was growing so we needed more space. Today I am constantly looking for a well-priced piece of real estate. One day of doing is worth more than 100 days of planning.

Q: What's your No. 1 best tip for those looking to build wealth with real estate investing?
Learn your basic real estate math so you can correctly evaluate a deal. If I can sneak in another related tip: Don't get emotional about real estate.

Q: Can you explain in more detail your post–financial independence income? How do you plan on living off of this income?
Another reason that real estate is so appealing to us, in particular, is that we love to travel. I manage the properties while we are local, but I

can easily outsource the property management of the properties if we choose to travel. An advantage of the vacation rental market is that property management infrastructure is already in place. This means we will have the ability to receive income from our rentals without a lot of day-to-day involvement. Also, since we only buy properties we are comfortable holding indefinitely, I also plan to stay involved in the real estate game indefinitely in ways that produce cashflow and generate happiness.

Q: What concerns do you have for the future related to retirement income? How will you address them?
I think I have all the same concerns most people do. My principal risk mitigation strategies are to invest in real assets in diversified markets. As long as I can finance my lifestyle with only the net cash flow from my investments, I sleep well at night.

Q: Do you plan to start selling your real estate holdings? If so, when and how?
No plans to sell at the moment.

Q: What's your No. 1 best tip for those looking to live off of investment income after retirement/financial independence?
Start early. If I have to name a regret, it's that I didn't jump off the cliff sooner. When you jump off the cliff, your most valuable asset—your time—truly becomes yours. And that can be the best feeling in the world.

PART 3

PREPARATIONS FOR THE CLIMB

---

*The Fundamentals of
Building Wealth*

CHAPTER 6
THE STORY OF
THE SAVINGS GAP

Real estate investing is a wonderful tool. But the basics of building wealth with real estate are the same as any other method:

1. Save money.
2. Invest the money wisely.
3. Harvest your wealth.

Later parts of this book will go into detail about items two and three. But before any of that can happen, the first step is figuring out how to save money.

The main concept to remember is something called your savings rate or savings gap. If you get this, you'll have an enormous head start when we talk about specific real estate strategies. But if you don't get it, no real estate strategy will be able to bail you out. The negative financial momentum will be too strong.

The fall after I graduated from college, I was trying to figure out what I wanted to do with my life. I was an above-average college football player, but the NFL didn't seem to want me. So that option was off the table. And I wasn't ready to begin a work career or follow through on my applications to medical schools. I decided to just take some extra classes at Clemson University for the fun of it, even though I was officially done with school. I loved to learn, and it would give me some time and space to think.

My classes during that extra semester included entomology (the study of insects), the philosophy of science (yeah, I'm a nerd), accounting, finance, and business management. I loved all my classes, but the professor in my business management class changed the course of my life.

That professor was named Dr. Louis Stone, and he eventually became my friend, mentor, and private investor in real estate. Soon after I met Louis, he told me a story about a simple formula to build wealth. The story stuck with me and gave me a basic formula for achieving financial independence relatively quickly in my own life.

How to Become Rich

When Louis was in his twenties working in North Carolina, he met an older, wealthy gentleman. One day the old man asked him, "Louis, do you want to know how to become rich?"

"Of course!" Louis enthusiastically said. (So did I when Louis asked me!)

"If you want to be rich, Louis, you need to learn to live on less than you earn. If you earn $40,000, live on less than $40,000. Got it, Louis?"

"Got it!"

"Next, you need to earn $80,000. But you need to still live on $40,000. Got it, Louis?"

"Got it!"

"Finally, you need to earn $120,000. But you need to still live on $40,000. Got it, Louis?"

"Yes, got it!"

"Louis, if you keep doing that, you can't help but become rich. And it will happen faster than you think."

The point of the story was to create a larger and larger gap between income and spending. This *savings gap* is the magic of building wealth quickly and steadily. And Louis's old mentor knew the natural tendency of young people in the workforce to inflate their lifestyle. And this, more than anything, destroys their chances to build wealth *very* quickly.

But Louis listened. So did I. And now it's your chance.

This simple idea of a savings gap has worked for many people. You can live simply, earn above-average income, and regularly save an enormous amount of money. Nothing fancy. But very powerful. And although the concept is simple, it also has some interesting math behind it, which I'll share in the next chapter.

GRAHAM STEPHAN

www.youtube.com/c/GrahamStephan
Location: Los Angeles, California
Chad's Favorite Quote from Graham:
"It doesn't matter how much you earn; it's how much you save that matters the most."

WEALTH-BUILDING STATISTICS

- **Profession/Career:** Real estate agent
- **Income During Wealth-Building Phase:** $200,000+/year
- **How Big a Role Did Real Estate Play in Wealth-Building?** Primary role
- **Primary Real Estate Strategy(ies):** Long-term buy and hold

FINANCIAL INDEPENDENCE STATISTICS

- **Age at Financial Independence:** 26 to 30
- **Annual Expenses in Retirement:** $30,000 to $50,000
- **Ideal Number of Rentals in Retirement:** 11 to 20
- **Primary Source of Retirement Income:** Rental income
- **Secondary Source of Retirement Income:** Dividends from public stocks; side hustles or part-time work
- **Ideal Debt Level of Real Estate Portfolio:** Between 51% to 75% loan to value

———————— Q&A ————————

Q: Can you explain in more detail how you built your current wealth?
Some of it was luck; some was strategy. I was always interested in saving money, so that came naturally to me. I'd get more enjoyment from saving money than spending it! I felt as if every dollar I invested was one step closer to being "free," and if I didn't absolutely need to spend it, I wouldn't. I began saving almost everything I made once I started working as a real estate agent. But I realized the income was fairly inconsistent, and that made me uneasy, the not knowing when

my next paycheck would come and how much it would be for. So, with the money I had saved up, I bought three rental properties—the only goal in this move was to establish a base income that I could build from. This ended up paying almost all my living expenses at the time, allowing me to save just about everything I made as a real estate agent. From there, I continued investing, and I now own five properties, three of which are paid off. I'm still working as a real estate agent, still saving all of that income, and still reinvesting all of it back into rental properties. All buy and hold—I have no intention of ever selling.

Q: What were the biggest obstacles and setbacks during your wealth-building stage? How did you overcome or push through them?
My biggest setback was when I *first* wanted to buy real estate, but I had zero credit score and no banks wanted to deal with me. Even though I was earning six figures at the time, I was worthless without any previous credit history. When I was a kid, my family was highly against credit cards. Everything was paid with debit or cash. Growing up with that mind-set ended up hurting me when it came time to buy real estate. I got my first credit card at 21. Had I gotten a credit card and begun building credit at 18, I could've doubled the number of properties I had bought early on. Lesson learned.

Q: What's your No. 1 best tip for those looking to build wealth with real estate investing?
Save. Save. Save. And build your credit as early as you can. It doesn't matter how much you earn; it's how much you save that matters the most. I know people making $250k/year who are broke, and people who are wealthy off $75k/year. And contribute to a 401(k)/Roth IRA—doesn't have to be a lot, but this gives you a little more flexibility and diversification later in life.

Q: Can you explain in more detail your post–financial independence income? How do you plan on living off of this income?
My rental income from five properties pays pretty much all my living expenses. This doesn't fund a glamorous lifestyle of sports cars and private jets, but it does pay the basic bills plus a little leftover for din-

ing out every now and then. My real estate agent income is all saved up and then reinvested at the end of the year. I also have YouTube ad revenue, which I'm continuing to reinvest back into the channel to continue to grow my brand. I pretty much just keep my lifestyle on par with my rental income. That way, everything else is profit, and each year as I invest, I can spend more.

Q: What concerns do you have for the future related to retirement income? How will you address them?
I've yet to rely 100 percent on rental income and I'm not sure I ever will, but finally scaling back might be a challenge because I'm so used to having other large sources of income if anything ever happens. Otherwise, with a six- to twelve-month emergency fund, I can't imagine there'd be anything that would happen that would cause concern.

Q: Do you plan to start selling your real estate holdings? If so, when and how?
Never. I plan to hold them as long as I can. There's no sense in selling unless I absolutely have to. I might consider it if the perfect opportunity came up, but it would have to be something incredible.

Q: What's your No. 1 best tip for those looking to live off of investment income after retirement/financial independence?
Downsize your life and find out what you really need and what really brings you the most enjoyment. Retail therapy gets old after a while. Many of the expensive toys get boring once you get used to them. There's a lot out there that's way more meaningful—friendships, for instance. Free hobbies are also amazing: working out, hiking, running, reading. Besides this, keep track of your expenses. You should know exactly how much you're spending and exactly how much you're making. Leave a buffer with your spending, just in case you need to go over for unexpected events.

CHAPTER 7
SIMPLE MATH = SHORTER PATH TO FINANCIAL INDEPENDENCE

Pete Adeney, the popular blogger "Mr. Money Mustache," retired at 30 after almost ten years of work as a software engineer. One of my favorite articles from Pete is titled "The Shockingly Simple Math Behind Early Retirement." In the piece, Pete shares that one factor, more than any other, allowed him to retire early.

The key factor was his savings rate, or the percentage of his take-home pay that he saved.

This, of course, is the same as the savings gap that Louis, I, and now *you* have learned. And the results of this math relationship Pete found look like this:

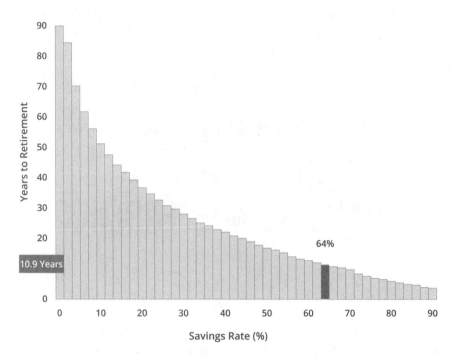

This is a graph of the relationship between savings rate and time until you retire. As you can see, the relationship is not a straight line. The time to retirement gets significantly shorter the more you save. Here are the same results in chart form:

SAVINGS RATE	YEARS OF WORK BEFORE RETIREMENT
5%	66
10%	51
20%	37
50%	17
64%	10.9
75%	7

There are, of course, assumptions to this math. For example, your expenses before and after retirement are assumed to be the same. Investment returns are 5 percent above inflation, and withdrawal rates after retirement are 4 percent. You can see all of the assumptions and download a full spreadsheet from Mr. Money Mustache's website.[12]

But the main point I'm trying to make using his math is this:

If you want to reach financial independence in a much shorter time than average, focus on becoming much better than average with your savings rate.

Being average as a saver is not good for your early retirement plans. The average savings rate in the United States as of December 2016 was only 5.04 percent. Switzerland's average rate was 18.79 percent, Canada's was 3.28 percent, and the United Kingdom's was -1.11 percent. [13]

Is it any wonder people are stuck at jobs their whole lives without being able to retire and take control of their money? The rate of 5.04 percent in the U.S. puts people on the *far* end of the graph, with more than sixty years to retirement (without outside government help). And if you want to retire earlier, even using incredible real estate strategies that somehow earn 25 percent returns won't help you without savings. You *first* need the savings rate, then you can focus on growing those savings.

So, do you know your savings rate? How much longer will it take you to retire based on these calculations? Whatever your savings rate happens to be, the point is not to judge you. The point is to offer you a wake-up call. If you have a goal to retire sooner than later, you need to improve your savings rate. And the variables of this math equation are fairly simple.

1. Decrease your expenses.
2. Increase your income.

It's important to focus on both of these savings levers at the same time. But in the next chapter, I want to begin with the one you have the most direct control over: decreasing your expenses.

---

12 Pete Adeney. "The Shockingly Simple Math Behind Early Retirement." Mr. Money Mustache. Last updated January 13, 2012. www.mrmoneymustache.com/2012/01/13/the-shockingly-simple-math-behind-early-retirement/.

13 "Household savings (indicator) doi: 10.1787/cfc6f499-en." OECD. Accessed on 14 November 14, 2017. https://data.oecd.org/hha/household-savings.htm.

PROFILE OF A REAL ESTATE EARLY RETIREE

JOE OLSON

adventuringalong.com
Location: Global Nomad
Chad's Favorite Quote from Joe:

"Rather than giving up after a mistake, I kept going, kept learning, and kept improving on my process."

WEALTH-BUILDING STATISTICS

- **Profession/Career:** Public school teacher (spouse was also a teacher)
- **Income During Wealth-Building Phase:** $75,000 to $99,999/year
- **How Big a Role Did Real Estate Play in Wealth-Building?** Primary vehicle
- **Primary Real Estate Strategy(ies):** Long-term rentals, fix and flip, private notes

FINANCIAL INDEPENDENCE STATISTICS

- **Age at Financial Independence:** 26 to 30
- **Annual Expenses in Retirement:** $30,000 to $50,000
- **Ideal Number of Rentals in Retirement:** 11 to 20
- **Primary Source of Retirement Income:** Rental income
- **Secondary Source of Retirement Income:** Interest from private notes, interest from bonds, dividends, stocks, periodic sale of stocks, Social Security income, annuities, side hustles or part-time work, privately owned business
- **Ideal Debt Level of Real Estate Portfolio:** Less than 25% loan to value

Q&A

Q: Can you explain in more detail how you built your current wealth?
We used a massive savings rate, combined with side gigs and a low cost of living, to plow most of our W2 income into real estate. We purchased buy and hold properties, did flips, and bought notes.

Q: What were the biggest obstacles and setbacks during your wealth-building stage? How did you overcome or push through them?
I have made a number of mistakes that cost tens of thousands of dollars throughout the course of my investing years. Underestimating costs, paying too much, trusting people without proper vetting, and investing in things I didn't fully understand. But each mistake was a lesson, and each investment I made was, on average, better than the last. Rather than giving up when I made a mistake, I kept going, kept learning, and kept improving on my process.

Q: What's your No. 1 best tip for those looking to build wealth with real estate investing?
Make sure you understand the important aspects of your investment and can properly calculate the risk-to-reward ratio of that investment.

Q: Can you explain in more detail your post–financial independence income? How do you plan on living off of this income?
We have rental income that more than covers our living expenses. Extra is reinvested.

Q: What concerns do you have for the future related to retirement income? How will you address them?
Inflation. I think too many people write off real estate as an inflation solution with the argument "real estate and rents will increase with inflation." This is not necessarily the case. It'll increase (or not) based on the local economy where your rentals are, which may lag behind actual inflation. You can't necessarily just live off all your rental income. Instead, you have to reinvest part of it in order to continue growing your wealth to keep up with inflation.

Q: Do you plan to start selling your real estate holdings? If so, when and how?
Every time a tenant moves out, we ask the question "sell or re-rent?" As we are long-term buy and hold landlords, almost every time so far the answer has been to rent the property again (only once have we sold what was going to be a long-term hold). I think having knowledge

and options to take advantage of opportunities, and flexibility to deal with market conditions, is better than having a rigid, fixed plan either way.

Q: What's your No. 1 best tip for those looking to live off of investment income after retirement/financial independence?
Plan for the rough times. Income and expenses fluctuate. There will be a time when income tips down on the low side (multiple tenants move out at once, either due to economic factors or coincidence) and expenses go up on the high side (multiple expenses all lining up to hit at once). Make sure you have the buffer and reserves needed to ride out these events.

CHAPTER 8
HOW TO CONTROL YOUR EXPENSES

Your personal finances work like pouring water into buckets. Your income fills the buckets, and your expenses are like holes in the bottom that drain the water out. If you have too many holes, you'll never have enough money left to save for investing. Your first job is to plug those leaks.

In personal finance, plugging the leaks starts by tracking your current expenses. I recommend eventually tracking your expenses for a full twelve-month period. But if you've never done this before, just start with one month. The process can seem daunting because there are hundreds of transactions each month. But technology or simple systems can help you.

My family tracks our expenses automatically online using free software like mint.com. This app and other similar ones pull data from your bank account and credit cards. Then it divides the spending into easy-to-follow categories such as housing, transportation, health care, etc. We have also tracked expenses the old-school way with cash envelopes, pen, paper, and spreadsheets. Both methods work as long as you're committed to the process.

The payoff of this exercise is awareness. Just knowing where your money is going will make it more likely that you will not waste it. When you see that you spent more than $1,500 eating out last month, you'll be less likely to just automatically eat out. And that will help you save money.

After tracking your spending, you'll also notice some money leaks that you didn't even realize you had. Money just seems to disappear. If you have a hard time controlling these leaks, I recommend going old school and using a cash envelope system, at least temporarily. For example, if you spend too much money eating out, just decide at the beginning of each month on an eating-out budget. Put that amount of cash in an envelope, and only take cash from the envelope to eat out. When the money runs out, you eat at home or take a lunch with you. It's the simplest form of discipline possible!

But probably the biggest expenses you'll notice fall into two categories: housing and transportation. And because they're so big, they deserve their own section.

Why You Should Cut the Big Expenses First

Going back to our bucket analogy, you'll likely notice two *enormous* holes. They are housing and transportation. The chart below from the 2016 U.S. Bureau of Labor Statistics Survey of Consumer Expenditures[14] shows just how much people spend on average, including housing and transportation.

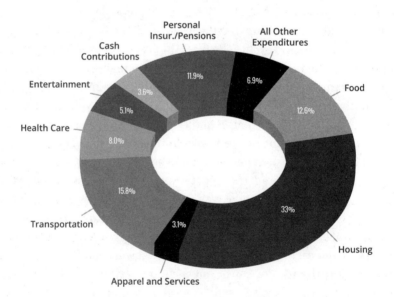

PER CONSUMER UNIT (2016 IN U.S.)

Average Expenditures

- Personal Insur./Pensions — 11.9%
- Cash Contributions — 3.6%
- All Other Expenditures — 6.9%
- Entertainment — 5.1%
- Food — 12.6%
- Health Care — 8.0%
- Transportation — 15.8%
- Housing — 33%
- Apparel and Services — 3.1%

Source: "Consumer Expenditures Survey - 2016" Bureau of Labor Statistics. 10/29/2017

---

14 "Consumer Expenditures Survey — 2016." Bureau of Labor Statistics. Last accessed on 10/29/2017.

According to this survey, housing is 33 percent, and transportation is about 16 percent of the total. Those two alone total almost 50 percent of all average expenditures! When you plug or reduce the size of these big holes, you get the highest return on your efforts.

One simple way to cut transportation costs is to live closer to work. If you can drive two miles instead of twenty, you'll save an enormous amount on gas and maintenance. You may even be able to eliminate your need for a car and simply walk or bike to work every day. This daily exercise will save you even more because you won't need a gym membership and you might reduce your health care costs by being more fit.

But even with owning a vehicle, let's say your options are to buy a decent used car for $10,000 or a new $30,000 car with $10,000 down and payments for five years. The initial cost difference is $20,000, which is big enough by itself. But after twenty years, if you bought the new car, the opportunity cost of lost potential investment returns at, let's say, 7 percent, is more than $77,000! Even if you would have had to buy another used car after the old one died, you would still have been ahead of the game.

While that $77,000 is huge, housing is a much bigger cost than your car. Finding ways to save on housing makes an even bigger difference in your early retirement plans. Let's say you could buy a house that costs a total of $150,000 with a mortgage payment of $750 per month. Or you could buy a house for $300,000 with a payment of $1,500 per month.

You would save *at least* $750 per month with the first house compared to the second. I say "at least" because this hypothetical doesn't include the higher cost of taxes, insurance, maintenance, or furnishings on a bigger house. But let's stick with just a $750 per month difference to make the point. If those savings are invested with a 7 percent annual return, they turn into more than $124,000 after ten years, and more than $368,000 after twenty years!

One car choice and one housing choice turn into $445,000 ($77,000 + $368,000) over twenty years. And I haven't even gotten to housing strategies like house hacking, live-in-then-rent, and live-in flips, which could reduce your housing costs even more (or even help you *make* money on your home). I'll tackle those topics in Part 4 on starter wealth-building plans.

But for now, the point is this: Concentrate on reducing expenses with the big-ticket items. You can also work on others like eating out less, buying fewer Starbucks lattes, etc. But your house and car will give you the biggest increase in your savings rate for time and energy invested. And don't forget that you're not just saving money; you're buying your freedom.

You Can Afford Anything, but Not Everything

This section has been about making choices with money. Some of these choices may be tough because you're taking money from one place and putting it in another (savings). Friends and family may even complain that you're not really enjoying life. It helps to remember that you're not depriving yourself by spending less. Instead, you're consciously choosing to "spend" it on something much better than "stuff"—your freedom!

More specifically, your increased savings are buying flexibility, free time, and an early escape from the money rat race. I love buying those. What about you? A fellow real estate investor and blogger whom I deeply respect named Paula Pant explains this beautifully with her motto at affordanything.com:

You can afford anything, but you can't afford everything.

You can't have it all right now. You have to choose. If you choose to spend 100 percent of your income on stuff, you are prioritizing that stuff over everything else. If you choose to save a large portion of that income and invest it, you're choosing to move toward freedom and flexibility as quickly as possible. There is no right or wrong here. There are only choices that either connect with your deeply held values or they don't.

And this doesn't mean you sacrifice enjoyment of life in the meantime. I've found the opposite to be true. Even during my growth stages when I saved the most, I've found the reduced focus on spending made me much happier. I learned a lot about myself and the precious things in life that money can't buy. And I knew as an investor that I'd have plenty of time and money down the road to enjoy every nice thing I could imagine. It's just a choice of which you want first—those fancy things or your freedom.

My hunch is that you've already chosen freedom. And that's going to give you a lot of firepower as you take the next steps toward financial independence. Speaking of firepower, let's take a look at the other side of your savings rate: increasing your income.

PROFILE OF A REAL ESTATE EARLY RETIREE

PAULA PANT

affordanything.com and the *Afford Anything* podcast
Location: Las Vegas, Nevada
Chad's Favorite Quote from Paula:
"Choose one niche and one strategy. Don't try to chase too many paths—just pick one and specialize there."

WEALTH-BUILDING STATISTICS

- **Profession/Career:** Freelance writer; spouse worked in the highway construction industry
- **Income During Wealth-Building Phase:** $60,000 to $150,000+/year
- **How Big a Role Did Real Estate Play in Wealth-Building?** Primary role
- **Primary Real Estate Strategy(ies):** Long-term buy and hold

FINANCIAL INDEPENDENCE STATISTICS

- **Age at Financial Independence:** 31 to 35
- **Annual Expenses in Retirement:** $30,000 to $50,000
- **Ideal Number of Rentals in Retirement:** 11 to 20
- **Primary Source of Retirement Income:** Business income (from blog, podcast, etc.)
- **Secondary Source of Retirement Income:** Rental properties
- **Ideal Debt Level of Real Estate Portfolio:** Between 26% to 50% loan to value

Q&A

Q: Can you explain in more detail how you built your current wealth?
I used house hacking for my first property—I bought a triplex, moved into one unit (with roommates), and rented out the other two. This brought my out-of-pocket personal housing costs to zero. After that, I bought single-family homes on a long-term buy and hold strategy. I'm using the Rental Snowball strategy—I use the cash flow from my

rentals to purchase more properties. Until now, I've acquired one property every one to two years on average.

Q: What were the biggest obstacles and setbacks during your wealth-building stage? How did you overcome or push through them?
In the beginning, my biggest obstacle was 1) believing I needed to do everything myself and my unwillingness to outsource/scale, and 2) lack of confidence. These days, my biggest obstacle is distraction.

Q: What's your No. 1 best tip for those looking to build wealth with real estate investing?
I have two tips. First, choose one niche and one strategy. Don't try to chase too many paths—just pick one and specialize there. For example, I specialize only in long-term buy and hold for residential rental properties. I intentionally decided not to foray into other fields like mobile home parks or tax liens. Narrowing my focus makes the task ahead less daunting. Second, when you're evaluating rental properties, ignore the cash-on-cash return (CoCR) and analyze rental properties solely on cap rate (the potential rate of return on the investment). CoCR is nothing more than a formula that rewards excessive debt.

Q: Can you explain in more detail your post–financial independence income? How do you plan on living off of this income?
In 2017, my rental properties produced a net income (after expenses, including PITI mortgage when applicable) of approximately $43,800. This is enough to cover my basic cost of living. However, this is not my only income. I also have a blog and podcast, and I do occasional freelance/coaching work. I enjoy this work more now that I don't have to worry about whether or not it'll pay the bills, and I don't need to "sell out" by accepting sponsored blog posts, or covering my website in Google ad banners, or doing any of those other types of things that I don't want to do.

Q: What concerns do you have for the future related to retirement income? How will you address them?

My biggest concern is that my own lifestyle tastes will escalate, and I will put myself back on the hedonistic discretionary-spending treadmill. I'd like to control that by occasionally "downscaling" into living in an RV or a camper, living in another country, etc., to remind myself that I don't need fancy things to be happy, and that voluntary simplicity is a great thing.

Q: Do you plan to start selling your real estate holdings? If so, when and how?
No, not at this time.

Q: What's your No. 1 best tip for those looking to live off of investment income after retirement/financial independence?
Buy rental properties based on cap rate. Don't worry about appreciation, and don't worry about cash-on-cash return. Just focus on the cap rate, and run the numbers as though you're outsourcing every task so that your math can be identity-agnostic.

CHAPTER 9
HOW TO INCREASE YOUR INCOME

Warren Buffett once told a classroom of Columbia business school students that he would pay $100,000 for 10 percent of their future earnings.[15] He also told them his offer meant they were each worth at least a total of $1 million dollars! Buffett's point was to remind them that their ability to produce income was an extremely valuable asset. And as a million-dollar asset, each of them should start prioritizing investments in themselves to improve their value even more.

I agree with Buffett's assessment. So my message to you in this chapter is that you're personally an extremely valuable asset. And you should prioritize investments of energy, time, and money to improve your ability to earn more income. Income isn't magic or something guaranteed by a boss or by the government. It's simply a return on *value* that you contribute to the marketplace. Therefore, if you want more income, you need to improve your ability to give value to others. This will not only improve your savings rate now, but it will be a source of inner security for the rest of your life after you reach financial independence. Here are a few of my favorite ideas to improve your ability to earn income.

Become an Expert
Our financial system tends to reward people who've gone deep in their chosen field to become experts. Medical doctors are a good example. Most doc-

---

15 "Warren Buffett's $100,000 Offer and $500,000 Advice for Columbia Business School Students," cnbc. com. Last updated March 18, 2010, www.cnbc.com/id/33891448.

tors study for at least ten years before beginning to receive large incomes. They spend four years at a university, four years in medical school, and two years at a residency. But they are rewarded with an average salary of over $200,000 on the *low* end.[16] And if a doctor continues to study and becomes an expert in a specialty field like orthopedics, she could expect to earn even more—$443,000 on average.

This principle of expertise holds in a wide variety of careers. The challenge for you is to find a skill or an area of expertise and go deep. And yes, it begins with formal education in some careers like medicine. But with information on any subject available on the internet, self-education is just as valuable and likely has a better return on investment. For example, if your business has a complicated technology system that you can study and master (on your own time), you'll make yourself much more valuable as an employee. And in a market-based system, being more valuable tends to be rewarded with more money.

Improve Your Communication Skills

During that same talk to Columbia business school students I referenced earlier,[17] Warren Buffett told the students they could improve on their $1 million value as income earners. He told them that learning communication skills would improve their value by 50 percent. That's an increase of $500,000 for one skill, as estimated by the greatest investor of all time.

Communication skills are so valuable because every type of career needs better communicators, yet few people have taken the time to improve theirs. The demand is high, and the supply is low. So all other things being equal, basic economics favor good communicators getting paid well.

I remember an example where my sister-in-law got a job at a computer software firm as an account manager for clients. She knew very little about computer software, but she has a warm, engaging, and confident communication style. The firm knew that this skill was very hard to teach, while some of the basic technical software skills could be taught over time. As a result, they hired her at a good starting salary.

To improve my own communication skills early in my career, I joined a local Toastmasters Club. Toastmasters is a network of local clubs whose

---

16 "Here's How Much Different Types of Doctors Are Paid," Fortune.com. Last updated April 4, 2016, fortune.com/2016/04/04/doctor-salaries/.

17 "Warren Buffett's $100,000 Offer and $500,000 Advice for Columbia Business School Students," cnbc.com.

sole purpose is to help its members improve their communication and public-speaking skills. The experience certainly improved my value as a real estate investor, and later as a teacher and public speaker. I also like Dale Carnegie books and courses. Warren Buffett actually started as a very awkward and ineffective communicator, but he took a Dale Carnegie course early in his career. If you see him speak in public now, he is very confident and has a down-to-earth, easy style that has been a big part of his success.

Become Invaluable Through Profound Service

I learned the term "profound service" from Steve Chandler in his book *Wealth Warrior*.[18] The basic idea is that wealth (and, in this case, income) comes back to you in direct proportion to how much service you give. That being the case, Steve encourages readers to set a standard of *profound* service.

I heard a perfect example of profound service on the BiggerPockets Money Podcast #12 with fellow real estate investor and BiggerPockets author David Greene.[19] David worked his way through college first busing tables and later as a waiter in a restaurant. He had no prior experience doing either job, but every day he looked for ways to better serve the restaurant customers, his boss, and his coworkers. For example, when he had a slow moment at his own tables, he would look for ways to help his coworkers by filling customers' water glasses or bringing something extra they needed. His profound level of service made him invaluable to everyone involved with the restaurant. As a result, he made more than $40,000 a year working part-time and actually saved $90,000 by the time he was done with college!

Profound service is an attitude and an approach to how you help people. It starts with enthusiasm and an earnest desire to serve others. When you bring that level of service to the workplace, you'll astonish those around you. And you'll earn a lot more money as a result.

Develop Real Estate Side Hustles

As a reader of this book, you are obviously already interested in real estate. So, a part-time job or small business (a side hustle) related to real estate can be a great way to increase your income. In the beginning, you can earn while

---

18 Steve Chandler. *Wealth Warrior: The Personal Prosperity Revolution*. Anna Maria, FL: Maurice Bassett, 2012.

19 "BiggerPockets Money Podcast 12: How to Become an 'Overnight' Success in 10 Short Years with David Greene." BiggerPockets.com. Last accessed on March 29, 2018, www.biggerpockets.com/renewsblog/ biggerpockets-money-podcast-12-overnight-success-10-short-years-david-greene/.

you learn. And later in your career, it's an easy way to leverage your real estate knowledge and skills into fun, part-time income generators. Here are some options:

- House flipper
- Real estate listing agent (representing sellers)
- Real estate buyers' agent (representing buyers)
- Leasing agent
- Airbnb property manager
- Property manager
- Project manager for remodels/construction
- Consultant
- Teacher
- Bookkeeper
- Handyman
- Carpenter
- Painter

Use your creativity and think of all the different skills you use as a real estate investor. I once wrote down more than twelve careers I could pursue just because I've invested in real estate for so many years.

It's also possible to turn your hobbies, involvement in the arts, teaching skills, and other interesting expertise into a side-hustle business. And you don't need to spend a lot of money up front to do it. You could start your own business. Sell a product online. If you enjoy doing it, you can make it happen.

You've now learned that a high savings rate is your foundational wealth-building tool. And you've also learned how to improve it by decreasing expenses and increasing income. But before we move on to the strategies to build wealth using real estate investing in the next chapter, let's take a look at the five wealth stages and figure out which one you're in.

—————— **PROFILE OF A REAL ESTATE EARLY RETIREE** ——————

LIZ SCHAPER

Location: San Diego, California
Chad's Favorite Quote from Liz:
*"Be bold and confident, and don't be afraid to
go your own way."*

WEALTH-BUILDING STATISTICS

- **Profession/Career:** Commercial banking
- **Income During Wealth-Building Phase:** $200,000+/year
- **How Big a Role Did Real Estate Play in Wealth-Building?** Other investing vehicles played a larger role
- **Primary Real Estate Strategy(ies):** Private lending/notes

FINANCIAL INDEPENDENCE STATISTICS

- **Age at Financial Independence:** 41 to 45
- **Annual Expenses in Retirement:** $30,000 to $50,000
- **Ideal Number of Rentals in Retirement:** Not applicable
- **Primary Source of Retirement Income:** Interest from private notes
- **Secondary Source of Retirement Income:** Dividends from public stocks
- **Ideal Debt Level of Real Estate Portfolio:** Not applicable (no debt on note portfolio)

—————— **Q&A** ——————

Q: Can you explain in more detail how you built your current wealth?
For most of the past twenty years, I built my wealth slowly but surely through stocks and bonds (mostly mutual funds). I also tended to save 50 percent or more of my income each year. However, I dabbled in one real estate vacation rental property (personal and rental use) without running the numbers to see if it made sense as an investment or not. I owned it for eleven years and sold in October 2016. In December 2014, I invested in a private equity fund that financed hard

money loans (I'm still invested in there). And in August 2015, I became an early investor in peerstreet.com, which is an online platform to invest in private lending notes. I invested the proceeds (not capital gains—just getting *part* of my investment back) from the sale of the vacation rental property into private notes with PeerStreet investors.

Q: *What were the biggest obstacles and setbacks during your wealth-building stage? How did you overcome or push through them?*
I went through a divorce and the 2008 economic meltdown simultaneously—both my personal and my financial life took an unexpected turn. There is a much more long-winded answer, but I'll touch on the high points. Lots of personal reflection, therapy, family, friends, an amazing community/neighborhood, persistence, having an infant who needed her mom to get her life together, patience, and exercise pulled me through. Despite having a lot that went wrong then, I was lucky and privileged to be employed, though my income fell to one-third of what I had made previously for a couple of years. A job opportunity came through in early 2010, which helped me stop treading water and begin to make forward progress, and ultimately enabled me to discover financial independence and pull off early retirement.

Q: *What's your No. 1 best tip for those looking to build wealth with real estate investing?*
Inadvertently, I did a live-in flip. To be honest, the townhouse was in good shape to start with, but I landscaped the yard, took down some wallpaper, and painted, and was able to sell for $220,000 more than I had purchased it for (net of real estate fees). I used that money as a down payment/renovation proceeds on my current house. This current house is in a much more central and desirable location, close to the water and to all the activities we like to do. I think if I had been more intentional about it, I might have been able to make more. But my No. 1 tip to build wealth is to live below your means and invest the difference. Eschew lifestyle inflation and spend money mindfully. I don't consider myself all that frugal, to be honest. I buy what I want, but somehow my wants are reasonable.

Q: Can you explain in more detail your post–financial independence income? How do you plan on living off of this income?

My primary income is interest from my private notes in the PeerStreet account, as well as the private equity investment (which is interest income as well). My secondary income is dividend income from my after-tax investment accounts (outside of 401(k)/IRA accounts). I don't plan on touching my retirement accounts for a long time, so I exclude those from the calculation. Tertiary source of income (as a former banker, I like having backup) are principal payments on loans in Peer-Street, but that's only if some extra unexpected expenses come up. Currently, there is still a gap between what I'm earning and what I'm spending. So I'm reinvesting the excess proceeds into their respective accounts.

Q: What concerns do you have for the future related to retirement income? How will you address them?

Sequence of returns risk (or sequence risk: The order of annual investment returns is important for retirees living off the income and capital of their investments) scares me, of course. This is why I don't want to sell any of the shares of stock and bonds in either my after-tax or retirement accounts. It's also the main reason I pursued alternative investments like private notes. My hope is that the private equity and PeerStreet private notes provide a hedge and some principal protection in a downturn. I have several notes paying back principal every month and lots of liquidity. The liquid nature of the PeerStreet notes' principal should help me make it through an economic downturn/retraction in stock prices. In theory, if the stock market falls below the historical mean, I do plan to shift some of the real estate note holdings into more shares of stock and reduce my alternative investment allocation. Of course, this is all a guess, and it's yet to be stress-tested.

Q: Do you plan to start selling your real estate holdings? If so, when and how?

I'll play my PeerStreet investment by ear. My private equity investment has a five-year commitment, so I plan to move that investment over to PeerStreet, index funds, or a combination thereof when the time comes. PeerStreet has turned out to be very liquid, and I think I'd give up some of the upside I'm getting (right now) for the flexibility. My primary residence is theoretically an investment, but I don't include it in my total assets because it's an expense to me. I don't plan on moving from San Diego, but I don't know what the future will hold. If needed, my home could always be sold for a tax-free gain down the road.

Q: What's your No. 1 best tip for those looking to live off of investment income after retirement/financial independence?
Be bold and confident, and don't be afraid to go your own way. Very few people pursue this lifestyle, so it can feel a little weird. It's OK; go for it anyway.

CHAPTER 10
THE FIVE WEALTH STAGES: WHAT'S YOURS?

It's now clear that saving a big portion of your earnings is the key to climbing faster up the mountain toward financial independence. But where are you starting from? The bottom of the mountain? Halfway up? Or near the top?

It's important to know this, because depending on where you are, some of the real estate strategies you'll learn later will make more sense than others. To help you identify your starting point, here are five wealth stages I have used to measure my own wealth-building progress.

The Five Wealth Stages

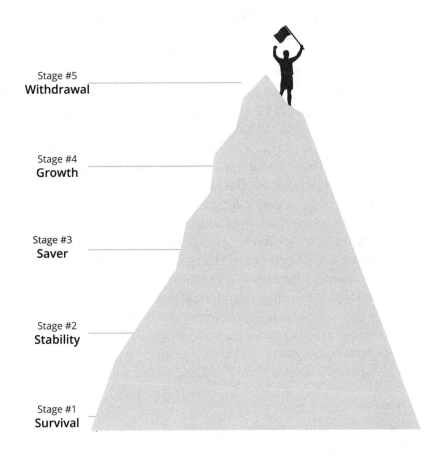

Stage #5
Withdrawal

Stage #4
Growth

Stage #3
Saver

Stage #2
Stability

Stage #1
Survival

I'll briefly explain each stage, and I'll give you examples of how real estate investing can fit into your plans.

1. Survival

This is the milestone of earning money and paying your bills. And if you're digging yourself out of financial holes of the past, you're also in survival stage. There's nothing wrong with being here. Most of us *have* been at some point. It's the place where you appreciate the basic satisfaction of supporting yourself financially. But it's not the ideal place to invest in real estate. You *need* to have extra cash instead of investing it into real estate. True investing starts at a later stage.

2. Stability

This is the stage where you move past survival and begin getting a financial cushion. Financial teacher Dave Ramsey suggests a series of baby steps:[20] build a cash emergency fund and pay off personal debts like credit cards, car loans, and student loans. And on the income side, you build marketable skills and lasting business relationships that give you more job security.

At this point, instead of sitting on the edge of a financial cliff, you've moved away from crisis mode. You have fewer debts pulling you down, and you can begin looking toward growth. But you're still not a true investor yet. Why? Because you don't have a lot of excess cash to invest or to provide a cushion in case of emergency. You still need to work on earning and saving more money.

Some of you at this stage may feel comfortable enough to begin the starter wealth-building plans in Part 4. But for many others at this stage, getting started with real estate could mean a full- or part-time job in the industry, or becoming a renter. For example, you could get your real estate license to learn the business as a buyer's or seller's agent. Or you could use your license to become a "bird dog" and find deals for other investors in exchange for a fee. This is how I began investing. You could also lease a house or an apartment and sublease bedrooms in order to reduce your housing bill. You'll need to negotiate what's called a master lease agreement from your landlord to do that. The point is that you need a career, not an investment vehicle, at this stage. If you can make money while learning real estate, even better.

3. Saver

This is the stage where you fully implement the power of your savings rate. Below-average wealth builders save 0–10 percent of their income, but above-average wealth-builders save 25 percent, 50 percent, and even 75 percent of what they bring in. By doing this, you accelerate your path to financial independence.

You increase your savings rate by maximizing your income with pay raises and side hustles (part-time businesses or jobs). And you simultaneously decrease your spending by reducing the big expenses: Maximizing

---

20 daveramsey.com/baby-steps.

contributions to tax-deductible retirement accounts allows you to reduce your income tax bill. And using real estate investing for your home reduces or even eliminates your housing expenses.

For example, you could "hack your housing" by renting out spare bedrooms, a basement apartment, or living in one unit of a small multi-unit building. This could reduce your housing costs and increase your savings rate as a result. You could also buy a modest home that needs repairs and move into it. After fixing it up and living there a couple of years, you could move out and keep it as a rental. I call this a "live-in-then-rent." Or you could resell (aka "flip") your residence after living there two or more years. As I'm writing this in 2018, the profit from these "live-in flips" can be kept tax-free up to $250,000 for an individual and $500,000 for a couple.

In Part 4, on starter real estate wealth-building strategies, I'll go into much more detail about how to use house hacking, live-in-then-rent, and live-in flips to jump-start your savings and your wealth-building.

4. Growth

This is the stage most of us think of as investing. It's taking your $50,000 nest egg and turning it into $1,000,000. The key to success with growth is maximizing compounding. You've got to earn solid returns on your savings, not touch those returns, and reinvest them wisely and with discipline.

In addition to the strategies I suggested in Stage 3, Saver, now you could also begin buying rentals or maybe start a real estate house-flipping business. Because you've learned to be a saver, you now have capital to invest either as down payments or to buy properties for cash. This is the perfect time to begin some of the real estate wealth-building strategies, like:

- The Rental Debt Snowball Plan
- The Buy and Hold Plan
- The Trade-Up Plan

I'll share examples of these plans in the section on primary real estate wealth-building strategies, Part 5, The Climb.

5. Withdrawal

This is the stage when you already have a large chunk of wealth (that is, equity). You may have built this equity from various sources, including a business, stocks, a 401(k) account, or previous real estate investments. You now want to begin withdrawing income from your wealth so that you can enjoy the fruits of your wealth-building labor. At this stage, you'll probably prioritize investing with less hassle, less risk, and more passive income.

Many of the same basic real estate strategies that worked to build wealth can work in the withdrawal stage. But the approach to using these strategies can be quite different. For example, I recommend a decent chunk of your rental portfolio be free and clear of debt at this stage. It increases your income, reduces your risk, and simplifies your life.

If you're approaching age 59.5, you can also begin taking out income from retirement accounts penalty-free. But even if you're not 59.5, you can continue growing your retirement accounts and perhaps do a Roth conversion to move more of your money into tax-free Roth IRAs before you reach age 70.5 and minimum required distributions.

I'll go into much more detail about the withdrawal phase in Part 6 on strategies to withdraw an unending supply of early retirement income.

For now, my main point in explaining the five wealth stages is that you need to have an idea of *your* stage first before you choose specific real estate strategies in the next chapters. If you just blindly start choosing strategies, you may find yourself wandering down the wrong path for years. And that could lead to frustration at best or financial disaster at worst.

So, which of the five wealth stages resonates most with you? Write down *the* one, and keep your stage in mind as we move on to the ultimate real estate wealth-building strategies.

———— PROFILE OF A REAL ESTATE EARLY RETIREE ————

SETH WILLIAMS

REtipster (retipster.com)
Location: Grand Rapids, Michigan
Chad's Favorite Quote from Seth:
"My single greatest asset has been my ability to find great deals on good properties ... that was where my business started to take off."

WEALTH-BUILDING STATISTICS

- **Profession/Career:** Commercial banking (wife was a CPA)

- **Income During Wealth-Building Phase:** $200,000+/year
- **How Big a Role Did Real Estate Play in Wealth-Building?** Equally important as other investing vehicles (stocks, bonds, businesses, etc.)
- **Primary Real Estate Strategy(ies):** Long-term rentals, land flipping, self-directed IRA (real estate, private notes, nontraditional assets)

FINANCIAL INDEPENDENCE STATISTICS
- **Age at Financial Independence:** 31 to 35
- **Annual Expenses in Retirement:** $75,000 to $100,000
- **Ideal Number of Rentals in Retirement:** 50+
- **Primary Source of Retirement Income:** Business income
- **Secondary Source of Retirement Income:** Rental properties

———————— Q&A ————————

Q: Can you explain in more detail how you built your current wealth?
My first successful real estate business was land investing. With the ability to buy land at a very low price and sell it quickly without taking on any debt in the process, I was able to generate large sums of cash, much faster than my day job could offer.

Once this business was sustainable, I decided to start funneling some of my profits into buying long-term rentals (because of the tax advantages, the diversification, and the long-term cash flow they would provide). Since my rentals were all managed by a property manager, that business didn't require much of my time or energy, and I could continue running my land business.

I then decided to start blogging at retipster.com , where I talk about my lessons and experiences with both land and rental properties, and I've been able to find opportunities to monetize that website as well.

Q: What were the biggest obstacles and setbacks during your wealth-building stage? How did you overcome or push through them?
In my land investing business, the biggest obstacles tend to come up when I'm trying to enter a new market for the first time. Figuring out

what offer prices will gain traction and how to get properties sold quickly usually starts with some preliminary research, then some educated guessing, and then some tweaking based on the results. Every market is different, and every market can work if the variables are dialed in just right, but it always takes time and patience to figure out those details. Sometimes, the desired results come about very quickly; occasionally, it takes more time and patience.

In my rental property business, the biggest challenge is managing my property manager. Since the manager is doing most of the hands-on work, my job as a landlord is significantly easier, but I still need to pay attention and monitor what's happening with my properties. Picking the right property manager is a big decision, and when you're working with a good one, they'll make everything easier. But every property manager requires oversight and must be accountable.

Q: What's your No. 1 best tip for those looking to build wealth with real estate investing?

Like any business, real estate investing is complex. There are a lot of things that need to be done right in order to be successful and profitable. However, for me, my single greatest asset has been an ability to find great deals on good properties. When I figured out where and how to find an endless supply of highly motivated sellers, that was the real turning point for my business starting to take off. When I'm able to acquire a property with tons of free equity, every other subsequent step usually falls in place without too much trouble.

It all starts with finding the right property at the right price (and luckily, there are many ways to find them). Figure out the best acquisition strategy for you and get to work! Every time you buy a good property, at a great price, from a highly motivated seller, you'll be writing yourself a massive future paycheck.

Q: Can you explain in more detail your post–financial independence income? How do you plan on living off of this income?

Part of what I love about my land investing business is that it's very feasible to generate a full-time (or larger) income while working at it on a part-time basis. My land business has always been a part-time gig that leaves room for me to do other things, which has been helpful in allowing me to diversify into rental properties and to pursue my blogging endeavors, among other things.

My rental property business is still relatively small, but my long-term plan is to continue growing this portfolio and making it a larger operation. It currently consists of multifamily residential properties, but I'd like to branch out into other types of less-conventional income-producing real estate, like self-storage facilities and farmland—preferably, areas that generate more income with less of an ongoing need for maintenance and upkeep.

Q: What concerns do you have for the future related to retirement income? How will you address them?
My greatest concern for any of my businesses is that one or more of them will become obsolete (for some unforeseen reason) or that the market will become overly saturated. However, after working these businesses for so many years, I've found that the fears are largely unfounded—at least for the immediate future. Nevertheless, this is part of why I've put so much effort into diversification and staying active in several different business ventures that are largely unrelated to one another. If one ever does start to lag (or if I just decide to retire from one of them altogether), it's OK, because my financial well-being isn't solely dependent on any one business.

Q: Do you plan to start selling your real estate holdings? If so, when and how?
My land business is always a revolving door of properties that I buy and sell. So yes, the plan is always to sell each property as soon as possible.

With every rental property I buy, the plan is to hold it for at least the foreseeable future. However, depending on the economics and opportunities that change with time, I'm not opposed to the idea of doing a 1031 exchange and redirecting my investment into larger properties, or perhaps moving into different types of properties that make more sense for my long-term direction.

Q: What's your No. 1 best tip for those looking to live off of investment income after retirement/financial independence?

When it comes to your personal living expenses, remember that frugality and simplicity are your friends. You don't need to be a millionaire to be financially free. You just need your sources of income to exceed your cost of living—and the less expensive your lifestyle is, the more options you'll have to retire early.

Financial freedom is *extremely* valuable, and in my opinion, it's easy to say no to a few unnecessary luxuries if it means I can choose how to spend my time each day (not to mention, the more free time I have, the more opportunities I'll have to create additional sources of income). If you're willing to make some small sacrifices, and you intentionally follow your action plan for building up independent sources of income, you might be surprised at how attainable it actually is.

PART 4
THE FIRST STEPS

Starter Real Estate
Wealth-Building Plans

*In preparing for battle I have always found that
plans are useless, but planning is indispensable.*

—DWIGHT D. EISENHOWER

In Parts 4 and 5, I will explain a menu of the best wealth-building real estate plans. Think of these plans as tools in your climbing backpack. Certain tools will work better than others in particular situations. For example, Part 4 is all about starter plans like house hacking, live-in-then-rent, live-in-flips, and BRRRR. Feel free to skip these starter plans and jump straight into Part 5 and the primary wealth-building plans if that's more useful for you at your stage.

Just remember that wherever you start, the tools work best when used *together* or *in sequence*. I will explain each strategy separately, as if it is a path by itself up the mountain. But in reality, the optimal path for you is usually a mix.

Veteran investor and one of the best real estate retirement minds I know, Jeff Brown, calls this "synergistic investing" because the tools complement and improve one another. This synergy will help you reach the top of the financial mountain with the best results.

Your job, then, is simply to learn about the wealth-building tools and identify the one or two plans that resonate the most with your situation *right now*. Don't fall into the trap of letting all the options overwhelm you.

Just choose one, get in motion, and *do something* to move forward. The purpose of a plan is to give you structure and direction. But once you're in motion, it's OK to adjust. And to help in that adjustment, you can seek the advice of mentors, colleagues, and professionals. And you can always refer back to this book as a guide as often as you need to. Now let's get started!

CHAPTER 11
THE HOUSE HACKING PLAN

The first real estate wealth-building plan I'll cover, the House Hacking Plan, is one of the most popular and effective strategies to get started in real estate. And there is no real estate topic that I evangelize and promote more than house hacking. For some of you, this may be the only strategy you need to make great strides toward financial independence.

House hacking simply means that you live in a residence that can also produce income. Although the concept has been around for a long time, the term was coined by an awesome real estate early retiree and fellow Bigger-Pockets author, Brandon Turner (see his Real Estate Early Retiree Profile at the end of Chapter 14).

I had my first experience with house hacking when I was still in my mid-twenties. I bought a fourplex apartment building, and I lived in one unit while renting out the other three (I'll share more details later in this chapter). The rent from the other three units paid all of my housing expenses for several years. It was a beautiful thing.

But a house hack doesn't have to be *that* good financially to be worthwhile. And there are other variations on the strategy. Here are ideas for property types you could use for a house hack:

Creative Use of Properties for House Hacking
- Duplex (two-unit) — one extra rental unit
- Triplex (three-unit) — two extra rental units
- Fourplex (four-unit) — three extra rental units

- House with a small extra rental unit (like a basement or garage apartment)
- House with spare bedrooms to rent, long-term or short-term (like Airbnb)
- House with extra land (and appropriate zoning) for RV or mobile home lot rentals
- House with space (and appropriate zoning) to rent parking
- *Rent* a house or an apartment and sublease extra bedrooms (with landlord's permission)

The main point is to think outside the box to generate income from your residence. When you do, there are a large number of benefits.

Intro

The first benefit of house hacking, as I've already said, is that it reduces your current housing expense. And as you learned in Part 3, on the fundamentals of wealth-building, cutting your housing expense is one of the best ways to increase savings and build wealth. Because housing is likely a *substantial* percentage of your total expenses, house hacking alone can supercharge your savings and wealth-building efforts.

And while house hacking to save money makes sense anywhere, it can be especially helpful if you are in higher-priced markets. House hacking may be an essential strategy just to keep you above water financially. In addition to saving money on your personal housing bill, house hacking also has several additional key benefits:

BENEFITS OF THE HOUSE HACKING PLAN	
Owner-occupied financing	Financing for a property you *occupy* is much easier to get than a pure investment property. As an occupant, you also receive the best terms possible, like low interest rates that are fixed for a long period of time (20 or 30 years).
Keep your mortgage	You also get to keep this attractive financing if you choose to move out later and keep the house hack as a rental.
Small down payment is possible	Some owner occupant loan programs have the smallest down payment requirements in all of real estate. For example, as a veteran you can purchase a house hack property with 0 percent down! And everyone else can use FHA and other owner-occupant loan programs with 3.5 percent to 10 percent down payments.
Learn how to manage properties	With house hacking, you live in the property while learning to manage it. Everyone makes mistakes while learning, but it's easier to recover when you're on site and personally involved.
Smooth transition to rentals	When you live in a property, you get to know it well. You also get to know the type of tenants your property attracts. So, once you move out, you will have an increased comfort level with the property, and as a landlord with your tenants. And with your low-interest loan, you'll likely also make the best possible cash flow from the property once it's fully rented.

Now that you know the basics of house hacking, let me show you an example with real numbers using my first fourplex.

My First House Hack—Merry Christmas to You

When I graduated from college and began investing in real estate, I lived in the cheapest situations possible. The first year, I lived at home with my parents. The second year, I crashed in the spare bedroom of my business partner's house. And eventually I had enough financial stability to go out on my own.

But I liked the idea of living for free! So, the house hack was my chosen strategy to get started on my own. Once I began looking for properties, a friend told me about a vacant foreclosed fourplex building. I went by to take a look and realized it needed *a lot* of fixing up. It was nasty!

In fact, I knew this property was nasty before I even got out of the car. When I looked through my car's windshield, I saw a friendly message greeting me in big letters across the entire second floor: "Merry Christmas"!

It didn't get any better inside. The walls had dark brown paneling, orange 1970s carpet, and wonderful aromas greeting me around every corner. I even found a chalk outline of a body in one of the living rooms. I can just imagine the reaction of the bankers who had foreclosed on this property the first time they inspected it. I bet they didn't even get out of the car.

But I knew my market. And the location was in a college town not far from campus. I thought it had potential. Plus, I follow the mantra of most experienced real estate investors that *the uglier and smellier the property, the better!* So I bought this nasty little fourplex, and I gave it some love. It became a wonderful home that actually *paid* me to live there. Here are the details after I turned it around and an "after" shot of the property.

The Fourplex Results After Some TLC (Tender Loving Care)

The property was in such bad condition before that it would never attract good tenants. I used a combination of financing from a local bank and a private money lender to fund my purchase plus about $45,000 in repairs and upgrades.

The repair work included four new central heating and air-conditioning units (plus new ductwork), replacement windows, exterior paint, landscaping, a community garden, dishwashers, interior paint, new lighting/fans, new back decks, and new floor coverings.

About six months later, the building was fully occupied and looking good. I then refinanced it with a low-interest thirty-year mortgage. And because I had improved the value of the building to $160,000, my new loan at 75 percent of the new value fully covered most of my funds from the purchase, remodel, and refinance of the property.

After the refinance, I had spent very little cash out of my pocket. This refinance technique actually has a name, the BRRRR strategy (Buy, Rehab, Rent, Refinance, Repeat), which I'll go over in detail later. The numbers looked like this:

REFINANCE OF MY HOUSE HACK	TOTAL
Purchase Price	-$70,000
Repairs	-$45,000
Holding/Closing Costs	-$6,500
Total Investment	**$121,500**
New Value After Improvements	$160,000
Refinance Loan @ 75% Loan to Value	$120,000
Cash Out of Pocket	**$1,500**

I realize that those of you reading this will have risk tolerance all over the map. Some of you will think my house hacking deal with only $1,500 cash out of pocket was awesome. Others will think refinancing and only having a small down payment is risky.

But whether you would refinance it exactly the same or differently, the main point is that I owned a property that basically paid me to live in it. Here are the rental income numbers after the refinance:

RENTAL INCOME	UNIT #1	UNIT #2	UNIT #3	UNIT #4	TOTAL
Rent/Month	$400	(my unit)	$400	$400	**$1,200**
2.5% Vacancy Reserve	-$20	n/a	-$20	-$20	**-$60**
Property Taxes/Month	-	-$162	-	-	**-$162**
Insurance/Month	-	-$50	-	-	**-$50**
Maintenance/Month	-$50	-$50	-$50	-$50	**-$200**
Business License/Month	-	-$5	-	-	**-$5**
Net Operating Income (NOI)/Month					**$723**
Mortgage Payment (Principal & Interest)		-$758			-$758
House Hacking Cash Flow/Month					**-$35**
House Hacking Cash Flow/Year					**-$420**

After all was said and done, my cost to live in this building every month was less than what most people pay for their internet! It was a very comfortable living arrangement that allowed me to save cash and build wealth for other real estate deals.

And I loved living in unit #2 of my own little apartment building. It was cozy and efficient, and I found tenant neighbors who also valued living there. Not too long after, I got married, and this was the first home for my wife and me in our first few years of marriage.

Now please understand that not all house hacking deals will be this good financially. It really depends on your market, your financing, and your ability to find very good deals. But the *concept* of using rental income to reduce or eliminate your housing expense works just about everywhere. And as I did, you can keep the property *and* the financing as a rental investment when you eventually move out.

The best part about house hacking is its flexibility with your big-picture wealth-building plan. Let's take a look at a few ideas of how you could transition after doing your first house hack.

The Next Steps After Your First House Hack

I shared an example of living in my house hack. But it doesn't stop there, does it? There are many interesting directions you could go after living in your house hack for a period of time.

For example, think about what would happen if you repeated the House Hack Plan three times. Using my fourplex example, after three properties you would own twelve rental units. And let's say it took you eight years to buy, renovate, rent, and repeat with those three properties.

After eight years, you could move into a regular house and stop house hacking. But if you bought the three house hack properties correctly, you'd now have solid rentals with positive cash flow. And that means they would make a solid investment for many years to come.

From there, you could just hold the rentals to see what happens. Or you could apply one of the other real estate wealth-building plans I'll share later in this section in order to accelerate your path to financial independence.

For example, you could begin saving and applying your excess cash flow and personal savings to one of the mortgages. If you do this strategically, you could quickly "snowball" the debt payoff on these properties. In many cases, within eight to twelve years you could have all the debt on the properties paid off. At that point, you'd own twelve rental units producing a lot of cash flow that you could live off of forever! See Chapter 15 on the Rental Debt Snowball Plan if that interests you.

In addition, you could take it one step further after house hacking and do what I did. After I finished my first house hack with the fourplex, I transitioned to a single-family house. But I didn't stop my wealth-building plan. I used the next house for the Live-In-Then-Rent Plan. I'll explain that next.

─────────── PROFILE OF A REAL ESTATE EARLY RETIREE ───────────

DREW N.
Guy on Fire (guyonfire.us)
Location: Washington, D.C.
Chad's Favorite Quote from Drew:
"Learn to love the business or move on to something else."

WEALTH-BUILDING STATISTICS
- **Profession/Career:** Commercial real estate, property management, rentals
- **Income During Wealth-Building Phase:** $100,000 to $149,999/year
- **How Big a Role Did Real Estate Play in Wealth-Building?** Primary vehicle
- **Primary Real Estate Strategy(ies):** Long-term rentals, rental debt snowball, 1031 tax-free exchange

FINANCIAL INDEPENDENCE STATISTICS
- **Age at Financial Independence:** 26 to 30
- **Annual Expenses in Retirement:** $30,000 to $50,000
- **Ideal Number of Rentals in Retirement:** 6 to 10
- **Primary Source of Retirement Income:** Rental income
- **Secondary Source of Retirement Income:** Interest from bonds, dividends from public stocks/equities, periodic sale of stocks/equities
- **Ideal Debt Level of Real Estate Portfolio:** 51% to 75% loan to value

—————— **Q&A** ——————

Q: Can you explain in more detail how you built your current wealth?
I am a firm believer in the long-term buy and hold strategy. After graduating college, I was fortunate enough to land an entry-level job as an analyst. Equally as fortuitous, I lived with my parents for a few months. During this time, I saved almost 100 percent of the income from my job.

Being young, hungry, and full of energy, I also had several side hustles. I lived off the income provided by these side gigs. After a few months of aggressive saving, I purchased a three-bedroom/two-bathroom house with a Federal Housing Administration (FHA) loan, which had a 3.5 percent down payment. I house hacked by renting out the extra rooms to two friends. Their rent largely subsidized my mortgage, and I basically lived for free. This was a great living arrangement, but I also wanted to own real estate that provided positive cash flow every month.

This desire led to my purchasing an old, run-down row home in a gentrifying neighborhood. The property required a complete gut renovation, but was worth the time and money. I rented out the four extra rooms, lived in the smallest room, and made a profit every month.

Four years of house hacking and aggressive savings allowed me to build a net worth of more than $500,000 and buy two additional rental properties. The cash flow from all my properties is likely enough for me to live on.

Q: What were the biggest obstacles and setbacks during your wealth-building stage? How did you overcome or push through them?
Saving up for a down payment is always a challenge for young investors. I was fortunate enough to live at home for a few months, which helped. Working side jobs also helped.

Q: What's your No. 1 best tip for those looking to build wealth with real estate investing?
Get a mentor. Learn from their mistakes. Learn to love the business or move on to something else.

Q: Can you explain in more detail your post-financial independence income? How do you plan on living off of this income?

Rental income will make up a large portion of my FI/retirement income. I will also diversify my income with dividends from brokerage accounts.

Q: What concerns do you have for the future related to retirement income? How will you address them?

I plan to have three years of living expenses in cash. This should get me through any downturns in the stock market, any major repair, or vacancy. During this time, I will not need the income generated by my stocks or rental property portfolio.

Q: Do you plan to start selling your real estate holdings? If so, when and how?

No.

Q: What's your No. 1 best tip for those looking to live off of investment income after retirement/financial independence?

I have not lived off of my investment income yet—but it is wise to leave some margin for error and have a safety net.

CHAPTER 12
THE LIVE-IN-THEN-RENT PLAN

I do love house hacking, but I know it's not for everyone. And that's OK. Because there is another plan that is very similar called the Live-In-Then-Rent Plan. It works like this:

THE 4 STEPS OF THE LIVE-IN-THEN-RENT PLAN

1. Move into a house
2. Live there for a reasonable time (1–2 years or more) while fixing the property up to be an ideal rental
3. Move out and keep the house as a rental with positive cash flow
4. Repeat (if desired)

This is the exact plan my wife and I used when we moved out of our house hack fourplex. We decided a small house would be better for us as we began to expand our family and have kids. But we still wanted the benefits of building wealth and using our home as an investment. As we did with house hacking, we moved into a house that we planned to someday keep as a rental. But unlike house hacking, we didn't rent part of our residence while we lived in it.

I love this plan because it has many of the same benefits as house hacking while also giving you more privacy and flexibility. Here are just a few of the benefits:

BENEFITS OF THE LIVE-IN-THEN-RENT PLAN	
Owner-occupied financing	Financing is easier to obtain, and you get better terms than with rental property financing.
Keep your mortgage	Most mortgages can stay on the property after you move out and begin renting. Just be sure you initially make it your residence and live there a reasonable length of time. And always be up front with your mortgage lender that renting may be part of your future plans.
Good rental locations	If you want to live there, it's also likely to be attractive to potential tenants.
Cost-effectively fix up the property	You have time while living there to save money by doing repairs yourself (if you want) and shopping patiently for materials.
Thoughtfully make rental improvements	While living in the property, you will notice repairs that will make the property a better rental, for instance, low-maintenance floor coverings.
Flexibility	You can stay in the house a short time, a long time, or even move back in later. The house is an asset you can always fall back on as a place to live.

But keep in mind that not just any house will bring you the benefits of the Live-In-Then-Rent Plan. A fancy 3,000-square-foot dream home likely won't work. Big, expensive, luxury homes do not make great rentals. A live-in-then-rent house should be low-maintenance, durable, and economically viable as an investment.

As with any other plan, you have to be strategic. You have to think ahead with your location, your type of house, your repairs, and your financing. But when it all comes together, you get the benefit of a nice place to live that can grow into a future investment.

Now let's look at an example of the Live-In-Then-Rent Plan to show you some realistic numbers.

Example of the Live-In-Then-Rent Plan

Let's say a young couple, Justin and Sarah, just got married, and after a year of renting they're ready to buy a house. But instead of following the herd to purchase a fancy new house, they want an older house they can fix up and eventually turn into a rental. They find a neighborhood they like. It has a lot of older houses with a mix of rentals and longtime owner occupants. It's near some hotter areas of town, but it hasn't become as popular yet.

They hire a real estate agent to help them do a search, and eventually they come across a single-family house that has promise. It's a one-story, 1,500-square-foot ranch-style house with brick siding. It has two bedrooms and 1.5 baths, but there seems to be space to turn an old dining room into a third bedroom. The half bath could be expanded to a full bath by adding a shower. There are hardwood floors under the 1970s carpeting, and the kitchen, bath, and cosmetics, in general, need updating. But Justin and Sarah love the setting, the yard, and potential for the house as a home and a future rental. The asking price is $125,000. The house is an estate sale, which means the owners inherited it when someone passed away. It's currently vacant.

Justin and Sarah know the house needs work, and they have cash saved up to do $10,000 to $15,000 in repairs. And they also run numbers as if they are going to rent the house (because eventually they will). They talk to a property manager in their agent's office, and she says the house could someday rent for between $1,350 and $1,450/month if they turn it into a three-bedroom, two-bath.

Justin and Sarah work backward from this rent and deduct all the likely rental expenses such as taxes, insurance, maintenance, capital expenses, management, and vacancy. They feel comfortable with a price of $115,000 because the net operating income as a rental could cover the mortgage plus give them about $100/month in positive cash flow.

They offer $115,000. After a negotiation, both sides agree to $120,000 if the seller pays most of the buyer's closing costs for an FHA loan.

The purchase costs look like this:

LIVE-IN-THEN-RENT HOUSE PURCHASE	
Purchase Price	$120,000
Buyer Closing Costs Out of Pocket	$1,000
Down Payment (3.5 percent)	$4,200
Loan (5 percent interest, 30-yr.)	$115,800
Total Cash Out of Pocket	**$5,200**

But the up-front cash isn't the entire story. After moving in, Justin and Sarah have a big remodel project list. Over the next year, they do much of the work themselves with the help of friends and family. They also hire out some of the work, like installing a new shower in the half bath, installing granite counters, and refinishing the hardwood floors.

When the dust settles, they have spent about $10,000 on materials and labor. But their old house has been transformed into an attractive, comfortable, low-maintenance place to live. It now has three bedrooms, two baths, hardwood floors, tile bathrooms, an updated kitchen with granite counters and tile floors, and wonderful landscaping and curb appeal.

Next Steps to a Live-In-Then-Rent Plan

Justin and Sarah enjoy the house for a second year, but they have their eye on another vacant fixer-upper house in the neighborhood that is very similar to their current one. They send a letter to the owners expressing their interest. After the owners call back, Justin and Sarah get to know them better and eventually make an offer to buy. The offer is accepted, and they make another move into a new house.

They quickly rent their original house for $1,400 a month to a highly qualified tenant. Here is what the income on the house looks like after it's rented:

LIVE-IN-THEN-RENT HOUSE RENTAL INCOME	
Gross Rent/Month	$1,400
Operating Expenses/Month (vacancy, tax, insurance, management, maintenance, capital expenses)	-$600
Net Operating Income (NOI)/Month:	**$800**
Mortgage Payment (Principal/Interest/PMI insurance)/Month	-$700
Net Income After Financing/Month	**$100**
Net Income After Financing/Year	**$1,200**

So, with Justin and Sarah's new fixer-upper, they start the entire process all over again. They work on fixing up the house, making it a nice place to live, and preparing it to be a rental someday.

If they're ambitious and have a vision, Justin and Sarah could do the same thing a couple more times. In the end, they'd have four solid rental houses with long-term financing and positive cash flow.

What would they do next? Well, they could use one of the primary wealth-building plans I'll discuss a little later, such as the Rental Debt Snowball, Buy and Hold, or Trade-Up Plan. But it will really depend on their overall early retirement plans, which is why I dedicated so much time to that subject earlier in the book.

But no matter what they choose after, the main point of the Live-In-Then-Rent Plan is that it got them started with investing. In this plan, you build a solid foundation with your property and with your financing. And if you work hard for five to ten years, you could set yourself up and be well on the way to your financial independence goals.

Let's take a look at one more plan to use your residence to build wealth. It's called the Live-In-Flip Plan.

————— PROFILE OF A REAL ESTATE EARLY RETIREE —————

TONY CRUMPTON
Tiger Solutions, LLC
Location: Clemson, South Carolina
Chad's Favorite Quote from Tony:
"Grind and hustle on a daily basis. Early bird gets the worm. Stop talking the talk and do it."

WEALTH-BUILDING STATISTICS
- **Profession/Career:** Sports writing; spouse, occupational therapist
- **Income During Wealth-Building Phase:** $150,000 to $199,999/ year
- **How Big a Role Did Real Estate Play in Wealth-Building?** Equally as important as other vehicles (stocks, bonds, etc.)
- **Primary Real Estate Strategy(ies):** Long-term rentals

FINANCIAL INDEPENDENCE STATISTICS
- **Age at Financial Independence:** 36 to 40
- **Annual Expenses in Retirement:** $30,000 to $50,000
- **Ideal Number of Rentals in Retirement:** 11 to 20

- **Primary Source of Retirement Income:** Business income
- **Secondary Source of Retirement Income:** Rental properties, interest from CDs, Social Security income, side hustles/part-time work
- **Ideal Debt Level of Real Estate Portfolio:** Zero percent—own everything free and clear

Q&A

Q: Can you explain in more detail how you built your current wealth?
I started with a mind-set that I wasn't excited about an average 9-to-5 job. I have an autoimmune disease called ulcerative colitis, and a normal job was not what I wanted for my life. In high school and college, I sold thousands of items on eBay and went to a local swap meet to find items to flip for a profit. This early lesson (pre–real estate) showed me the value of hard work while getting up early, out-hustling other people to find deals, the importance of negotiating so you could buy items at a low cost to sell for a profit, and analyzing the numbers on potential deals.

After graduating from a top 25 public college, instead of getting a high-paying computer science job, I managed a run-down trailer park. I learned real estate lessons on picking the right tenant, building rapport with my tenants, and learning about the myriad of repair issues and the value of a skilled, reliable, and honest handyman. After cutting my teeth with the trailer park, I bought several properties from tax sales over the years. I have rented several of them, and I have also purchased a few nicer properties in the town where I live. Everything is paid off free and clear on the properties, including my primary residence.

Q: What were the biggest obstacles and setbacks during your wealth-building stage? How did you overcome or push through them?
My biggest obstacle was tuning out the naysayers who didn't understand why I wasn't getting a "9-to-5 job" like they had. Once I genuinely didn't care what others thought about the details of my life, I was free and able to get to work on making a life the way that I wanted for my family and me.

Another obstacle was spreading myself too thin with different revenue streams: my web work among multiple websites, real estate investing and management, eBay selling, home hacking with a basement rental, etc. In the past few years, I have hired a property manager to help with the day-to-day management, started working with a trustworthy financial adviser, and hired a talented CPA to help me with my taxes and overall business structure.

Q: What's your No. 1 best tip for those looking to build wealth with real estate investing?
Honestly, I wouldn't buy old millhouses in dangerous areas, because it's just a road of misery for a lot of property managers (including myself!). You need a decent rental to attract a respectable tenant who won't trash your property. I know a low price seems exciting, but the headaches are usually not worth it. Try to find single-family homes in decent areas that you would live in. Walk around different neighborhoods and understand what is actually happening in the areas and talk to people there. Reach out to those who know more than you in real estate and find a mentor like Coach Carson.

In day-to-day living, stop buying so much junk and invest your money instead. The quicker you get your (or your spouse's) spending under control, the sooner you can live life every day without as much stress.

Q: Can you explain in more detail your post–financial independence income? How do you plan on living off of this income?
On a daily basis, I plan to work on my website and be involved in real estate until I don't have the passion for it anymore. However, I think I am fortunate to be able to do this, so I have no plans on stopping anytime soon. I don't really think the real estate story is over for me, and I hope to do several more deals in the future.

Q: What concerns do you have for the future related to retirement income? How will you address them?
My wife and I aren't crazy spenders, so I think we will be fine.

Q: Do you plan to start selling your real estate holdings? If so, when and how?

I have no intention of selling any property, but if the market gets extremely hot, I would be naive not to think about it. Moving away from the area might be one reason I would sell some properties.

Q: What's your No. 1 best tip for those looking to live off of investment income after retirement/financial independence?

Grind and hustle on a daily basis. Early bird gets the worm. Stop talking the talk and do it.

CHAPTER 13
THE LIVE-IN FLIP PLAN

Turning a residence into a rental is the core strategy of the prior two plans. But rentals are not the only way to make money in real estate. You can also flip (that is, resell for a profit) your residence using something called the Live-In Flip Plan. Here's how it works:

THE 4 STEPS OF THE LIVE-IN FLIP PLAN

1. Move into a house with potential for repairs that will increase the value
2. Live there 2 of the last 5 years
3. Sell and earn tax-free profits
4. Repeat

This strategy takes advantage of a tax law that rewards owner occupants who stay in a home for two years or more. The reward is that you don't pay federal income tax on the gain (on the profit) when you resell the house for more than you invested. There are some limits, and there are basic rules to follow. For example, U.S. laws, as of 2018, limit tax-free gains to $250,000 for an individual and $500,000 for a couple filing taxes jointly. I recommend you read more at the IRS website to stay up-to-date with any changes.

Tax-free gains of that size are a *big* deal when you're building wealth. Compounding your profits (that is, reinvesting them from one property to the next) grows your wealth faster than almost any other method. Therefore, this strategy is an enormous wealth-building lever if you use it well.

My friends Carl and Mindy are bloggers at 1500days.com (you can see their Real Estate Early Retiree Profile at the end of this chapter). And they used the Live-In Flip Plan successfully by flipping five houses, paying no taxes, and earning more than $400,000 in the process. This chunk of money early in their career became the nest egg that eventually grew into more than $1,200,000 and allowed them to retire early in their forties. This stuff works if you apply it correctly!

Here are some of the benefits of the Live-In Flip Plan.

BENEFITS OF THE LIVE-IN FLIP PLAN	
Tax-free compounding	Tax-free profits are rare, so this is a big benefit that allows you to compound and grow your net worth quicker.
Lower risk than normal house flips	The flipping you see on TV shows is speculative. The house is vacant and the investors *must* sell before expenses eat them alive. With a live-in flip, you are living there (you have to live somewhere), which gives you patience and flexibility.
Cost-effectively fix up the property	You have time while living there to save money by doing repairs yourself (if you like) and shopping patiently for materials. Some repairs must be done by licensed contractors. Check with your local municipality.
Thoughtfully make improvements	During your two-year waiting period, you can thoughtfully line up the improvements that will help the house sell for top dollar.
Flexibility	You don't *have* to sell. You could stay there longer. You could also turn it into a rental (aka Live-In-Then-Rent). The choice is yours.

As with the other plans, the Live-In Flip Plan has tips and strategies that can make or break your success. Here are a few of the top tips I received from Carl at 1500days.com:

- Buy the ugliest home in a nice neighborhood.
- Focus on homes that are cosmetically ugly, but structurally sound.
- Do some of the work yourself (if possible) to make more profit.
- Learn new skills from friends, family, free classes at the big-box home improvement stores, and YouTube videos.
- Focus on one or two high-value skills, like installing tile and cabinets.
- Know when to hire a job out, such as putting up rough sheetrock, installing HVAC, and doing big concrete jobs.
- Have fun! Add your touches and character to a job—that's what makes your home stand out.

Now let me share an example of how this could work to build wealth over about six to seven years.

Example of the Live-In Flip Plan

Rich and April are friends of our other couple, Justin and Sarah. They like the idea of building wealth with their residence, but the Live-In Flip Plan appeals to them more than rentals. They want to live in a bigger house, and the rent does not make as much sense given the prices in their area.

Like Justin and Sarah, Rich and April begin by studying their market. They find the fringe neighborhoods on the cusp of being more popular. These older neighborhoods are turning over to younger owners who are willing to invest time and money to make them like-new again.

After a month of searching with the help of a real estate agent, they find their cosmetic fixer-upper property that needs some love. The house is 2,000 square feet with 3 bedrooms and 1.5 baths. It was built in 1982, and few things have been updated since then. The asking price is $225,000, but they end up buying it for $200,000. The purchase numbers for House #1 look like this:

PURCHASE — LIVE-IN FLIP HOUSE #1	
Purchase Price	-$200,000
Buyer Closing Costs	-$3,000
Down Payment (20%)	-$40,000
Loan (4.5% interest, 30-yr.)	$160,000
Reserves for Repairs/Materials	-$30,000
Total Cash Out of Pocket	**$73,000**

Rich and April work hard and carefully spend their repair money during the first two years in the house. But they also enjoy living in a vibrant, up-and-coming neighborhood. They even make friends with others nearby and take turns at one another's houses for painting and pizza parties.

And as they get close to the end of the two-year time frame, they keep their eyes out in the neighborhood for their next purchase. They find a very similar property (House #2), which has been rented by a landlord for a long time and needs improvements. After talking with the owner, they negotiate a purchase price of $215,000 (the neighborhood is appreciating). The owner also gives them sixty days to close on the purchase.

So just around two years from the original purchase, House #1 is spotless and looks ready to sell. April has obtained her real estate license and with the help of her broker, she puts the house on the market at $300,000. Several buyers view it right away, and they negotiate a purchase contract with one at the full asking price of $300,000. The final net proceeds from the sale of House #1 look like this:

RESALE — LIVE-IN FLIP HOUSE #1	
Sales Price	$300,000
Commissions/Closing Costs (5%)	-$15,000
Mortgage Payoff	-$154,500
Total Cash Proceeds	$130,500

Rich and April celebrate for a moment and take a deep breath after the closing. But then five minutes later they sit down to close and purchase House #2. And they have a hectic afternoon moving their stuff from one house to the next (with another pizza party for their friends who help). The purchase numbers for House #2 look like this:

PURCHASE — LIVE-IN FLIP HOUSE #2	
Purchase Price	-$215,000
Buyer Closing Costs	-$4,000
Down Payment	-$50,000
Loan (4.5% interest, 30-yr.)	$165,000
Reserves for Repairs/Materials	-$35,000
Total Cash Invested	$89,000
Excess Cash Available ($130,500–$89,000)	$41,500

I'll fast-forward the story a little because this two-year period is very much like the last one. They find another similar fixer-upper (House #3) to buy before they sell this one. And at the end, Rich and April get House #2 beautiful and put it on the market. The overall market has appreciated at about 3 percent a year. So although House #2 is similar to House #1, which they sold for $300,000 two years earlier, House #2 is now worth about $320,000.

Here are the numbers from the sale of House #2:

RESALE — LIVE-IN FLIP HOUSE #2	
Sales Price	$320,000
Commissions/Closing Costs (5%)	-$16,000
Mortgage Payoff	-$159,000
Total Cash Proceeds	**$145,000**
Total Cash, Including $41,500 Reserve	**$186,500**

I'm going to pause the story here for a moment because this is a very interesting place. It's only been four years since Rich and April began. Yes, there have been some hassles. And yes, they've had to work hard. But after their second flip, they're sitting on $186,500 in cash, they owe nothing in taxes, and they began with $73,000.

How hard would you have to work at a second job or overtime to generate an extra $113,500 in *after tax* money over four years? Or would it even be possible? Live-in flips synergize the benefit of a side job, your residence, and efficient tax strategy.

Now back to the story. Let's finish their journey with the purchase and then resale of House #3.

PURCHASE — LIVE-IN FLIP HOUSE #3	
Purchase Price	-$230,000
Buyer Closing Costs	-$4,500
Down Payment	-$60,000
Loan (4.5% interest, 30-yr.)	$170,000
Reserves for Repairs/Materials	-$40,000
Total Cash Invested	**$104,500**
Excess Cash Available ($186,500–$104,500)	**$82,000**

In order to simplify their situation (and my math!), I'm going to assume Rich and April decide to take a sabbatical or mini-retirement and not buy another house after they sell House #3. My personal favorite way to celebrate after six years of hard work is a nice mini-retirement trip for six to twelve months! So, after two years owning House #3, here are the sales numbers:

RESALE — LIVE-IN FLIP HOUSE #3	
Sales Price	$340,000
Commissions/Closing Costs (5%)	-$17,000
Mortgage Payoff	-$164,000
Total Cash Proceeds	**$159,000**
Total Cash, Including $82,000 Reserve	**$241,000**

Rich and April are sitting on $241,000 cash after beginning with $73,000 six years earlier! Let's look at some potential next steps for Rich and April and their big cash nest egg.

Next Steps of the Live-In Flip Plan

In a nutshell, the Live-In Flip Plan allows you to build a nest egg more quickly by taking advantage of favorable tax laws and your ability to improve a house's value. After six or seven years, you may be like Rich and April with

$241,000 or more in your bank account. But what do you do next?

Because you have that cash in the bank, all sorts of options are available. You could invest it outside of real estate in assets like stocks or index funds. This is what my friends Carl and Mindy did to grow to a net worth of more than $1,200,000. But you could also move to one of the primary wealth-building plans that I'll cover in Part 5.

For example, you could use the money as down payments on multiple rental houses. Or you could just pay cash for a smaller number of rental houses. This initial capital can be the momentum that keeps your wealth-building plans moving. And just as important, you will have learned a lot about remodeling, buying properties, financing, and tracking the market. You're no longer a rookie! You could begin flipping houses as a business. And you can proceed with these next steps with much more confidence.

Now let's move beyond strategies that use your residence to something called the BRRRR Plan. This is a strategy that helps you buy multiple rental properties without needing a full down payment for each one.

———— PROFILE OF A REAL ESTATE EARLY RETIREE ————

MINDY AND CARL JENSEN

1500 Days to Freedom (1500days.com)
And *How to Sell Your Home* by Mindy Jensen
Location: Longmont, Colorado
Chad's Favorite Quote from Mindy and Carl:
"Louis Pasteur said, 'Fortune favors the prepared mind.' This is incredibly true in real estate investing."

WEALTH-BUILDING STATISTICS
- **Profession/Career:** Stay-at-home mom, computer programmer, respectively
- **Income During Wealth-Building Phase:** $100,000 to 149,999/year
- **How Big a Role Did Real Estate Play in Wealth-Building?** Equally important as other strategies
- **Primary Real Estate Strategy(ies):** Live-in flips, self-directed retirement account with real estate investments

FINANCIAL INDEPENDENCE STATISTICS

- **Age at Financial Independence:** 41 to 45
- **Annual Expenses in Retirement:** $30,000 to $50,000
- **Ideal Number of Rentals in Retirement:** 2 to 5
- **Primary Source of Retirement Income:** Side hustle/business or part-time work
- **Secondary Source of Retirement Income:** Interest from private notes
- **Ideal Debt Level of Real Estate Portfolio:** 26% to 50% loan to value

Q&A

Q: Can you explain in more detail how you built your current wealth?
My wife and I built the core of our nest egg with live-in flips. It all started when we fixed up a small home that we lived in right after we were married. To our surprise, we made $100,000 in profit from the sale. We decided that we'd repeat the process, so we looked for outdated but structurally sound homes. We would install new tile, hang modern cabinetry, and replace the pink toilets and tubs. After two years, we'd sell and start another project.

One wonderful aspect of this strategy is that if you live in the flip for at least two years, you probably won't pay any taxes on the gains. See IRS 2-out-of-5-year rule for more information.

Q: What were the biggest obstacles and setbacks during your wealth-building stage? How did you overcome or push through them?
We did most of the work ourselves, which was overwhelming at times. We had full-time jobs, so we'd come home from work and then put on tool belts and switch to construction mode. We had almost no free hours in the day. It was a lot of hard work, but it was always worth it when we got the big check at the end. When times were hard, we'd focus on the payoff.

Q: What's your No. 1 best tip for those looking to build wealth with real estate investing?

There are many ways to invest in real estate, including flipping, renting, and investing in deals with others. The common thread is that you must do your research. Unless you buy a REIT (real estate investment trust), no form of real estate investing is passive. This shouldn't scare you, though. Real estate can be rewarding and lucrative for the investor who puts in the time. Read books, study the markets you're interested in, and find a mentor.

Louis Pasteur said, "Fortune favors the prepared mind." This is incredibly true in real estate investing.

Q: Can you explain in more detail your post–financial independence income? How do you plan on living off of this income?
Our investment portfolio is split between the stock market and real estate. On the stock market side, we have index funds and individual stocks (I don't advocate this, but I used to buy them when I was younger). On the real estate side, we are invested in a trailer park, syndication deals, and private loans. The stock market investments are growth-oriented while the real estate is income and growth.

We'll draw down our investments with whatever is appropriate, given market conditions. For example, stock valuations are unreliable, so if we needed money now, we'd sell those. However, if the stock market were to have a big correction, we might choose to live off of income from the real estate.

Q: What concerns do you have for the future related to retirement income? How will you address them?
It's amazing to consider what humans accomplished in the twentieth century. We went from riding on horses to landing on the moon. But the advances in the twenty-first century will be even greater and will happen at a faster pace.

Technologies like artificial intelligence (AI), autonomous vehicles, and CRISPR (a form of genomic editing) will remake society. What will happen to us when AI can do our jobs? These changes will affect the stock market and real estate in ways that we don't understand and can't predict. The best insurance is to attain financial independence and always remain flexible.

Q: Do you plan to start selling your real estate holdings? If so, when and how?

I like Warren Buffett's quote: "My favorite holding period is forever." My syndication deals have an end date, but I hope to hold our trailer park for decades.

Q: What's your No. 1 best tip for those looking to live off of investment income after retirement/financial independence?

Be flexible and frugal. If the stock market crashes or your apartment building burns down the day after you retire, tighten your finances, get a roommate, or start renting your car out on a sharing site. Flexibility ensures that you'll be able to adapt when times get tough. And if you're frugal, it doesn't take much to move the financial needle, so just a short-term side hustle may get you through a hard time.

Also, stop worrying. Everything is going to be all right.

CHAPTER 14
THE BRRRR PLAN

In the chapters that follow, I will show you various wealth-building plans that use rental properties. But one of the limitations of all these plans is that when you run out of cash for down payments, you're stuck. No more new purchases for a while. But the BRRRR Plan can help you with that by recycling your up-front cash. That makes it very useful both if you're starting your wealth building or if you're trying to conserve cash for whatever reason.

BRRRR stands for buy, rehab, rent, refinance, repeat. Like flipping houses, it's all about finding fixer-upper properties, rehabbing them, and increasing their value. This could be a single-family house or multi-unit apartments. But instead of selling, you keep the property as a rental and refinance to pull out some or all of your cash.

This is a technique that many investors have used for a long time (myself included), but my friend and fellow BiggerPockets author Brandon Turner was kind enough to name it several years ago so that we could all remember it. Here's the BRRRR Plan:

THE 5 STEPS OF THE BRRRR PLAN	
B	Buy a property that has potential to increase its value with repairs. Typically, you'll use short-term purchase financing, like cash, a line of credit, private money, or hard money.
R	Rehab the property to increase its value and make it rentable.
R	Rent the property to a quality tenant (or tenants).
R	Refinance using a long-term mortgage.
R	Repeat (if desired).

This plan is most useful when you're trying to grow your rental portfolio rather quickly, but you don't have enough cash for down payments and repairs on multiple properties. By *carefully* refinancing to pull out your cash, you can recycle the funds and buy several properties in a row. Let me show you an example of the BRRRR Plan in action so that you can see how it works.

Example of the BRRRR Plan

Do you remember my fourplex from the House Hacking Plan? The property was *definitely* a fixer-upper, but I used BRRRR to pull out my cash and secure a long-term loan on the property.

When I bought the fourplex, I used a combination of a local bank commercial loan, private money, and my own funds. Then, after it was repaired, I rented out three of the units and moved into the fourth. After a seasoning period (typically six months, but it depends on who does the refinance loan), I then refinanced the property to pay off the lenders and recoup my personal funds.

The essential part of this strategy is using both short-term and long-term financing. Short-term funds are great for moving quickly to capture a good deal without all the normal hassles of mortgage loans. Long-term mortgage financing has the best interest rates, payments, and terms so that you can rent the property more profitably.

Here's what the refinance numbers looked like in my case:

REFINANCE OF FOURPLEX	TOTAL
Purchase Price	-$70,000
Repairs	-$45,000
Holding/Closing Costs	-$6,500
Total Investment	**$121,500**
New Value After Improvements	$160,000
Refinance Loan @ 75% Loan to Value	$120,000
Cash Out of Pocket	**$1,500**

How many deals could you do with $1,500 out of pocket? The answer is a lot! The practical limitation for most investors is when your mortgage lender cuts you off for new refinance loans at five to ten properties. This number fluctuates, depending upon policy from mega mortgage companies like Fannie Mae and Freddie Mac.

If you want to keep growing beyond that number of properties, you'll have to switch plans or switch your financing source to commercial loans or private lenders, or simply pay off your loans before buying more (see the Rental Debt Snowball Plan).

But as you'll see in some of the rental plans that follow, five to ten rental properties may be all you need to accomplish your financial goals. And even for those who want more properties, the BRRRR Plan is a great jump-start to the rest of your wealth-building plans.

Now let's move from the starter wealth-building plans to the primary wealth-building plans. As I said earlier, in real life many of these plans work together synergistically. But in general, these next plans are for those of you in the growth phase of your wealth-building journey. You've built savings, you're financially stable, and you're ready to accelerate your progress toward an early retirement. We'll start with a useful strategy to build wealth and end up with free-and-clear, cash-flowing rental properties in a relatively short period of time. It's called the Rental Debt Snowball Plan.

—————— PROFILE OF A REAL ESTATE EARLY RETIREE ——————

BRANDON TURNER
BiggerPockets.com
Author of *The Book on Rental Property Investing*
Location: Montesano, Washington
Chad's Favorite Quote from Brandon:
*"From the beginning, I've had two goals in mind: collect
cash-flowing units and scale."*

WEALTH-BUILDING STATISTICS

- **Profession/Career:** Banker (like, at a branch ... not a glamorous job); wife was a barista
- **Income During Wealth-Building Phase:** $50,000 to $74,999/year
- **How Big a Role Did Real Estate Play in Wealth-Building?** Primary vehicle
- **Primary Real Estate Strategy(ies):** Long-term and short-term hold rentals, fix-and-flip, rental debt snowball, 1031 tax-free exchange, live-in flip, private lending/notes, apartment syndications

FINANCIAL INDEPENDENCE STATISTICS

- **Age at Financial Independence:** 26 to 30
- **Annual Expenses in Retirement:** $75,000 to $100,000
- **Ideal Number of Rentals in Retirement:** 50+
- **Primary Source of Retirement Income:** Privately owned business
- **Secondary Source of Retirement Income:** Rentals, private note interest, side hustles
- **Ideal Debt Level of Real Estate Portfolio:** Between 51% to 75%

——————— Q&A ———————

Q: Can you explain in more detail how you built your current wealth?
I've been slowly building my rental portfolio for 11 years now. I started with a single-family house, then bought a duplex, some more singles/small multi, and eventually a 24-unit. Recently, after some addi-

tional smaller purchases, I sold the 24-unit and did a 1031 exchange into a couple more properties (another 24-unit and a 46-unit mobile home park). From the beginning, I've had two goals in mind: collect cash-flowing units and scale. In other words, I didn't want to buy units linearly, like one per year; I wanted to buy exponentially (one, two, five, ten, twenty). More or less, I've done this. I'm at ninety-six units now.

Q: What were the biggest obstacles and setbacks during your wealth-building stage? How did you overcome or push through them?
Learning to buy the right deals was the toughest thing for me. I could always find something to buy, but not always the *right* thing. I could always find the financing, but not every property is worth buying. What helped was regularly sitting down and asking myself: *What am I trying to do, and why am I trying to do it?* These two questions helped me to reframe what I was doing, to step back and look at the big picture. I still struggle here, but I've gotten a lot better.

Q: What's your No. 1 best tip for those looking to build wealth with real estate investing?
Learn how to analyze deals. Everything else is secondary, in my opinion.

Q: Can you explain in more detail your post–financial independence income? How do you plan on living off of this income?
I make decent income from rentals, and if I had to live off that income, I could. But instead, I "recycle" that money and I live off other income, primarily from my job at BiggerPockets, book sales, and the occasional house flip.

Q: What concerns do you have for the future related to retirement income? How will you address them?
The market could crash, people could stop buying my books, I could quit my job. But I'm not really worried about much of this, because I've diversified my income streams in so many ways, and I have thirty-year fixed mortgages on most of my properties. I also believe that if the market does crash, it's going to hurt the bottom 50 percent of

landlords a lot more than the top 50 percent ... so I just need to be one of the best at filling vacancies.

Q: Do you plan to start selling your real estate holdings? If so, when and how?
Yes, I sell when I know I can buy something that gets me a higher return *and* is easier to handle.

Q: What's your No. 1 best tip for those looking to live off of investment income after retirement/financial independence?
Make sure you have a lot more investment income coming in than you think you need. The market is really good right now, and rents are high. This won't always be the case.

PART 5
THE CLIMB

---

*The Primary Real Estate
Wealth-Building Plans*

CHAPTER 15
THE RENTAL DEBT SNOWBALL PLAN

The Rental Debt Snowball Plan is a way to relatively quickly own a free-and-clear (that is, no debt) portfolio of rental properties that produces enough income to cover some or all of your financial independence number. The mechanism that makes this plan work is simple: Reinvest all your net rental income into debt paydown. But when this simple concept is applied strategically as part of an overall financial independence plan, the results are very powerful.

Here is how the plan works in six steps:

THE 6 STEPS OF THE RENTAL DEBT SNOWBALL PLAN

1. Save cash for down payments.
2. Purchase several income properties using conservative, low-interest loans (or buy and then refinance, like in the BRRRR Plan).
3. Save 100 percent of the net rental income, plus add in extra savings from a job.
4. Use all savings and apply that cash toward *one* of the loans each month until that loan is paid off early.
5. Use all savings, plus new free-and-clear income, to apply toward another loan until it's paid off early (this is where the snowball starts rolling faster).
6. Repeat until all loans are paid off.

The power of this strategy is concentrated savings. The alternative is spreading extra savings over several different loans. But doing that takes much longer to actually get one loan paid off. With the Rental Debt Snowball Plan, you get a property paid off quickly and then add in that extra cash flow to the next loan. As this happens over and over, the snowball effect gets stronger and stronger, resulting in steady, progressively faster equity buildup. It's very satisfying psychologically, and it's quite effective as an early retirement plan. Here is an example of the Rental Debt Snowball Plan in action.

Example of the Rental Debt Snowball Plan

Let's say you want to end up with three properties free and clear. You could do as many properties as you want, of course, but this will keep the math simple as an illustration. You decide to buy easy-to-manage duplexes in good locations. Your target properties might be those with two-bedroom, two-bath apartments in a walkable location close to parks, coffee shops, and local attractions.

Let's say each apartment rents for $750, and the entire duplex rents for $1,500. After subtracting $600 in operating expenses (taxes, insurance, management, maintenance, capital expenses, vacancy), which does not include your mortgage payment, your net operating income will be $900 per month.

Since you have good credit, you plan to put 20 percent down and get a 5 percent, 30-year mortgage. You then work hard and, during one year, you buy all three investment properties for the same price (remember, I'm keeping it simple to illustrate!). Here are the numbers:

CASH INVESTED	DUPLEX #1	DUPLEX #2	DUPLEX #3
Purchase Price	-$150,000	-$150,000	-$150,000
Loan (Debt)	$120,000	$120,000	$120,000
20% Down Payment	-$30,000	-$30,000	-$30,000
Closing/Holding Costs	-$5,000	-$5,000	-$5,000
TOTAL CASH	-$35,000	-$35,000	-$35,000

To purchase these three duplexes, you needed $105,000 cash and good credit. If that much cash seems beyond your reach, reread the earlier chapter on the BRRRR Plan. It's an approach you can combine with the Rental Debt Snowball Plan in order to use less up-front cash out of pocket. But back to this deal. Here is what your positive cash flow would look like once you get all three properties rented:

POSITIVE CASH FLOW	DUPLEX #1	DUPLEX #2	DUPLEX #3	TOTAL
Net Operating Income (NOI)/Month	$900	$900	$900	**$2,700**
Mortgage Payment/ Month	-$644	-$644	-$644	**-$1,932**
Cash Flow/Month	$256	$256	$256	**$768**

As you can see, your rentals produce $768 per month in positive cash flow. Because depreciation will likely shelter most of your income from tax while you still have mortgages, I am not considering income taxes yet. But that is something you will need to calculate in real life. I also assume you can save an extra $1,000 per month from a job or other income source in order to accelerate your plan.

The Amazing Momentum of Debt Snowballs

The main point is to snowball your mortgages (that is, pay them off faster and faster over time) by eliminating one mortgage as quickly as possible, and then the next, and the next. To do this snowball, you use every bit of the positive cash flow and extra savings to make an extra-large monthly payment on one mortgage. Here is what that would look like in this case:

+$768 ... positive cash flow from rentals
+$1,000 ... extra savings from job
+$644 ... regular mortgage payment (Loan for Duplex #1)
= $2,412 per month ... extra-large mortgage payment

This massive extra payment begins the snowball. Each time a mortgage is paid off, the additional savings are then added to the next loan—the snowball gets bigger and bigger. How fast does your debt snowball accumulate in this case? Take a look at this infographic for the big picture.

The Rental Debt Snowball Plan

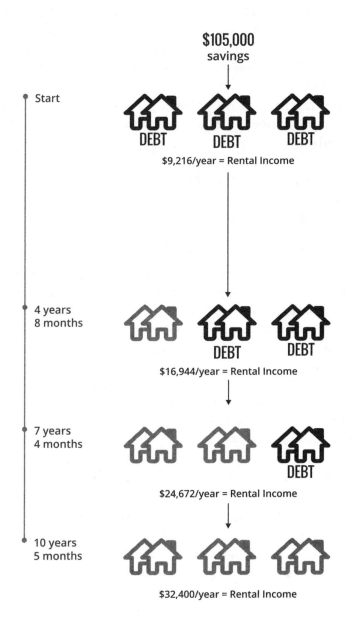

$105,000
savings

Start

DEBT   DEBT   DEBT

$9,216/year = Rental Income

4 years
8 months

DEBT   DEBT

$16,944/year = Rental Income

7 years
4 months

DEBT

$24,672/year = Rental Income

10 years
5 months

$32,400/year = Rental Income

So, in a total of ten years and five months (125 months), you own your three duplexes free and clear of any debt. This means all $2,700/month or $32,400 per year of net operating income from the rentals goes into your bank account. You have essentially started with a $105,000 investment, added $1,000/month for 125 months ($125,000), and ended up with $32,400 per year of income for life (or more, as rents could have increased during those ten-plus years). And this amount of money from free-and-clear properties can make a steady, consistent income stream that allows you to retire early or reach one of the other milestones, like a mini-retirement or semi-retirement.

Pretty exciting, isn't it? And if $32,400 per year is not enough, you can buy more properties in the beginning, buy more properties at the end, or use other non-real estate strategies to fill the income gap.

Benefits of the Rental Debt Snowball Plan

No plan is perfect. But, I think you'll find that the Rental Debt Snowball Plan has several big benefits.

Benefit #1: Control

Success with a Rental Debt Snowball Plan does not depend upon inflation, luck, speculation, or a Wall Street expert. What does it depend upon?

- Buying good properties, up front.
- Financing with good loans, up front.
- Remaining a disciplined saver for longer than a decade.

These can all be accomplished with a little education, focus, and soul-searching.

Benefit #2: Visible, Measurable, and Steady Progress

The progress you make in the Rental Debt Snowball Plan is visible, measurable, and steady. You can literally track your progress month by month as you pay off your mortgages. Each chunk that is taken out of your mortgage is one step closer to your end goal. The psychological benefit of this visible progress is *enormous*.

Personal finance teacher Dave Ramsey often says that success with money is 80 percent behavior and only 20 percent math. In other words, you are not a robot, no matter how rational and intelligent you think you are. Visible and measurable progress (especially for long-term goals) gives you a little reward that reinforces the message: "You're on your way. Keep going!"

And while appreciation of real estate, or even stock and index funds, can also give you visible and measurable feedback, the prices often roller-coaster up or down and unsettle even the most self-disciplined of us. Instead, progress with the Rental Debt Snowball Plan is steady and gets better and better over time.

Benefit #3: Flexibility
Real life is unpredictable, and your plans should be flexible to reflect that reality. The Rental Debt Snowball Plan can be slowed or stopped as needed. If you hit a major job crisis that cuts your extra savings, you can temporarily hold off on the full snowball until you get back on your feet. You will actually continue making progress, just a little slower.

You are also flexible on deciding how many or how few properties you want in the end. A bigger portfolio of free-and-clear properties will require more cash and more time invested, but you'll have a bigger cash flow in the end. The decision all goes back to your destination, your financial independence number, and how big a part real estate investing will play in your plans.

Now that you've seen the benefits of using a debt snowball to get rentals free and clear, let's take a look at a similar alternative plan for those who don't want to use any debt in the first place. Even though this next plan is more conservative, you'll see that it functions very well and can still meet your financial independence goals.

The All-Cash Rental Plan
This plan is more conservative than the Rental Debt Snowball Plan because it involves no debt from the start. But the end result is still the same: a portfolio of free-and-clear properties. And the primary mechanism is also the same: reinvesting 100 percent of net rental income. Because this variation on the Rental Debt Snowball Plan is so simple, it actually reminds me of the championship strategy used by National Football League Hall of Fame coach Vince Lombardi.

Coach Lombardi's team, the Green Bay Packers, ran two basic plays on offense—a sweep left and a sweep right. The sweep play is as simple as it gets in football. His players would practice these two plays over and over and *over*! They became sick of the endless and boring repetition. But you can probably guess what happened. His players executed these simple plays to perfection and won championships.

Just as the football players did, I have found that simple, conservative real estate plans executed consistently and with discipline will often outperform more debt-filled, "intelligent" plans. This doesn't mean you should never use debt in real estate (I have in my business). But if a no-debt approach appeals to you, then just go execute it to perfection and win your financial independence!

The All-Cash Rental Plan works like this:

THE 4 STEPS OF THE ALL-CASH RENTAL PLAN

1. Save enough cash to buy one income property.
2. Save 100 percent of the rental income, plus extra savings from a job.
3. Buy another income property.
4. Repeat until your goal for free-and-clear properties is met.

Sounds simple, doesn't it? But will simple work? Let's see.

Example of the All-Cash Rental Plan

Like we did in the Rental Debt Snowball Plan, in this example I'll use duplexes. But these properties will be a little lower priced. First, you save up $100,000 cash. This might come from your impressive savings rate and high earnings from a job. It could also come from selling other assets, like stocks or other real estate. Next, you buy a duplex that needs some repair work. The purchase numbers look like this:

DUPLEX #1 — PURCHASE	
Purchase Price	$80,000
Remodel/Holding/Closing Costs	$20,000
Total Investment	**$100,000**

The income on the property after remodeling and renting looks like this:

DUPLEX #1 — RENTAL INCOME	
Gross Rent/Month	$1,200
Operating Expense/Month (vacancy, tax, insurance, management, maintenance, capital expenses)	-$500
Net Operating Income (NOI)/Month	$700
Net Operating Income(NOI)/Year	**$8,400**
Income Tax (assume 25% rate and some depreciation shelter)	-$1,373
Net Rental Income After Tax/Year	**$7,027**

The duplex in this example gives you $7,027 in after-tax cash flow per year. I also assume that you can save $12,000 per year from your job or another source. So, each year you'll accumulate a total of about $19,000 in cash that you can save for the next purchase (I rounded down to make math easier).

After about five years, four months, you'll have another $100,000 saved. This means you can now buy Duplex #2 for $100,000. Yes, I know prices could go up over that time. But they could also go down or stay flat. And if rents go up, you could also get more than $19,000 a year. So, to keep the math simple and let you focus on the concept, I'm just keeping prices the same.

The purchase numbers for Duplex #2 look like this:

DUPLEX #2 — PURCHASE	
Purchase Price	$80,000
Remodel/Holding/Closing Costs	$20,000
Total Investment	**$100,000**

Now that you own two rentals, your rental income looks like this:

RENTAL INCOME — 2 DUPLEXES	DUPLEX #1	DUPLEX #2	TOTAL
Gross Rent/Month	$1,200	$1,200	$2,400
Operating Expense/Month (vacancy, tax, insurance, management, maintenance, capital expenses)	-$500	-$500	-$1,000
Net Operating Income (NOI)/Month	$700	$700	$1,400
Net Operating Income(NOI)/Year	**$8,400**	**$8,400**	**$16,800**
Income Tax (assume 25% rate)	-$1,373	-$1,373	-$2,746
Net Rental Income After Tax/Year	**$7,027**	**$7,027**	**$14,054**

You now receive $14,054 in after-tax rental cash flow per year. I also assume that you continue to save $12,000 a year from your job or another source. You'll now accumulate a total of $26,054 in cash per year. And after another three years, eleven months (nine years, three months after starting), you'll have another $100,000 saved. So you buy Duplex #3.

If this plan seems to start slowly, it's because it does! But the pattern keeps going on and on, and the money accumulates faster and faster over time.

The Overall Results of the All-Cash Rental Plan

If you want to see the big picture using the same assumptions, in just under fifteen years (fourteen years, ten months) you would own five duplexes (ten units) that produce more than $35,000 per year in net after-tax rent, free and clear of any debt! You began with $100,000 cash, and you contributed an extra $180,000 over fifteen years for a total investment of $280,000. Here is an infographic that shows the entire plan over time and the financial results:

The All-Cash Rental Plan

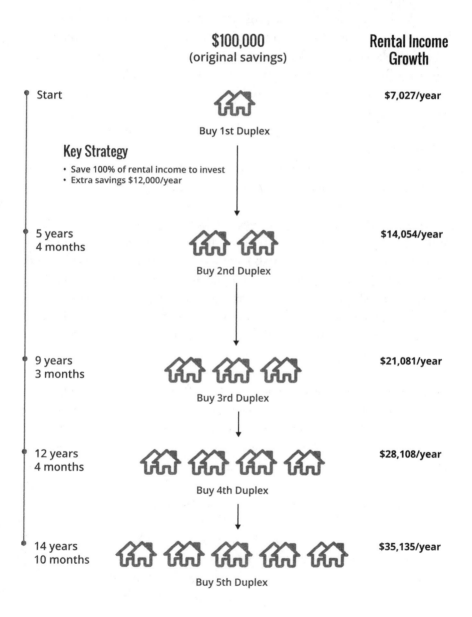

$100,000
(original savings)

Rental Income Growth

Start — Buy 1st Duplex — $7,027/year

Key Strategy
- Save 100% of rental income to invest
- Extra savings $12,000/year

5 years 4 months — Buy 2nd Duplex — $14,054/year

9 years 3 months — Buy 3rd Duplex — $21,081/year

12 years 4 months — Buy 4th Duplex — $28,108/year

14 years 10 months — Buy 5th Duplex — $35,135/year

In terms of building a safe retirement income, these are solid results. And I like that this plan depends primarily upon your ability to do three things:

1. Save money.
2. Purchase good deals.
3. Manage a small number of properties (or hire a manager).

I acknowledge No. 1 and No. 2 will not always be easy. But are you looking for easy or achievable? The point is that your results, in this plan and in the others, are largely dependent on your efforts up front. It's that control and positive influence on your investment success that attracted you to real estate in the first place, right? We'll leave the "easy," completely passive, no-hard-work paths to others.

Objections to the All-Cash Rental Plan

There are four primary objections that I have heard in the past when discussing the All-Cash Rental Plan. I will try to address them here.

Objection #1: "I can't find these great deals in my area."
You might say that these deals have incredible cash flow numbers, but you'll never be able to find any like that. I agree that the numbers are very good, yet in the right markets, these types of deals can be found consistently. If you are in a high-priced market where you're unlikely to find these kinds of deals, you can just go buy in other markets. But remember the principle still works, even with different numbers and higher prices. The timetable just might be a little longer.

Objection #2: "I don't have enough cash. It will take too long to get started."
My first response is patience. If you don't have enough cash yet, you have an earning and savings problem, not an investing problem. That was exactly why I began this part of the book with the importance of your savings rate. However, if you want to use the All-Cash Rental Plan earlier, you might consider thinking outside the box.

Do you have a big chunk of savings in an IRA or a 401(k)? These types of accounts can be self-directed to buy real estate. Although I personally prefer to lend money from my retirement account to reduce risk and hassle, you can also buy rentals. And the rent would compound tax-free. You may also be able to partner with someone else. If you have $50,000 and another person has $50,000, together you could buy the property in the example.

Objection #3: Debt leverage is a good thing, especially if we have inflation.
Yes, using debt leverage and owning more properties can be a solid hedge to future inflation. For example, if our economy experiences inflation (which it has and likely will continue to), then paying back debt in the future will be with cheaper dollars. This benefits you as the borrower. And there is nothing quite as financially beautiful to me as having a fixed major expense for decades (interest) while my primary source of income increases (rent). The growing spread between income and expense can make you wealthy.

But just because this is an attractive scenario does not mean the All-Cash Rental Plan is somehow flawed. Free-and-clear rental properties *also* benefit from inflation if their rent and prices go up, but it's just not as magnified as with leveraged properties. Last I checked, if a plan actually *works* and gets someone to early retirement safely, that's a good thing. Half the battle is finding a plan *you* are comfortable with so that you can stick with it. If you're comfortable with the lower-risk approach of no debt, then go for it.

Objection #4: What if there are good deals available and I haven't finished saving money?
To me, this is probably the most relevant objection. Waiting until you have enough cash could cause you to miss some good buying opportunities. For example, what if your five years of saving for Duplex #2 is in years like 2008–2013? You would miss out on some of the best buying opportunities of a lifetime.

If you find yourself in a situation where you have more real estate deals available than you have money, you may want to consider using safe leverage (long-term mortgage, fixed interest, good cash flow) and then shifting to something like the Rental Debt Snowball Plan to pay the debt off quickly. You could also find a partner. I would rather have 50 percent of something than zero percent of nothing.

Now that you've seen the benefits of the Rental Debt Snowball Plan and its cousin, the All-Cash Rental Plan, let's move on to one of the most common strategies to build wealth with rental properties: the Buy and Hold Plan.

RICHARD CAREY

Rich on Money (richonmoney.com)
Location: Seoul, South Korea
Chad's Favorite Quote from Richard:
"Don't buy unless you have the cash flow. Appreciation may or may not happen."

WEALTH-BUILDING STATISTICS

- **Profession/Career:** U.S. Military
- **Income During Wealth-Building Phase:** $50,000 to $74,999/year
- **How Big a Role Did Real Estate Play in Wealth-Building?** Primary Role
- **Primary Real Estate Strategy(ies):** Long-term buy and hold

FINANCIAL INDEPENDENCE STATISTICS

- **Age at Financial Independence:** 41 to 45
- **Annual Expenses in Retirement:** $75,000 to $100,000
- **Ideal Number of Rentals in Retirement:** 20 to 50
- **Primary Source of Retirement Income:** Rental income
- **Secondary Source of Retirement Income:** Pension (military)
- **Ideal Debt Level of Real Estate Portfolio:** None—own everything free and clear

—————— Q&A ——————

Q: Can you explain in more detail how you built your current wealth?
I got started by living frugally and saving money up. I had the cash for my first down payment, enough cash to finance a few fix-and-flips, and plenty of cash saved up when it came time to buy rental properties. My approach evolved as I made mistakes and figured things out. I'm in the military, so I move every two to three years. I started off buying my primary residence in Washington, D.C.—a townhouse for $280,000 in 2003. I tried to buy a second property but couldn't find any good deals. Prices were rising too fast. So I also did a flip of new construction

property. This means I bought before construction started and then flipped it as a new property when construction finished. I thought I would make a fortune, but it was the peak of the bubble, and I barely got away with a couple thousand for my trouble. I then flipped six houses in D.C. with a partner while I lived in Japan. This was mostly successful. Then I bought a few houses with cash in Alabama and made them long-term rentals. I realized this was making good money, so I sold my D.C. property and bought more Alabama rentals.

These rentals are single-family homes that I buy and fix up for about $50,000, and rent out for about $900 a month. I stuck with this long-term buy and hold rental plan to build most of my wealth.

Q: What were the biggest obstacles and setbacks during your wealth-building stage? How did you overcome or push through them?
I wasn't local with the properties, since I was moving every two to three years and going overseas for my job. I solved this by using very competent property managers local to my properties. I also had a fear of making a financial mistake that would ruin me. I pressed through the fear, overcame some significant obstacles, made it work, and learned a ton in the process.

Q: What's your No. 1 best tip for those looking to build wealth with real estate investing?
Don't buy unless you have the cash flow. Appreciation may or may not happen. And don't jump on the bandwagon. When I flipped new construction in D.C., it was because others had been flipping new construction for years and making a fortune. The belief that would continue is naïve.

Q: Can you explain in more detail your post–financial independence income? How do you plan on living off of this income?
My twenty rental properties are all paid off, so I have a large passive income. I also have a military pension.

Q: What concerns do you have for the future related to retirement income? How will you address them?

I'd like to live in an expensive area, like Monterey, California, so I will need some additional income to live comfortably there.

Q: Do you plan to start selling your real estate holdings? If so, when and how?
I would sell the worst-performing properties off slowly, but I would probably wait ten years to start doing this.

Q: What's your No. 1 best tip for those looking to live off of investment income after retirement/financial independence?
If you can pay it all off, it'll make things a lot easier.

CHAPTER 16
THE BUY AND HOLD PLAN

This plan is very popular among real estate early retirees. It means you buy an income property and simply hold it as a rental. If the location and the property are good, then you benefit from the compounding of the I.D.E.A.L. real estate benefits discussed in Chapter 1, like income, depreciation, equity buildup, and appreciation. There are *many* viable variations of the Buy and Hold Plan. I'm going to share two major sub-strategies in this chapter:

- The Long-Term Buy and Hold Plan
- The Short-Term Buy and Hold Plan

As with all plans, these are rarely used in isolation. You build the most wealth by using them together synergistically. But I will explain each by itself so that you can see its benefits and challenges. I'll begin with the Long-Term Buy and Hold.

The Long-Term Buy and Hold Plan

In Warren Buffett's 1988 letter to shareholders of Berkshire Hathaway, he said that his favorite holding period was forever.[21] He had recently purchased a major stock position in Coca-Cola (unpopular at the time), and he wanted to explain that quality companies with excellent management only get better over time. The same goes for real estate long-term holds. If you can find a quality income property in an improving location and secure it with attractive financing, time is your friend. You will likely make a lot of money off of that property over time.

---

21 Warren Buffett. "Chairman's 1988 Letter to Shareholders," Berkshire Hathaway. Last updated February 28, 1989. www.berkshirehathaway.com/letters/1988.html>

I like to think of the Long-Term Buy and Hold Plan as planting and caring for an apple tree orchard. The progress starts slowly as the young trees are planted and begin growing. They initially don't produce a lot of fruit. But if you're patient and care for your trees as they mature, they can feed you with abundance for the rest of your life. So the basic steps of creating this orchard of a Long-Term Buy and Hold Plan work like this:

THE 5 STEPS OF THE LONG-TERM BUY AND HOLD PLAN

1. Choose a quality location with good long-term prospects.
2. Buy a property with solid income (*at least* break-even cash flow) and low-maintenance construction (like solid surface floors and brick exteriors).
3. Obtain a fixed interest, long-term mortgage of 15 to 30 years.
4. Build management systems to handle the tenant and maintenance cycles (either third party or do it yourself).
5. Hold, hold, hold! This means 10, 20, or even 30 years or more so that you can ride up the waves of real estate cycles.

To show you how this entire Long-Term Buy and Hold Plan can work, let's look at a more detailed example.

Example of the Long-Term Buy and Hold Plan

I'm going to keep the example simple. In your version of this plan, you're welcome to buy more properties. But let's say you start by purchasing three single-family houses. Each house is 3 bedrooms, 2 baths, 1,500 square feet, with a garage and a small, but cozy, backyard. They are newer construction properties in older neighborhoods that have seen a revitalization because of their proximity to major parks and good schools.

Although you live on the West Coast, you buy these three houses out of state in Nashville, Tennessee. You purchase each house for $200,000, which was not a bargain price. But the houses are well-built and perfectly fit your criteria for low-maintenance. You put 20 percent down ($40,000 each) and get a 30-year mortgage at 5 percent interest with an $859 per month principal and interest payment.

Each house rents for $1,800 per month using a local third-party manager you vetted for professionalism and reliability. Your operating expenses (management, vacancy, taxes, insurance, maintenance, and capital expense reserves) are $800 per month. So, the initial net operating income (that is, before deducting a mortgage payment) is $1,800 – $800 = $1,000 per month.

Here is what the initial purchase numbers for all three properties look like:

CASH INVESTED	HOUSE #1	HOUSE #2	HOUSE #3	TOTAL
Purchase Price	-$200,000	-$200,000	-$200,000	**-$600,000**
Loan (Debt)	$160,000	$160,000	$160,000	**$480,000**
20% Down Payment	-$40,000	-$40,000	-$40,000	**-$120,000**
Closing/Holding Costs	-$5,000	-$5,000	-$5,000	**-$15,000**
TOTAL CASH	-$45,000	-$45,000	-$45,000	**-$135,000**

So to purchase these three houses, you needed $135,000 cash plus good credit. If that much cash seems beyond your reach, you could just buy one at a time and save up to buy more. You could also use less cash by purchasing fixer-upper properties and implementing the BRRRR Plan that I explained earlier. Here is what your positive cash flow would look like once you get all three properties rented:

POSITIVE CASH FLOW	HOUSE #1	HOUSE #2	HOUSE #3	TOTAL
Net Operating Income (NOI)/Month	$1,000	$1,000	$1,000	**$3,000**
Mortgage Payment/ Month	-$859	-$859	-$859	**-$2,577**
Cash Flow/Month	$141	$141	$141	**$423**
Cash Flow/Year	$1,692	$1,692	$1,692	**$5,076**

Now $423 per month or $5,076 per year is not an exciting cash flow on an initial investment of $135,000. The cash-on-cash return before considering taxes is only 3.76 percent ($5,076 / $135,000). And there is no equity from the purchase other than your down payment. But this plan was about buying quality and benefiting over the *long-term*. You'll have to be patient. And because you purchased well on the front end, you're positioned to benefit from this patience.

Results of the Long-Term Buy and Hold Example

One of the big advantages you have with your long-term hold rental portfolio is that you fixed your biggest expense (interest) even while your income increases. No one can predict appreciation of real estate rents or values, but let's say the rents appreciate at about 3 percent per year. Here is how the net rental income improves over a fifteen-year period:

NEW CASH FLOW (15 YRS.)	HOUSE #1	HOUSE #2	HOUSE #3	TOTAL
Rent/Month	$2,800	$2,800	$2,800	**$8,400**
Operating Expenses/Month	-$1,247	-$1,247	-$1,247	**-$3,741**
Mortgage Payment/Month	-$859	-$859	-$859	**$2,577**
Cash Flow/Month	$694	$694	$694	**$2,082**
Cash Flow/Year	$8,328	$8,328	$8,328	**$24,984**

So, because your mortgage expense has stayed the same, the total cash flow has increased along with the rents and the operating expenses. And after fifteen years, the equity in the property (difference between the value and the loan balance) looks like this, even paying the minimum monthly mortgage payments.

NEW EQUITY (15 YRS.)	HOUSE #1	HOUSE #2	HOUSE #3	TOTAL
Value	$311,000	$311,000	$311,000	**$933,000**
Mortgage Balance	-$108,615	-$108,615	-$108,615	**-$325,845**
Equity	$202,385	$202,385	$202,385	**$607,155**

Your $135,000 initial investment has turned into $607,155 of equity after fifteen years simply because of loan amortization and appreciation. That's more than a 10 percent annual return—not counting any reinvestment of rental income. But in reality, you could have easily used the net rental income ($423/month) and some extra personal savings (let's say, $1,000/month) to implement the Rental Debt Snowball Plan and pay off the mortgages in the same amount of time or less.

The calculation for adding increasing rents each year to the debt snowball was more than I wanted to tackle in this example. But even applying the extra savings from the beginning ($423 + $1,000 = 1,423/month) would have paid off all three mortgages within fifteen years. Using the same appreciation rate of 3 percent per year, the new rental income at the fifteen-year point with paid-off properties would look like this:

NEW CASH FLOW (15 YRS. FREE-AND-CLEAR HOUSES)	HOUSE #1	HOUSE #2	HOUSE #3	TOTAL
Rent/Month	$2,800	$2,800	$2,800	**$8,400**
Operating Expenses/Month	-$1,247	-$1,247	-$1,247	**$3,741**
Mortgage Payment/Month	$0	$0	$0	**$0**
Cash Flow/Month	$1,553	$1,553	$1,553	**$4,659**
Cash Flow/Year	$18,636	$18,636	$18,636	**$55,908**

After fifteen years, you now own three quality properties free-and-clear of debt, which produce $4,659/month or $55,908/year in positive cash flow (pre-tax)! And your equity in the properties looks like this:

NEW EQUITY (15 YRS. FREE-AND-CLEAR HOUSES)	HOUSE #1	HOUSE #2	HOUSE #3	TOTAL
Value	$311,000	$311,000	$311,000	**$933,000**
Mortgage Balance	$0	$0	$0	**$0**
Equity	$311,000	$311,000	$311,000	**$933,000**

You turned an investment of $135,000 plus $12,000 per year for fifteen years into $933,000 of wealth. My financial calculator shows that's about a 9.89 percent return. Also not bad! But remember how I said this was a long-term game? And with quality properties in quality locations, it just keeps getting better.

For the next fifteen years, you could use the net rental income to pay for some or all of your early retirement lifestyle. But look what happens to the rent and value at the same rate of 3 percent appreciation:

NEW CASH FLOW (30 YRS.)	HOUSE #1	HOUSE #2	HOUSE #3	TOTAL
Rent/Month	$4,369	$4,369	$4,369	**$13,107**
Operating Expenses/ Month	-$1,942	-$1,942	-$1,942	**$5,826**
Mortgage Payment/ Month	$0	$0	$0	**$0**
Cash Flow/Month	$2,427	$2,427	$2,427	**$7,281**
Cash Flow/Year	$29,124	$29,124	$29,124	**$87,372**

And your equity in the properties after another fifteen years looks like this:

NEW EQUITY (30 YRS.)	HOUSE #1	HOUSE #2	HOUSE #3	TOTAL
Value	$485,000	$485,000	$485,000	**$1,455,000**
Mortgage Balance	$0	$0	$0	**$0**
Equity	$485,000	$485,000	$485,000	**$1,455,000**

Of course, you might correctly point out that all the other prices in society might have also inflated by 3 percent over the same time. So $1,455,000 in equity and $87,372 of income are not as valuable as those same amounts today. But the main point is that quality real estate *can* keep up with inflation. In the meantime, you're living your life and doing what matters.

And although it's not guaranteed, quality locations and properties over the *last* thirty years have often appreciated at higher rates than inflation. If you are fortunate and experience 5 percent average appreciation, you'll be much better off than this.

How to Successfully Harvest Your Long-Term Buy and Hold Properties

When you execute the Long-Term Buy and Hold Plan, time will allow you to amortize your loan, reinvest your income (like into a Rental Debt Snowball Plan or into down payments on more properties), and wait on appreciation of the rent and property values. And once you see these benefits on paper, you can then begin harvesting your winnings. Here are a few options to do that:

- Live off of the net rental income
- Refinance to pull out tax-free cash (I plan to do this to pay for my kids' college)
- Sell to capture equity (and pay taxes)
- Sell and trade up using 1031 tax-free exchanges (see the Trade-Up Plan coming next)
- Sell with owner financing to receive passive principal/interest payments while maintaining the property as collateral (security)

But as with trees in an apple orchard, one of the keys to successfully harvesting from your long-term rental properties is *pruning*. You need to constantly evaluate and improve your properties and your overall portfolio as time goes on. For example, you can:

- Replace suboptimal properties with more optimal ones. These suboptimal properties may have below-average income production, too much tenant turnover, high-hassle tenants, or ongoing maintenance issues.
- Reduce debt levels, either by completely paying them off or reducing overall loan-to-value levels. If you do maintain debt, rather than keeping debt at 40 percent on every property, for example, keep 80 percent on some and zero percent on others. This can increase income and lower your risk profile.
- Reinvest money to make capital improvements as needed, like new roofs, new heating and air units, and repairs to avoid functional or cosmetic obsolescence.

Now that you've seen the benefits of a Long-Term Buy and Hold Plan, let's look at a different but complementary buy and hold strategy called the Short-Term Buy and Hold Plan.

The Short-Term Buy and Hold Plan

Not every property, market, financing, or personal situation works with long-term buy and holds. In some cases, it can make more sense to hold your rentals short-term, which just means you don't keep a rental property for fifteen to thirty years. Instead, you resell a property sooner—like in three to five years. Why would this make more sense? There are many reasons and benefits, including:

- You can generate cash and equity quickly to reinvest and grow.
- You'll be able to cash out of a bargain-priced purchase as the market cycle heats up.
- You can harvest your increased value from income property where you raised the rents, improved the management, and/or reduced expenses.
- Local market demographics or economics are not ideal for a long-term hold, like the price/rent ratio is too high.
- A property is not low-maintenance or efficient enough for a long-term hold.
- You can't get good long-term financing.
- You just don't want to hold or manage rentals long-term.

Any of these reasons (or others) could be valid. And if that fits you, here's a basic plan you could follow.

5 STEPS TO THE SHORT-TERM BUY AND HOLD PLAN

1. Buy properties *well below full value* (key!)
2. Rent for a short time (1–5 years)
3. Sell at an optimal time (which could mean optimal for tax savings and/or optimal because it's a good selling market)
4. Harvest your equity at the closing
5. Reinvest—either in more real estate, debt paydown, or other investments

There are many variations of this basic Short-Term Buy and Hold formula beginning at Step #5. For example, you could use your harvested equity to accelerate paydown of debt like in the Rental Debt Snowball Plan. Or you could use the equity to expand your portfolio like in the Trade-Up Plan, which I'll cover in the next chapter. Or you could just do several rounds of short-term holds to churn and build equity. That's exactly what I suggested in the Live-In Flip Plan covered earlier.

A short-term hold is like a powerful lever. You can use it whenever you need to boost your savings and long-term wealth-building plan. But the consistent theme is to harvest the equity you created over a relatively short period of time. What you do with that equity will depend on your situation and overall plan.

But to show you one specific way to use the Short-Term Buy and Hold Plan to build wealth alongside the Long-Term Buy and Hold Plan, I'll share an example I've put into practice called Buy-3-Sell-2-Keep-1.

Short-Term Buy and Hold Example: Buy-3-Sell-2-Keep-1 Plan

When my business partner and I began our real estate business, we primarily fixed and quickly flipped houses for cash to pay the bills. But whenever possible, we started holding properties as short-term rentals in a parallel business. The margins were better than fix-and-flips because we saved on commissions and holding costs. And it allowed us to transition away from simply making a living to wealth-building.

Because we were working hard at finding deals, we ended up with more properties than we needed to meet our long-term financial goals. This also meant we had higher levels of leverage than we felt comfortable with long-term. So the natural next step was to sell off some of these buy and hold properties, harvest their equity, and pay down debt on the properties we wanted to keep long-term (as with the Long-Term Buy and Hold Plan). The end result was a safer, simpler long-term portfolio. Here's a simplified version of what we did:

1. Buy three income properties (or some multiple of three).
2. Use small down payments plus loans for purchases.
3. Rent for a short period of time (1–5 years).
4. Sell two of the three properties and keep the third.
5. Use the net sales proceeds from the two sales to pay off the third keeper property.

As I said earlier, the key part of this plan is to buy properties at a discount. This builds in a profit and a margin of safety from the beginning. If you pay too much, you'll get stuck with them long-term whether you like it or not! Let's look at an example to demonstrate the basics of what we did.

The Acquisition of Three Properties

An investor named Kyle buys three single-family houses for $175,000 all-in. The full value of each is $250,000, so he is able to find bargains at 70 percent of the full value. Kyle also finds a private lender to loan $150,000 on each house, meaning he makes a $25,000 down payment per property. The purchase numbers look like this:

PURCHASE OF 3 HOUSES	HOUSE #1	HOUSE #2	HOUSE #3	TOTAL
Full Value	$250,000	$250,000	$250,000	**$750,000**
Total Purchase Price	$175,000	$175,000	$175,000	**$525,000**
Down Payment	-$25,000	-$25,000	-$25,000	**-$75,000**
Loan (Debt)	$150,000	$150,000	$150,000	**$450,000**
Equity at Purchase (includes down payment)	**$100,000**	**$100,000**	**$100,000**	**$300,000**

So Kyle needs $75,000 of his own cash to control all three properties. And as was with my actual situation, I assume he does not have the ability or desire to get bank financing. Each of the $150,000 loans comes from private lenders. And I'll assume he borrows on terms of 7 percent interest with interest-only payments (no amortization) of $875/month. Plus, all principal must be repaid in ten years.

Who has this kind of money to lend, you may ask? Plenty of people, I've found. This is especially true when you keep the lender's risk low and offer a reasonable return. The loan in this example is $150,000, and the full value is $250,000. That's a low-risk 60 percent loan to value. And the interest rate of 7 percent will satisfy many knowledgeable real estate people who understand real estate (at least as I write this in 2018, when bank CD rates are below 1 percent).

But remember this is still a rental property. Let's look at the rental numbers for this short-term hold purchase.

Rental Income for the Three-House Purchase
The rental income for the purchases of Kyle's three houses looks like this:

RENTAL INCOME FOR 3-HOUSE PURCHASE	HOUSE #1	HOUSE #2	HOUSE #3	TOTAL
Rent/Month	$1,500	$1,500	$1,500	**$4,500**
Operating Expenses/ Month	-$600	-$600	-$600	**-$1,800**
Mortgage Payment/ Month	-$875	-$875	-$875	**-$2,625**
Cash Flow/Month	$25	$25	$25	**$75**
Cash Flow/Year	$300	$300	$300	**$900**

I hope you're scratching your head by now. Only $75/month or $900/year in positive cash flow? On an investment of $75,000? Is Kyle crazy to do this deal? Actually, maybe not. And this is the main point of the example.

The properties Kyle bought don't cash flow that well. This is a very common phenomenon in high-priced markets or in higher price ranges of any residential market. If he were simply buying these properties for rental income or to reinvest in a debt snowball, he'd be right not to be excited about $25/month of cash flow each. And in the real world, that can very easily turn into negative cash flow (and probably will).

But remember the point of short-term holds? It's to harvest equity. And that's what Kyle is going to do next.

Sales Proceeds from Reselling Two of the Three Houses

Because Kyle is savvy and wants to maximize his profits, he had begun thinking about his exit strategy from the very beginning. And he realizes that the most efficient way to resell a property is to sell it to the tenants living there (no real estate commissions, no vacant holding period, less haggling on price).

With this plan in mind, Kyle decides that two of the three houses are not ideal long-term holds. They're not built for low-maintenance (they're too big and fancy), and the locations are not as good as the third property. So when he rents those two properties, he screens for tenants who may be interested in buying the house down the road. In both cases, the tenants need time to save up a down payment and work on their credit. And Kyle is willing to wait a couple of years for that to happen.

Kyle could give them what's called a lease with an option to buy. But to keep things simple, he just tells them verbally that he'd like to sell it to them at the market price at the time of the sale. Kyle asks them to come talk with him when they're ready.

It just so happens that both tenants get ready to buy at the exact same time three years later (how convenient for my math). But being aware of tax strategy, Kyle negotiates for one to buy at the end of one year and the other to buy at the beginning of the next year in order to separate the impact on his income tax liability.

Kyle's houses appreciated at a rate of 3.23 percent from $250,000 to $275,000, which is the price he's willing to sell for. He also agrees to contribute 3 percent toward closing costs to help his tenants get the deal done. The sales proceeds look like this:

SALES PROCEEDS RESALE OF 2 HOUSES	HOUSE #1	HOUSE #2	HOUSE #3	TOTAL
Sales Price	$275,000	$275,000	n/a	$550,000
Closing Costs	-$8,250	-$8,250	n/a	-$16,500
Mortgage Payoff	-$150,000	-$150,000	n/a	-$300,000
Net Proceeds (Pre-Tax)	$116,750	$116,750	n/a	**$233,500**
Depreciation Recapture Tax	-$3,750	-$3,750	n/a	-$7,500
Capital Gains Tax	-$18,350	-$18,350	n/a	-$36,700
Net Gain After Tax	**$94,650**	**$94,650**	n/a	**$189,300**

Depreciation Recapture Tax [22]

Capital Gains Tax [23]

Your third keeper property has a loan balance of $150,000. You can now use the $189,300 to pay that off, and you still have $39,300 to put in the bank. This entire process from beginning to end looks like this in graphic form:

---

[22] The assumption is that each property's building value basis was $137,500. When depreciated over 27.5 years, this created a $5,000 per year depreciation expense per property for three years. Thus, $15,000 of depreciation had to be recaptured and the assumed tax rate was 25 percent. 25% x $15,000 = $3,750.

[23] The capital gains tax rate was assumed to be 20 percent. The taxable gain was $275,000 – $175,000 – $8,250 = $91,750. $91,750 x 20% = $18,350.

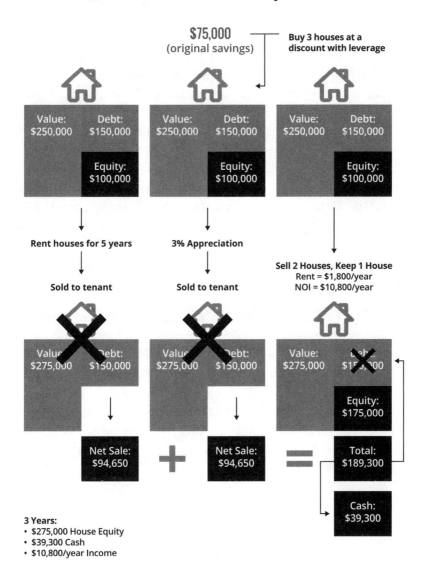

REAL ESTATE EARLY RETIREMENT

Buy-3-Sell-2-Keep-1 Plan

$75,000
(original savings)

Buy 3 houses at a discount with leverage

Value: $250,000   Debt: $150,000
Equity: $100,000

Value: $250,000   Debt: $150,000
Equity: $100,000

Value: $250,000   Debt: $150,000
Equity: $100,000

Rent houses for 5 years

3% Appreciation

Sell 2 Houses, Keep 1 House
Rent = $1,800/year
NOI = $10,800/year

Sold to tenant

Sold to tenant

Value: $275,000   Debt: $150,000

Value: $275,000   Debt: $150,000

Value: $275,000   Debt: $150,000
Equity: $175,000

Net Sale: $94,650

+

Net Sale: $94,650

=

Total: $189,300

Cash: $39,300

3 Years:
- $275,000 House Equity
- $39,300 Cash
- $10,800/year Income

Final Results of the Buy-3-Sell-2-Keep-1 Plan

The end result is that within three years, Kyle turns a $75,000 initial investment into free-and-clear property equity of $275,000 plus $39,300 cash, for a total $314,300 in wealth. The third property is still rented, and without a mortgage, it now produces $900/month or $10,800 per year, assuming there was no rental appreciation.

This is just a 3.9 percent return on Kyle's equity of $275,000 ($10,800 / $275,000). Therefore, it may be reasonable to decide that instead of paying off the third property's mortgage he may want to reinvest the $189,300 into something else. Kyle could do another round of short-term holds or invest in one of the other wealth-building plans in this book. And if House #3 is worth keeping in the long run (like if the rent and value are appreciating nicely), he may also consider refinancing the third house to get better terms and cash flow.

The good thing at this stage is that the choice is up to Kyle! And he's built the skill of using short-term holds, which he can use again whenever he needs to. One specialized application of the Short-Term Buy and Hold Plan is the topic of the next chapter. It's called the Trade-Up Plan, and it's a way to take advantage of special tax laws in order to rapidly grow your real estate wealth tax-free.

———— PROFILE OF A REAL ESTATE EARLY RETIREE ————

GREG AND HOLLY JOHNSON
Club Thrifty Media, LLC (clubthrifty.com)
Location: Noblesville, Indiana
Chad's Favorite Quote from Greg and Holly:
"[A] buy and hold strategy is a great way for most people to make money over the long term. Slow and steady tends to win the race."

WEALTH-BUILDING STATISTICS
- **Profession/Career:** Blogging/freelance writing; formerly a funeral director
- **Income During Wealth-Building Phase:** $200,000+/year
- **How Big a Role Did Real Estate Play in Wealth-Building?** Equally as important as other vehicles (stocks, bonds, businesses, etc.)

- **Primary Real Estate Strategy(ies):** Long-term rentals; rental debt snowball

FINANCIAL INDEPENDENCE STATISTICS
- **Age at Financial Independence:** 51 to 60 (goal)
- **Annual Expenses in Retirement:** $100,000 to $150,000
- **Ideal Number of Rentals in Retirement:** 6 to 10
- **Primary Source of Retirement Income:** Proceeds from periodic sale of public stocks
- **Secondary Source of Retirement Income:** Rental properties, Social Security, private business income
- **Ideal Debt Level of Real Estate Portfolio:** None—own everything free and clear

Q&A

Q: Can you explain in more detail how you built your current wealth?
We've always been very interested in real estate as an investment vehicle. After buying our first house in our mid-20s (primary residence), we decided that we also wanted to get into the rental market. At the time, we had saved about $10,000 and used that to make the down payment on our first rental property. Roughly a year later, we decided to upgrade our primary residence and turn our first house into a rental as well. It was about that time that we decided to eliminate all of our consumer debt. After paying off about $50,000 in consumer debt, we then decided to start paying extra toward the mortgage on our first rental property.

Over the years, our personal income has increased significantly. It took us about nine years to pay off our first rental, which we did in late 2016. We then used the rental money from that house to help pay off our primary residence in March 2018. At the moment, we are saving up cash to purchase at least two more properties in our area. We're also using the rental income from Rental #1 to help us pay off Rental #2. By the time we are ready to retire, we expect to have about six paid-off properties.

The majority of our stock market investing is done through our individual 401(k) accounts. Last year, we were able to max out our individual contributions, plus add an "employer" contribution from our business.

Q: What were the biggest obstacles and setbacks during your wealth-building stage? How did you overcome or push through them?
Thankfully, we haven't had that many problems. The only issue we had was a family who rented from us for three years and ended up doing some major damage to one of our houses. (They were great renters for 2.5 years. The couple went through a divorce near the end of their stay on our property, and their teenage kids were left home alone a lot, destroying the house.) We ended up spending our anniversary gutting the house and getting it ready to rent out again.

Q: What's your No. 1 best tip for those looking to build wealth with real estate investing?
Plan to be in it for the long haul. A lot of people see big dollar signs in flipping houses, so they want to get in and get out quickly. Don't get me wrong, some people can make that work and cash in … but it also presents a lot of risk. Just like investing in the stock market, a buy and hold strategy is a great way for most people to make money over the long term. Slow and steady tends to win the race.

Q: Can you explain in more detail your post–financial independence income? How do you plan on living off of this income?
We plan to use a variety of sources of income during retirement. I said our primary source of income would be from our retirement accounts. However, it would be ideal if we rarely needed to touch those.

We have a business that will continue making money into the foreseeable future, so that could be part of our income. Additionally, we'll have rental income that will first help us pay for our children's college. Then, we'll use that as income during retirement. Additionally, I'm sure we'll have Social Security to draw from.

Furthermore, we have very few expenses and zero debt (except the mortgage on Rental #2, which the tenants more than pay for with monthly rent).

Q: What concerns do you have for the future related to retirement income? How will you address them?

To be honest, I'm not really concerned at all. Because we've already built several streams of retirement income, we think we are in pretty good shape.

Q: Do you plan to start selling your real estate holdings? If so, when and how?

At the moment, no. If we do decide to sell them, it will be deep into our retirement years.

Q: What's your No. 1 best tip for those looking to live off of investment income after retirement/financial independence?

Keep your expenses as low as possible, and pay off all your debt well before you are ready to retire.

CHAPTER 17

THE TRADE-UP PLAN (COMPOUNDING WEALTH TAX-FREE)

The Trade-Up Plan is a specialized version of the Short-Term Buy and Hold Plan that grows your wealth in a tax-optimized way. Using this strategy, you can build a portfolio of cash-flowing rental properties starting with a relatively small amount of capital.

It works by beginning small with rental properties and then strategically selling them. You then reinvest the profits into a larger number of properties or one higher-priced property after each sale. This "trading-up" broadens your base of assets and income with each transaction. I'll start by explaining a few ways to minimize taxes as you trade up.

Three Techniques to Minimize Taxes as You Trade Up

The most well-known technique to minimize taxes on a sale of real estate is called a 1031 tax-free exchange. This technique allows you to sell properties and defer the payment of income taxes if you reinvest all the profits in a way that follows tax laws (section 1031) regulated by the IRS.

A second, more specialized technique is to use something called a cost segregation study that generates a *large* amount of short-term depreciation expense by separating a property into its component parts (like appliances, carpet, cabinets, etc.).[24] Because most of you won't be classified as real estate professionals, this large excess of depreciation expense cannot be used in the short-term to offset any of your normal, active income.[25] It's carried forward until the time of the property sale, when it can be used to shelter some or all of the gains from this property *plus* ordinary income from your job. This allows you to buy, hold, sell, and then experience a large tax savings in the year of the sale.

A third tax-efficient technique is to sell when you are personally in a lower tax bracket. Capital gains tax, like regular income taxes, has different rates for different income levels. As of 2018, the lowest two income tax brackets pay zero percent capital gains tax! The highest tax bracket pays 20 percent, and everything between pays 15 percent.

Depending on your income and the number of deductions you have, you may have years in the zero percent capital gains bracket. Those would be excellent times to sell a property, harvest a gain, and reinvest the proceeds without paying capital gains tax (you'd likely still have depreciation recapture tax).

Reducing or eliminating taxes on a sale gives you a *tremendous* potential boost moving toward financial independence. Without taxes taking a bite out of your profits, you can compound and grow your wealth even faster. To explain the Trade-Up Plan and to show the power of tax-free compounding, I'll share the following detailed example using the most common technique, 1031 tax-free exchanges.

Example of the Trade-Up Plan
It works like this:

6 STEPS TO THE TRADE-UP PLAN (WITH 1031 TAX-FREE EXCHANGES)

1. Save up cash for a down payment, closing costs, and cash reserves.
2. Buy a rental property at a slight discount (10–15 percent or more).

---

[24] These kinds of components have shorter lifespans than the typical residential property (3 to 10 years instead of 27.5 years). This dramatically increases the initial amount of depreciation expense that can be claimed. Because the process is very detailed, you usually need to hire third-party companies that specialize in this technique to execute the study.

[25] This is a complex tax topic that your CPA needs to help you with, but the main point is that depreciation expense that creates a loss can only offset *passive* income. Rental income is passive, but it's usually much smaller than the depreciation created by the cost segregation study. And unless you're a real estate professional who spends more than half your time materially participating in real estate activities, you can't use this passive depreciation loss to offset your regular job income or other investment portfolio income. The excess loss is simply carried forward unused until you sell the property. Then you can use it to offset active and passive income in the year of the sale, which is the key payoff of this technique.

3. Rent the property, pay down the mortgage, and save cash for a period of time (say, 2 years).
4. Sell the property.
5. Use a 1031 tax-free exchange to purchase a larger property, also at a slight discount.
6. Repeat and continue growing until you meet your financial goals.

Your equity and cash flow grow and compound quickly as you repeat these steps over and over. In this example, you will buy a property, rent it for two years, resell it with a 1031 tax-free exchange, and purchase a replacement property. Then the process will be repeated over and over, compounding your gains tax-free.

Each property will be a little bigger (that's the trade up), and by the end you'll have a much larger net worth and rental income. The key to success in this example will be a few criteria that need to be met when acquiring the deals:

- Each unit must produce $100+/month in net rental income (before tax).
- The purchase price must be at least 10 percent below full current value (or the value can be quickly increased with minimal cost by increasing rent, decreasing expenses, or both).
- There will be no major remodels.
- Class B or C+ property types only. This means no old or cheaply built properties and no war-zone locations. But it also means you won't be buying brand-new buildings in the best locations, because they're harder to get at a discount.
- All loans must be twenty- to thirty-year amortizations.
- There are no loan balloon payments shorter than ten years.

Because there are more moving parts than in the other plans, I'll explain each step in more detail.

Years 1 & 2: Preparation for the First Purchase
To make it more realistic, I assume in this example that you're starting from scratch. You spend the first two years preparing to get started. Here are the things you do to get ready:

Save Cash
I spent a lot of time earlier in Part 3 discussing the importance of saving

cash to build wealth. This plan is no different. You might work on these ideas during this saving period:

- Cut personal expenses.
- Sell stuff (say, in yard sales, on eBay, Craigslist, etc.).
- Sell assets (cars, stocks, other properties).
- Work overtime and earn bonuses at your regular job.
- Flip a house or start another side-hustle business.
- Sell your principal residence, save the equity tax-free, then downsize and/or rent.
- Borrow from a 401(k). This is not ideal; I'd explore other options first, if possible. You typically have to pay back the loan in a short time. But if it's the difference between executing the plan or not, you may want to consider it.
- Borrow money on a HELOC (home equity line of credit). I'd use this as a last resort. If anything goes wrong, you are also risking your personal residence. Plus, you have to make monthly payments on the borrowed cash.
- Bring in a partner. Partnerships add complexity and risk (from potential breakups). Enter them carefully (like a marriage). Partnerships also reduce your share of the profit on the back end. But if you don't have the cash and/or credit, part of something is better than all of nothing.

Study Your Target Market
While you're saving cash, you'll also become an expert in your target real estate market. This will give you a *big* advantage and intuitive feel for values when you put your deals in motion.

Prepare Purchase Financing
Purchase financing is a key part of the Trade-Up Plan. You know you need to prepare for two different types:

1. **Traditional mortgage financing:** Only available for one- to four-unit residential properties, usually thirty-year amortizations and fixed interest rates.
2. **Commercial financing:** Available for smaller or larger properties, usually fifteen- to twenty-five-year amortizations, and often have balloon notes (all principal due) within five to ten years.

So, you network on BiggerPockets in the forums and at local real estate meetups to find the most qualified lenders. You then get prequalified for loans before you start hunting.

Hunt for Deals

Finally, you begin looking for deals, even as you're still preparing the other items. You know this is the part of the process that takes the most time to get up and running.

You network with local agents, wholesalers, and referral sources. You also build a list of all the investment-grade properties in your target area, including the owners and their mailing addresses. You find this information by digging around on the local tax assessor website. By the end of the two-year period, you have been sending out personal letters to these owners, and you have several good prospects to make offers on. Which brings us to the next step.

End of Year 2: Purchase a Duplex

All of your hard work pays off. One of the letters you send to an owner of a duplex turns into a deal. By the way, you are allowed to celebrate and do a happy dance at this stage! Buying your first property is exciting. The purchase numbers for your first duplex look like this:

PROPERTY #1 — PURCHASE PRICE & VALUE	
Full Value	$235,000
Purchase Price	$210,000
New Equity	**$25,000**

The cash requirements for the purchase look like this:

PROPERTY #1 — CASH REQUIREMENTS	
Closing Costs	$3,000
Down Payment (20%)	$42,000
Reserve	$5,000
Total Cash	**$50,000**

The financing of Property #1 looks like this:

PROPERTY #1 — FINANCING	
Loan Amount	$168,000
Interest Rate	5%
Term Length	30 years
Principal/Interest Payment	$902/month

Years 3 & 4: Collect Rent and Sell the Duplex

The duplex is a nice property. It is already rented when you buy it, but the owner has kept the rents a little low after a long ownership period. You increase rents and keep the property spruced up.

By the way, this strategy of increasing income or decreasing expenses will be a common theme in each step of the Trade-Up Plan. Spying these opportunities during the purchase process is how you add at least 10 percent of value above the price you paid. The rental income for the duplex looks like this:

PROPERTY #1 — RENTAL INCOME	
Gross Rent (2 units)	$2,100/month
Operating Expenses (vacancy, taxes, insurance, management, maintenance, and capital expenses)	-$900/month
Net Operating Income	$1,200/month
Mortgage Payment (Principal/Interest)	-$902/month
Net Income After Financing (Monthly)	**$298/month**
Net Income After Financing (Yearly)	**$3,576/year**

I assume the rental income is completely sheltered by depreciation, which means you pay no taxes on the net rental income. So, during these two years you save 100 percent of the rental income that you collect. This rental income savings totals $7,152 over two years. You also save $12,000 per year from your day job for a total of $24,000 over two years. **Including the $5,000 cash reserve from your first deal, you save a total of $36,152 to use for your next purchase.**

And you are sure to continue hustling to put this cash to good use. Another one of your letters to a rental property owner also turns into a deal. You find a small four-unit apartment building (aka a fourplex) with an owner willing to sell at an attractive price. She'll also give you an option to purchase the property in six months, which means you have time to sell your other property.

You put your duplex on the market with a real estate agent. You agree to a 5 percent commission at the time of sale, and you also assume you'll pay 1 percent in seller closing costs. Before you put the property on the market, you also reconnect with your 1031 exchange intermediary who is prepared to walk you through the process. The intermediary's fee will be included in the closing costs of the next purchase.

Fortunately, your duplex sells relatively easily. At the time of the sale, your funds available for the next purchase look like this:

PROPERTY #1 — SALES PROCEEDS	
Sales Price	$235,000
Sales Agent Commission (5%)	-$11,750
Seller Closing Costs (1%)	-$2,350
Loan Balance at Closing	-$163,000
Net Sales Proceeds	**$57,900**

With the $36,152 cash savings and the $57,900 sales proceeds, you now have $94,052 to use for the next purchase.

End of Year 4: Purchase Fourplex

Just as the sale of the duplex is finished, you execute your option to purchase the fourplex that you had under contract. The purchase numbers look like this:

PROPERTY #2 — PURCHASE PRICE & VALUE	
Full Value	$450,000
Purchase Price	$405,000
New Equity	**$45,000**

The cash requirements for the purchase look like this:

PROPERTY #2 — CASH REQUIREMENTS	
Closing Costs	$5,000
Down Payment (20%)	$81,000
New Reserve	$8,052
Total Cash	**$94,052**

The financing of Property #2 looks like this:

PROPERTY #2 — FINANCING	
Loan Amount	$324,000
Interest Rate	5%
Term Length	30 years
Principal/Interest Payment	$1,739/month

Years 5 & 6: Collect Rent and Sell the Fourplex

Like the duplex, the fourplex is a nice property. And as you did with the duplex, you increase rents and keep the property maintained and looking good. The rental income for the duplex looks like this:

PROPERTY #2 — RENTAL INCOME	
Gross Rent (4 units)	$4,000/month
Operating Expenses (vacancy, taxes, insurance, management, maintenance, and capital expenses)	-$1,688/month
Net Operating Income	$2,312/month
Mortgage Payment (Principal/Interest)	-$1,739/month
Net Income After Financing (Monthly)	**$573/month**
Net Income After Financing (Yearly)	**$6,876/year**

Again, I assume the rental income is completely sheltered by depreciation, which means you pay no taxes on the net rental income. And just like last time, you save 100 percent of the rental income that you collect. The total rental income savings is $13,752 over two years. You also save $12,000 per year for a total of $24,000 over two years. **Including the $8,052 cash reserve, you save a total of $45,804 to use for your next purchase.**

During the two-year holding period, you reconnect with your commercial lender. You know it's time to make a big jump, so you want to be preapproved and prepared. Of course, you also continue to work daily looking for a new deal. And this time an agent brings you a twenty-unit property that meets your criteria perfectly.

The negotiation with the twenty-unit owner is tough, but because it was an off-market deal (not listed on the Multiple Listing Service, known as MLS), you are able to get some flexibility on the closing time so you can execute your 1031 exchange. You give the seller a big earnest money deposit to make him feel more comfortable.

You quickly put your fourplex on the market to sell with the same agent as before. Your 1031 exchange intermediary again agrees to handle the details of the exchange. A buyer quickly jumps on the opportunity to buy your fourplex. This is a smart, eager new investor who wants to do a house hack (living in one unit and renting out the other three). Perhaps she also read this book! Your sales proceeds from the fourplex look like this:

PROPERTY #2 — SALES PROCEEDS	
Sales Price	$450,000
Sales Agent Commission (5%)	-$22,500
Seller Closing Costs (1%)	-$4,500
Loan Balance at Closing	-$314,200
Net Sales Proceeds	**$108,800**

With the $45,804 cash savings and the $108,800 sales proceeds, you now have $154,604 to use for the next purchase.

End of Year 6: Purchase Twenty-Unit

Right after the sale of the fourplex, you purchase the twenty-unit apartment complex. The purchase numbers look like this:

PROPERTY #3 — PURCHASE PRICE & VALUE	
Full Value	$600,000
Purchase Price	$515,000
New Equity	**$85,000**

The cash requirements for the purchase look like this:

PROPERTY #3 — CASH REQUIREMENTS	
Closing Costs	$10,000
Down Payment (25%)	$129,000
New Reserve	$15,604
Total Cash	**$154,604**

The financing of Property #3 looks like this:

PROPERTY #3 — FINANCING	
Loan Amount	$386,000
Interest Rate	5%
Amortization Length	20 years
Balloon Payment Year	10 years
Principal/Interest Payment	$2,547/month

Years 5 & 6: Collect Rent and Sell the Twenty-Unit

Your experience managing and increasing rents on the duplex and fourplex pay off. You're able to increase the rents a small amount, and you're also able to decrease several property expense items (like the property tax bill, which had an excessive tax value). Both of these increase your cash flow, but more important, increase the value of the property. The rental income for the twenty-unit property looks like this:

PROPERTY #3 — RENTAL INCOME	
Gross Rent (20 units)	$8,400/month
Operating Expenses (vacancy, taxes, insurance, management, common utilities, maintenance, and capital expenses)	-$3,500/month
Net Operating Income	$4,900/month
Mortgage Payment (Principal/Interest)	-$2,547/month
Net Income After Financing (Monthly)	**$2,353/month**
Net Income After Financing (Yearly)	**$28,236/year**

Because of your success building rental income, it appears on the surface that you may have more income than you have depreciation tax shelter. This means you could owe taxes on some of your rental income, which would decrease how much you could save.

But your highly qualified CPA brings up the idea of segregating some of your building's cost into components. This means separating the cost of twenty refrigerators, twenty dishwashers, and twenty HVAC units from the building cost because they all depreciate faster than the building itself. The CPA helps you prepare documentation that gives you extra depreciation that's more than sufficient to shelter the extra income and avoid paying income taxes for now.

The total rental income savings is $56,472 over two years. You once again save $12,000 per year for a total of $24,000 over two years. **Including the $15,604 cash reserve, you save a total of $96,076 to use for your next purchase.**

You once again reconnect with your commercial lender to prepare for your next deal. And because you've been hunting in your target market for more than five years, you've built a reputation as a solid professional investor who can be trusted to follow through. As a result, the same agent who brought you the twenty-unit building brings another seller with a nearby thirty-unit apartment complex.

This time the negotiation is much smoother because the agent knows and trusts you. The seller is again flexible with your timetable to sell the property. Now that the thirty-unit is under contract, you put the twenty-unit building on the market. Unlike the duplex and fourplex, the twenty-unit takes a little longer to sell. But after six months of marketing, you find a buyer. Your sales proceeds from the twenty-unit look like this:

PROPERTY #3 — SALES PROCEEDS	
Sales Price	$600,000
Sales Agent Commission (5%)	-$30,000
Seller Closing Costs (1%)	-$6,000
Loan Balance at Closing	-$362,000
Net Sales Proceeds	**$202,000**

With the $96,076 cash savings and the $202,000 sales proceeds, you now have $298,076 to use for the next purchase.

End of Year 8: Purchase Thirty-Unit

Because the twenty-unit is sold, you use the proceeds from the sale along with your cash savings to purchase the thirty-unit property with the help of your 1031 exchange intermediary. Here are the numbers from the purchase of the thirty-unit building:

PROPERTY #4 — PURCHASE PRICE & VALUE	
Full Value	$1,000,000
Purchase Price	$875,000
New Equity	**$125,000**

The cash requirements for the purchase look like this:

PROPERTY #4 — CASH REQUIREMENTS	
Closing Costs	$12,000
Down Payment (30%)	$266,000
New Reserve	$20,076
Total Cash	**$298,076**

The financing of Property #4 looks like this:

PROPERTY #4 — FINANCING	
Loan Amount	$609,000
Interest Rate	5%
Amortization Length	20 years
Balloon Payment Year	10 years
Principal/Interest Payment	$4,019/month

Final Results of the Trade-Up Plan Example

It's been a focused, intense eight years! But after it's all done, you look up to notice what you've accomplished. Here is your final rental income on the thirty-unit:

PROPERTY #4 — RENTAL INCOME	
Gross Rent (30 units)	$13,800/month
Operating Expenses (vacancy, taxes, insurance, management, common utilities, maintenance, and capital expenses)	-$6,300/month
Net Operating Income	$7,500/month
Mortgage Payment (Principal/Interest)	-$4,019/month
Net Income After Financing (Monthly)	**$3,481/month**
Net Income After Financing (Yearly)	**$41,772/year**

This infographic gives you an overview of the entire journey and the final results of the Trade-Up Plan example.

REAL ESTATE EARLY RETIREMENT

The Trade-Up Plan

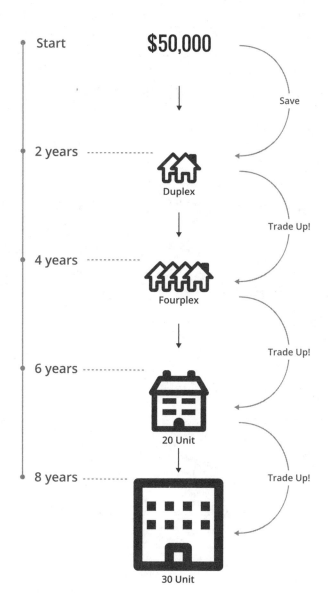

Start — $50,000

Save

2 years — Duplex

Trade Up!

4 years — Fourplex

Trade Up!

6 years — 20 Unit

Trade Up!

8 years — 30 Unit

You began with little cash, and you scraped together $50,000. Then you compounded and turned your $50,000 into a $1 million property. And this final property produces $41,772/year in net rental income, has $391,000 in equity, and reduces the principal on the loan by more than $18,000 per year.

Yes, it took some hustle to find good deals and execute big purchases and sales. But if you can live on less than $41,772 a year, you've made it to a new level of financial independence! And that means you can make a major life shift if you want. After all, that's what you did all of this work for, right?

And even if $41,772 isn't enough to pay all your bills, now may be a good time for the mini-retirement or semi-retirement milestones I talked about in the beginning of the book. You've earned a break! This can also be a time to think about what's next. Is there anything else that can be done to make this Trade-Up Plan a little better or safer?

Final Thoughts on the Trade-Up Plan

Remember in the beginning of this book when I wrote that massive real estate empires are not always better? I shared this graph about business growth:

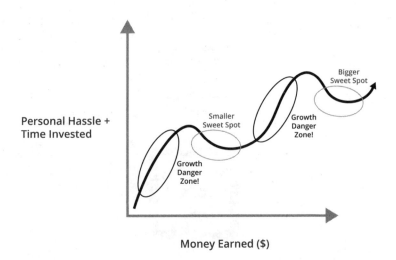

Business Life Cycle

Personal Hassle + Time Invested

Smaller Sweet Spot

Bigger Sweet Spot

Growth Danger Zone!

Growth Danger Zone!

Growth Danger Zone!

Money Earned ($)

The last eight years of this Trade-Up Plan example were one of the steep inclines of the graph. You certainly had personal time, hassle, and risk involved. If you want to keep getting bigger, you're welcome to keep applying the principles and climb the growth curve even more. If it all goes well, you will certainly make more income and build a larger net worth in the end.

But I'd also encourage you to consider your overall risk and your life goals. Is there a way to both reduce your risk and also increase your income? This might be an opportunity to stay in a sweet spot with less hassle while still meeting your personal goals.

One way to do this is transition to debt acceleration and payoff, much like I wrote about in the Rental Debt Snowball Plan. You could use the extra rental income, your $12,000/year job savings, and perhaps some extra short-term hold profits to make enormous mortgage payments and cut the total loan term down significantly.

In five to ten years (depending on how much extra you save) you could own the thirty-unit property free and clear of debt. Many commercial mortgages have prepayment penalties, so you'll have to negotiate or find a lender without that penalty. But in the end, your free-and-clear property would produce about $90,000 a year in rental income (assuming no rent appreciation)! And you'd have lower risk and more flexibility with no debt on the property.

As you can see, the Trade-Up Plan has real potential to build wealth. But it also is not easy. It's a plan for the more entrepreneurial real estate investors who can juggle deal finding, financing, and transaction details while staying disciplined over a number of years.

And please remember that this example isn't an exact recipe for how the plan will work in your life. It's simply meant to make the concept come alive. The specifics will inevitably be different in your situation. It's the principles and the core benefits of the plan that matter.

I hope that it got you thinking and expanded your toolbox of real estate wealth-building options. I trust that you'll use your own intelligence and creativity to learn more and to turn these ideas into reality for yourself.

In the next chapter, I'll summarize all the wealth-building plans we've covered and help you figure out which one (or ones together) are right for you.

PROFILE OF A REAL ESTATE EARLY RETIREE

ELIZABETH COLEGROVE

The Reluctant Landlord (reluctantlandlord.net)
Location: Hanford, California
Chad's Favorite Quote from Elizabeth:
"Build as much as you can so you have the most options later!"

WEALTH-BUILDING STATISTICS

- **Profession/Career:** Worked for commercial real estate companies (property manager, financial analyst); now a blogger (husband is Navy pilot)
- **Income During Wealth-Building Phase:** $100,000 to $149,999/year
- **How Big a Role Did Real Estate Play in Wealth-Building?** Primary vehicle
- **Primary Real Estate Strategy(ies):** Long-term rentals, rental debt snowball, 1031 tax-free exchanges

FINANCIAL INDEPENDENCE STATISTICS

- **Age at Financial Independence:** 41 to 45 (still working toward the goal)
- **Annual Expenses in Retirement:** $100,000 to $150,000
- **Ideal Number of Rentals in Retirement:** 11 to 20
- **Primary Source of Retirement Income:** Rental income
- **Secondary Source of Retirement Income:** Military pension
- **Ideal Debt Level of Real Estate Portfolio:** Not sure

Q&A

Q: Can you explain in more detail how you built your current wealth?
My husband is active duty military, and we got married right out of college at 22/23. We quickly realized that a normal career for me was going to be impossible because we moved around so much. At the same time, we wanted financial independence when he had the opportunity to retire at 44. Therefore, we quickly realized that the buy

and hold strategy was the best for us. We could live on one income and invest the other income when I could find work (I have a master's degree).

As we move frequently (to date, six times in eight years of marriage), we realized we could buy a personal property and turn it into a rental when we moved. The goal was to turn a negative into a positive. The goal of these investments was that, over time, this could become my permanent job, allowing us the flexibility of staying home with our kids while still building equity and growth.

While this was never the "plan," we have always been *determined* proponents of looking through every door that is opened. You never know when something will be a big asset, even if it seems to be an obstacle at first. For example, we never wanted to come to Hanford, California. It ended up being the best decision the Navy made for us. And because we got out here at a low in the market, we have been able to really grow our portfolio in a way we never dreamed.

Q: What were the biggest obstacles and setbacks during your wealth-building stage? How did you overcome or push through them?
We started buying in 2011. We saw the deals, but in 2013 when we got to California and saw the low prices, we knew this was the time to stock up on buy and holds. Honestly, the most frustrating part was knowing there were tons of buy and hold deals and not being able to take advantage of them (the reality is, being young and having a stunted career made it really hard to obtain a lot of buy and holds). The market really wasn't for flippers; it was long-term buy and holds.

That being said, we learned a lot and were still able to get to eight houses. Now it's all about turning the great equity we made during the recession into the best uses. For example, we have recently done a huge portfolio shift now that we can support more expensive houses. We have sold our cheaper homes that have upcoming maintenance issues and traded them for brand-new, expensive, higher-rent homes. Many of these are on fifteen-year loans, something we couldn't do before. We are also getting into some furnished rentals.

Q: What's your No. 1 best tip for those looking to build wealth with real estate investing?

Turn your frustrations into advantages. For us, we have turned moving into a way to buy personal properties. Cheaper properties (because that was all we could afford) helped us build equity and flip them into larger properties. This has allowed us to continue to increase our rent and potential growth using the same equity, only better leverage.

Q: Can you explain in more detail your post–financial independence income? How do you plan on living off of this income?

Our primary source of FI income is the houses' rental income. Our goal is to leverage as much as possible to grow as large as possible in equity with the highest income possible. Our secondary source is a fixed health care expense through the military and a pension.

Q: What concerns do you have for the future related to retirement income? How will you address that?

Our largest concerns have been health care. We have alleviated that through the military health care and pension.

Q: Do you plan to start selling your real estate holdings? If so, when and how?

Yes and no. We have started to sell our real estate holdings but not to get rid of them. Instead, we're selling to upgrade them and use our equity better. The goal, for example, is to go from $1,500 to $2,100 of income with pretty much the same equity. For us, the goal is cash flow in our 40s. We want to grow our portfolio as much as possible to provide the largest cash flow. And we want to have the biggest amount of equity to allow us the most options.

Q: What's your No. 1 best tip for those looking to live off of investment income after retirement/financial independence?

Build as much as you can so you have the most options later!

CHAPTER 18
HOW TO CHOOSE THE RIGHT WEALTH-BUILDING PLAN FOR YOU

You've just made it through the real estate wealth-building plans. For some of you, I hope the lightbulbs went off in your head with one of the plans and you immediately said, "This plan is for me!" If so, put away the map and start climbing. The purpose of a plan is simply to help you make smart decisions and keep moving toward your goal. Actually applying the plan in real life is where your wealth is built.

But I've coached enough investors to know that many of you will be overwhelmed by the different wealth-building options. And that's OK. It's easy to get stuck at a crossroads because you don't want to make the wrong decision. After all, more than one of the plans could be promising. This chapter is designed to help you focus and choose the right real estate wealth-building plan to keep you moving forward.

It helps to think of yourself in one of three general situations:
1. Ready to Start or Just Getting Started
2. Own Some Properties, But Not Yet at Financial Independence Number
3. Own Enough Properties or Already Have a Large Chunk of Wealth

In the following sections, I'll give you some ideas for good wealth-building plans for each situation.

Ready to Start or Just Getting Started

When you're just getting started with real estate investing, the next step is simply to buy your first property or two. This important first step helps you learn, gain momentum, and start climbing. And depending on your financial goals, you may only need one or two properties to accomplish everything you need.

All the wealth-building plans I shared in "Part 4: The First Steps" are ideal for new investors. But the House Hacking Plan is always my first suggestion. It accomplishes multiple financial goals, and it is where many of the real estate early retirees profiled throughout this book got started. Long-term house hacking can easily transition into any of the primary wealth-building plans like the Rental Debt Snowball, Buy and Hold, or Trade Up. It's very flexible.

But perhaps you don't want to live next to your tenants. Or maybe your family can't fit in an apartment. I'd first encourage you to think creatively about house hacking. You could instead buy a house with a garage apartment or a separate accessory dwelling unit to rent as a house hack. I'd also encourage you to remember that house hacking does not have to be a forever plan. Just look at it as a stage of your life where you get started and then move on (which is what I did). The end results are well worth it! And if you buy in the right locations, the types of tenants you attract can be people who make great neighbors.

But if house hacking still isn't right for you, just begin with a regular house that you can convert to a rental (Live-In-Then-Rent Plan) or a flip (Live-In Flip Plan). Many of the real estate early retirees profiled in this book also got started with these strategies. Like house hacking, these plans will transition well into the primary wealth-building plans. And you still get some of the same owner-occupant financing benefits of house hacking that make it easier to get started.

If you are happily in a home or don't want to use any of these owner-occupied starter strategies for some reason, you can just start with purchasing a straight rental property. But my same advice applies: Just focus on the first one or two deals. You likely have a lot to learn about the business, so taking it slow early on will allow you to absorb the real-world education that these properties will teach you.

And if you have limited up-front cash for purchases, use the BRRRR Plan to conserve your cash. Buying low, rehabbing, renting, and then refinancing to pull out some or all of your cash will allow you to purchase more than one property. Since you don't have a lot of cash, you'll need to build a competitive advantage of being good at finding lower-priced fixer-upper properties. And this can get you started and moving toward one of the primary wealth-building plans, which I'll talk about next.

Own Some Properties, But Not Yet at Financial Independence Number

Some of you have already gotten started, but maybe you don't yet have enough properties to meet your financial independence number. For example, you may own three rental properties that each produce $350/month in net rental income after a mortgage payment of $400/month. This means you have a total of $1,050/month of net rental income, but you need $5,000/month to reach your financial independence number. Which plan should you choose?

For many of you, the decision in this situation is between the Buy and Hold Plan and the Trade-Up Plan. You still need to grow, so it's just a question of *how* you grow. The Buy and Hold Plan is all about using net income and/or appreciation to grow. The Trade-Up Plan uses quick forced appreciation (like fixing up a property and raising the rents) and periodic selling/exchanging of properties in order to grow. Both plans can work, but it often comes down to what you're comfortable with.

Use the Buy and Hold Plan to Buy More Rentals

The Buy and Hold Plan allows you to patiently collect rent, save cash flow, and accumulate extra savings from other sources (like your job, a side business, or even a fix-and-flip property). When you have enough cash for another down payment, you can then purchase your next property. This works especially well when you own properties that you don't want to sell. They may be great buildings, great locations, or both; you just want to let them sit and grow while you accumulate their cash flows.

In her Real Estate Early Retiree Profile at the end of Chapter 8, Paula Pant described doing this exact plan. She already owns properties, but she isn't selling the properties to trade up or using the cash flow to pay off debt. Instead, she's holding her rentals and every couple years, enough cash piles up to buy another rental. It's a safe, disciplined way to grow.

Use the Trade-Up Plan to Buy More Rentals

On the other hand, the Trade-Up Plan involves a few more moving parts. But if done successfully, you can quickly compound and grow your equity like no other plan. Using a 1031 exchange will require entrepreneurial skills and a team to execute everything successfully. You have forty-five days from the sale of the original property to identify a replacement property, and you have 180 days from the original sale to buy the replacement property.

The Trade-Up Plan is especially good if you're looking to transition from one property type (like houses or small multi-unit apartments) to a larger property type (larger multi-unit apartments or a large group of properties). One or two trades done well could have you in a position with all the cash flow you need to reach financial independence. But it's important to identify your personal temperament. The people I know successfully doing the Trade-Up Plan are entrepreneurs who get excited about wheeling and dealing. If that's not you, just stick with the Buy and Hold Plan and patiently grow.

There is also nothing wrong with combining these two plans in a sequence. For example, you may want to first trade up to exchange your equity to a better cash flow property. Then you can use the Buy and Hold Plan, save the cash flow, and continue growing from there.

Don't Buy Any More Rentals (For Now)

Finally, I have to mention one other possibility for those in this situation. Even if you're not at your financial independence number, some of you may want to push toward an intermediate financial milestone (such as a financial plateau described in Chapter 5). This means you want to get to a temporary stopping point and put growth on hold for a little while. For example, you may want to do a mini-retirement to travel for a year or more like I have. Or you may want to transition into semi-retirement, go part-time at your job, or just transition to a more interesting job that pays less.

In the earlier example of this section, you have three rentals that each produce $350 per month net income after paying a $400 per month mortgage. If you paid off all three mortgages using a Rental Debt Snowball, you'd have $750 per month of positive cash flow (pre-tax) per property or $2,250 per month total. That doesn't reach your full financial independence goal of $5,000 per month, but it gets you part of the way there. And that income, simplicity, and safety may serve you well during that financial plateau in your life. You can later begin growing again using the Buy and Hold Plan (accumulating more rentals) or even the Trade-Up Plan.

Now let's look at one more scenario: You have enough properties or wealth but need to make a few more moves to reach financial independence.

Own Enough Properties or Already Have a Large Chunk of Wealth

Once you have enough wealth to *theoretically* reach your financial independence number, you may find yourself in a few different scenarios. In a best case, you may have plenty of net rental income to pay for your early retirement expenses. If so, well done! As long as you're comfortable with your portfolio as it is, move on to Part 6 to learn how to build a retirement withdrawal that lasts.

In another case, you may have enough properties to reach your financial independence number, but you don't have enough rental income to fully support your lifestyle until your mortgages are paid off. This is the *perfect* scenario for the Rental Debt Snowball Plan. Just start concentrating your cash flow and savings, earn as much extra money as you can from other sources, and topple those debts like dominos. If you have an excess number of properties, you can also use the buy-3-sell-2-keep-1 concept to liquidate a couple of properties and use the net proceeds to accelerate debt paydown on a keeper property.

Finally, you may be in a situation with enough wealth to achieve financial independence, but you don't own any real estate assets. Your money may be currently invested in stocks, bonds, or some other traditional asset class, but you want to transition some of that money into real estate properties. This way you can produce enough income for part or all of your early retirement needs.

In this case, you may have a lot of wealth, but you're still a real estate rookie! Be careful. Go back and read my recommendations in this chapter for those ready to start or just starting. You may or may not want to buy a house hack property, but you can still take your first steps with a rental property *slowly*. You'll learn more on your first deal than you could ever learn in a real estate book. Take enough time to let those lessons sink in before buying your next deals.

And consider becoming a private lender. The subject is not a primary topic of this book, but it's an excellent way to generate passive income from real estate–based investments. You can make loans directly to borrowers, through a mortgage broker or hard money lender, or through one of the new crowdfunding platforms. The Real Estate Early Retiree Profile at the end of Chapter 9 with Liz Schaper is a perfect example of this path. Liz generates a large enough income from interest on her private loans to support her early retirement lifestyle.

Don't Overthink. Just Go Build Some Wealth

We've come to the end of the section on building wealth using real estate investing. Have you decided which wealth-building plan makes the most sense for you? The key is not to overthink everything.

Although you want to consider the big picture, you don't have to figure out every detail right away. That would be like trying to view your entire route up the mountain before you've even set foot on the trail! Your job, instead, is to think about your situation *right now*. Focus on the next steps. Which one of the plans excites you the most and seems to make the most sense? Do some journaling, take a walk, and give it a little time for reflection. If you're still stuck, consult with a mentor or other investors on places like BiggerPockets. com and local meetups. Sometimes just talking it through can clarify your situation.

Just like when you're climbing a mountain, your first steps don't have to be perfect. They just need to go up! If you choose a plan, buy a property, and begin building wealth, then you are moving up. You will have plenty of chances to stop and reflect. Keep this book by your side and return to it during a break from climbing. But if you stand still and never start, there are no adjustments to be made. Get in motion doing that next step!

Now let's move on to Part 6, where you figure out how to create an unending stream of income after you've reached the peak of financial independence.

———— PROFILE OF A REAL ESTATE EARLY RETIREE ————

ERIC BOWLIN
Ideal Real Estate Investing (idealrei.com)
Location: Worcester, Massachusetts
Chad's Favorite Quote from Eric:
"Make decisions with risk mitigation in mind ... some people focus entirely on the risks and forget to make a decision. ... Others dive in headfirst and don't protect the downside."

WEALTH-BUILDING STATISTICS
- **Profession/Career:** Graduate student and part-time Army, then Realtor and contractor

---

- **Income During Wealth-Building Phase:** $49,999 or less/year
- **How Big a Role Did Real Estate Play in Wealth-Building?** Primary role
- **Primary Real Estate Strategy(ies):** Long-term buy and hold, BRRRR plan, live-in flip, and more recently 1031 tax-free exchange and apartment syndication

FINANCIAL INDEPENDENCE STATISTICS
- **Age at Financial Independence:** 26 to 30
- **Annual Expenses in Retirement:** $50,000 to $75,000
- **Ideal Number of Rentals in Retirement:** 50+
- **Primary Source of Retirement Income:** Rental income
- **Secondary Source of Retirement Income:** Dividends from public stocks, period sale of stocks/equities, business income, income from syndications
- **Ideal Debt Level of Real Estate Portfolio:** 51% to 75%

——————— Q&A ———————

Q: Can you explain in more detail how you built your current wealth?
My wife and I focused on long-term buy and holds using a variation of the BRRR method. We'd pay cash for properties, stabilize and add value, and then we'd refinance them and cash out. I did this for a few years until we had enough rental income to pay all our bills, then we moved up to syndication.

Q: What were the biggest obstacles and setbacks during your wealth-building stage? How did you overcome or push through them?
The biggest obstacle was probably myself, and my setbacks were always related to losing focus on the core of the business. For example, I started a contracting company one year and didn't lose money, but wasted a whole year on that instead of just buying more property. If I had just stayed focused, I could have gotten a lot further, I believe.

Q: What's your No. 1 best tip for those looking to build wealth with real estate investing?

It's important to make decisions with risk mitigation in mind. This is important because some people focus entirely on the risks and forget to make a decision (and never get started). Others dive in headfirst and don't protect the downside.

Q: Can you explain in more detail your post–financial independence income? How do you plan on living off of this income?
Rental income is our primary source. My goal is to have my website be the secondary source. The idea is to have at least a few streams of revenue that are not entirely related to each other so if one isn't doing well, the other can pick up the slack.

Q: What concerns do you have for the future related to retirement income? How will you address them?
Our biggest issue is trying to make our investments more passive. Our portfolio requires a bit of our time to manage, and my wife and I would like to leverage that up into bigger deals and stop dealing with the day-to-day management. We don't really have a specific way to fix this issue.

Q: Do you plan to start selling your real estate holdings? If so, when and how?
We don't feel comfortable enough to sell yet. We don't have a time-line.

Q: What's your No. 1 best tip for those looking to live off of investment income after retirement/financial independence?
Focus on your goals up front and invest based on those specific goals. For example, if you want to travel a lot, structure your business so you can leave.

PART 6
THE PEAK AND BEYOND

*Strategies to Withdraw an
Unending Supply of Early
Retirement Income*

CHAPTER 19
AN EARLY RETIREMENT WITHDRAWAL PLAN THAT LASTS

You've arrived at the peak of the financial mountain. Congratulations! You now have enough wealth to cover your personal expenses with investment income during an early retirement. Enjoy the scenery for a while, but also realize that this new achievement brings its own set of challenges.

When climbing, the goal was to build wealth. Now the challenge is *keeping* that wealth and *withdrawing it* wisely to support your lifestyle for the rest of your life. Some early retirement nerds (that includes me!) call this financial stage the withdrawal or drawdown phase.

Your age and risk tolerance will influence what a good early retirement withdrawal plan looks like. For example, early retirees in their 30s, 40s, or 50s likely have a *long* time horizon of forty to sixty years to live off of their investments. It's very difficult to accurately predict economic, political, and social trends over these long periods. This means it's also difficult to give 100 percent foolproof withdrawal formulas. So, the general strategy for early retirees is to just stay flexible. This applies to your investment portfolio, your lifestyle, and your attitude about working for income (at least part-time) as a backup plan.

But if you're retiring at 65, for example, your priorities and timelines will likely be different. You will probably have Social Security or other pension income, secure health insurance through Medicare, and perhaps less desire (or ability) to work for income in a pinch. Your priorities could be weighted more toward a secure income and less risk, even if it sacrifices a bit of growth and flexibility.

It's important to get clear on where you are in life so that you can set priorities. Then you can build a withdrawal plan that works for you. But as with the rest of this book, my focus here will be primarily for people who plan to retire at an earlier age than traditional retirement (for example, 30 to 50). The rest of this chapter will summarize real estate–centered ideas to create an early retirement withdrawal plan that lasts.

Goals and Risks of the Withdrawal Phase

In the withdrawal phase, your wealth is like a big lake or reservoir full of water. You worked hard to fill the lake up, and now you want to make sure the reservoir of money lasts for your entire life as you withdraw from it. A good early retirement withdrawal plan helps you manage your wealth reservoir levels for the long run. And, more specifically, your withdrawal plan should be oriented around two primary goals:

Primary Withdrawal Plan Goals

1. Your portfolio pays for all your living expenses (now and in the future).
2. Your portfolio never runs out of money.

As we discussed in Part 2 with your financial independence number, living off your investments is basically a function of three factors:

- Your wealth or net worth (W)
- Your annual expenses (E)
- The cash return on your wealth (r)

Here's the formula I shared earlier:

$$W \times r = E$$
or
$$E \div r = W$$

If your wealth (W) is substantial, your expenses (E) can also be higher, even with a lower return (r). For example, if you have a $10 million net worth, even a low 2 percent cash return will produce $200,000 per year! But the smaller your wealth (W), the larger your return (r) needs to be in order to cover a minimal amount of expenses (E). However, if you have $1 million in wealth, you would need a 20 percent cash return to produce the same $200,000 per year.

But chasing high returns during early retirement exposes you to excessive risk of losing your savings. Remember that the second primary goal of an early retirement plan is that it never runs out. Maintaining (and even growing) your savings means that you can't just focus on maximizing your rate of withdrawal. You have to address the financial risks that could prematurely drain your hard-earned wealth.

To learn how to ensure that your wealth lasts, let's begin by looking at traditional retirement planning and something called the Four Percent Rule.

The Four Percent Rule and Traditional Retirement Planning

The Four Percent Rule says you can withdraw about 4 percent of your total investment portfolio without fear of running out of money in a traditional retirement period of about thirty years. For example, if you plan to live off of $100,000 per year, you'd need $2,500,000 in retirement savings to meet the 4 percent threshold ($100,000 / 4% = $2,500,000). William Bengen, a retired financial adviser, studied historical markets and first articulated the 4 percent concept in 1994.[26] He used it as a rule of thumb to advise his clients during their retirement withdrawal phase.

The 4 percent rule of thumb typically applies to a traditional portfolio of stocks, bonds, and mutual funds. And with interest and dividends at historic lows, it assumes the money for the 4 percent withdrawal will come from a combination of dividends, interest, *and* some sales of assets. The success rate of the Four Percent Rule is complicated and depends on several factors. But perhaps the biggest challenge to the 4 percent withdrawal strategy is that it depends, at least in part, on selling assets. And this makes you vulnerable to something known as the *sequence of returns risk*, the risk that if you sell at the wrong time, like right after a major stock market crash, you could permanently disable your portfolio.[27] And in that scenario, you risk a rapidly falling balance of wealth when you most need it.

---

26 William P. Bengen. "Determining Withdrawal Rates Using Historical Data." *Journal of Financial Planning*. October 1994.

27 The "Ultimate Guide to Safe Withdrawal Rates" by Karsten Jeske at earlyretirementnow.com has been my favorite resource to understand the nuances and limitations of the sequence of returns risk and the 4 percent rule. I encourage you to read his work if you're interested in the topic.

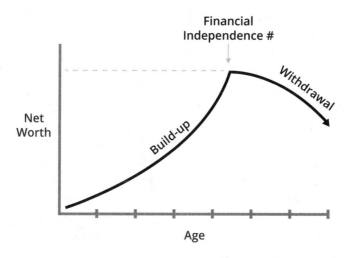

Financial
Independence #

Net
Worth

Build-up

Withdrawal

Age

You don't want the withdrawal arrow to hit $0 before you run out of years!

While I'm fascinated with the Four Percent Rule and the sequence of returns risk, as a real estate investor, these luckily need not be your major focus. Real estate isn't perfect, but it does have an important advantage when used as a primary early retirement withdrawal source. The advantage is that real estate investments tend to produce income at a much higher rate than other popular assets like stocks, bonds, annuities, and bank CDs. And real estate also offers a reasonable inflation hedge if you choose locations well.

This helpful combination of high income yields and a good inflation hedge allows you to build a simple real estate portfolio where you never have to sell or eat into your principal. I'll explain why that's so useful.

Don't Touch the Principal

In recent times, broadly diversified stock and bond portfolios produce dividends or interest at less than a 4 percent rate. Selling the stocks or bonds has been necessary to meet the 4 percent withdrawal strategy. This works as long as the prices go up, but a more conservative approach is to own assets that produce income at a rate greater than 4 percent so that you can live off of your investment income. Real estate investing is ideal for that.

For example, remember the seven free-and-clear rental houses in Chapter 4? They produced income of about $58,800/year after operating expenses. In my experience, a well-trained real estate investor can eventually find properties like these that produce between 5 percent and 10 percent rental income yields even with no debt. So the right real estate investments allow you to have a withdrawal strategy of more than the traditional Four Percent Rule for the same money invested. This way you can pay for your lifestyle expenses with more ease (goal No. 1 of a good withdrawal plan).

At the same time, you're not eating into any of your principal, which makes it kind of hard to run out! And not running out was goal No. 2 of a good withdrawal strategy. With your rental income safely covering your expenses, you don't need to sell investments. You may choose to sell for other reasons, like improving your portfolio. But overall you can be a patient, opportunistic investor who can avoid selling when property values drop.

Covering all your expenses and avoiding principal reduction are critical first steps in an early retirement. But there are other risks to think about, particularly inflation and an unpredictable economic future. This is especially true the longer you have to live off of your investments as an early retiree. In the next chapter, I'll share one of my favorite ways to address these priorities by using something called an "income floor + upside investing."

──────── **PROFILE OF A REAL ESTATE EARLY RETIREE** ────────

RICKY CAMERON

Cameron Realty (cameronrealty.net) &
The Diversified Doc (diversifieddoc.com)
Location: Quitman, Texas
Chad's Favorite Quote from Ricky:
"Many say to specialize; I say be open to any real estate investment that makes sense."

WEALTH-BUILDING STATISTICS

- **Profession/Career:** ER physician
- **Income During Wealth-Building Phase:** $200,000+/year
- **How Big a Role Did Real Estate Play in Wealth-Building?** Primary role
- **Primary Real Estate Strategy(ies):** Long-term buy and hold, short-term buy and hold, fix-and-flip, 1031 tax-free exchange

FINANCIAL INDEPENDENCE STATISTICS

- **Age at Financial Independence:** 46 to 50
- **Annual Expenses in Retirement:** $100,000 to $150,000
- **Ideal Number of Rentals in Retirement:** 50+
- **Primary Source of Retirement Income:** Rental Income
- **Secondary Source of Retirement Income:** Business income, side-hustles/part-time work
- **Ideal Debt Level of Real Estate Portfolio:** 51% to 75%

---------- Q&A ----------

Q: Can you explain in more detail how you built your current wealth?
After completion of medical school, I moved back to my hometown to begin my medical practice and I bought a 26-acre parcel of land. After cleaning the place up a bit, I received an unsolicited offer that allowed a nice profit of about $20,000. This seemed to be a nice side hustle, so I began buying, improving, and selling parcels of land in East Texas. I utilized 1031 exchanges and carried the notes on many properties either in the first or second lien position. Around 2008, I was able to liquidate my last tract of land before the real estate market slowed. Since the vacant land provided very little cash flow while holding, I decided to move into the rental market, as bank-owned homes were available on every corner. I used a combination of long-term and short-term buy and hold strategies to build a portfolio of properties as well as 1031 exchanges. I carried the notes on several of the homes but only have one left, as I refinanced the others later to pay off my higher-interest notes. Over the last several years, I've bought a couple of small apartments with a partner and syndicated a deal, and am currently working on a residential development.

Q: What were the biggest obstacles and setbacks during your wealth-building stage? How did you overcome or push through them?
Learning to delegate was my biggest obstacle. In the beginning, I felt as if I had to handle all steps in the process. When I learned to delegate, the wealth-building process shifted into overdrive. Not only did it allow me to accomplish more in a given amount of time, but my

team members were often better at the task than I was, creating a better end result.

Q: What's your No. 1 best tip for those looking to build wealth with real estate investing?

Many say to specialize; I say be open to any real estate investment that makes sense. If I had stuck with vacant land development, I would have done my last deal in 2006. The fundamentals of investing are the same. This isn't brain surgery. Keep an eye open for good deals, whether they be single-family homes, duplexes, commercial property, land, etc. Find partners that complement your skill set.

Q: Can you explain in more detail your post–financial independence income? How do you plan on living off of this income?

My primary source of FI at this point is still part-time ER shift work. I'm not dependent on the income, but I'm still a little anxious to walk away in my 40s from a career that's pretty malleable and took me twelve years to obtain the skills. My secondary sources of income are from positive cash flowing rentals, real estate notes, and a therapy staffing business I partnered with. The staffing opportunity was created by networking with real estate investors and being open to other investment vehicles.

Q: What concerns do you have for the future related to retirement income? How will you address them?

Real estate is my favorite investment class and currently the most tax-favored asset. However, the rules can change at any time, and the appeal of real estate could be tarnished if many of the tax advantages were to change. I still believe that diversification is critical to protecting your retirement income. You can diversify within real estate (single-family homes versus commercial triple net lease versus first lien notes, etc.) or keep a percentage of your wealth in other asset classes (index funds, businesses, etc.).

Q: Do you plan to start selling your real estate holdings? If so, when and how?

I'm accumulating both single-family homes and apartments so that I have options in my later years. There are proponents in each camp. Some say apartments are the only way to go; others say buy nothing but single-family homes. The truth is they are different and both have unique features. I'm planning to keep my apartments long-term, but start to sell my single-family home portfolio with long-term owner-financing in my 60s to give me stable income for thirty years. Be the bank.

Q: What's your No. 1 best tip for those looking to live off of investment income after retirement/financial independence?
Diversify your holdings and have multiple backup plans if the rules of the game are changed.

CHAPTER 20
BUILD AN INCOME FLOOR, THEN INVEST FOR THE UPSIDE

In his excellent book *Can I Retire Yet?* early retiree Darrow Kirkpatrick explains a hybrid approach to a withdrawal strategy.[28] Essentially, he recommends first building a safe and steady income floor to cover your expenses. This is similar to the concept of the financial independence number I first referenced back in Chapter 3. But once that income floor is secure, Darrow also recommends upside investing to help address future uncertainties and inflation.

Darrow is not a real estate investor, so his recommended income floor comes from safe, consistent income generators like annuities, pensions, and Social Security income. If you have access to these types of income streams, they can also be the first part of your income floor. You can then fill the remaining gap with real estate income properties.

I first learned about the equivalent of a real estate–based income floor from a long-time teacher and mentor of mine named John Schaub. In his book *Building Wealth One House at a Time,*[29] John explains something I've nicknamed "the free-and-clear real estate plan." The idea is to own a small portfolio of safe, easy-to-manage rental properties (likely single-family houses in quality neighborhoods) that have their mortgages paid off.

Why no mortgage debt? First of all, because it reduces your exposure to deflation risk (another Great Depression, like the 1920s). If market rents

---

28 Darrow Kirkpatrick. *Can I Retire Yet?* Chattanooga, TN: StructureByDesign, 2016.

29 John Schaub. *Building Wealth One House at a Time*. New York: McGraw-Hill, 2016.

were to fall off a cliff—it's possible!—your no-debt portfolio would give you a cushion to lower your rents without the concern of losing everything because you can't pay your mortgage. And beyond that, having no debt simplifies your investments so that you can focus on the many other things that matter in your life after financial independence.

But remember that in the long run, an income floor isn't enough. It's also wise to invest for the upside. This means your investment portfolio also needs to grow to keep up with inflation and to provide a financial cushion for unpredictable events. You have several options to do this, but I always like to start with the simplest solution. John Schaub's free-and-clear house plan actually does quite well serving double duty.

Houses in quality neighborhoods have the bonus benefit of being more than an income floor. As I said earlier, if you choose your location well, there is a good chance the price and rents will increase with inflation over time. And unlike apartments and commercial real estate, house prices aren't always correlated with the property's rent. A house's value is determined by demand from owner-occupant house buyers and the supply of competing homes on the market, meaning the house price could sometimes increase even if rents stay flat. If this income floor + upside rental portfolio works out, your early retirement withdrawal plan would look more like this over time:

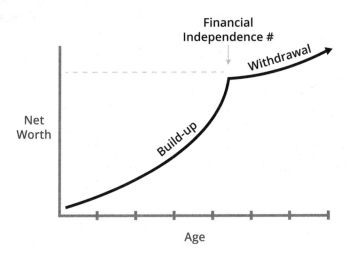

Having said all of this, properties free and clear of debt aren't the only way to create an income floor and invest for the upside. Your priorities, age, risk tolerance, and personal preferences might push you to still carry some debt.

And houses aren't the only good property type for an early retirement investment portfolio. In many areas (mine included), small multi-unit buildings (two, three, fourplexes) have similar long-term benefits over houses. Let me share an example of an income floor + upside investing portfolio with both free-and-clear and leveraged properties.

Sample Real Estate Income Floor + Upside Investing Portfolio

Let's say that during your wealth-building phase, you began with a combination of several plans from Parts 4 and 5. First, you use the Trade-Up Plan to quickly acquire seven duplexes and four fourplexes (eleven buildings, or thirty units in total). Each apartment unit rents for $600/month. And while the full value of each unit is $60,000, you are able to acquire them for less at $50,000/unit. In other words, the full value of your portfolio is $1,800,000 ($60,000 x 30 units) and the total acquisition cost is $1,500,000 ($50,000 x 30 units). This $1,500,0000 basis in the property is broken down between building cost ($1,100,000) and land cost ($400,000). With a depreciable lifetime of 27.5 years, this means you also get a depreciation shelter of $40,000/year total ($1,100,000 / 27.5) or $1,333/unit.

In the beginning, you use the BRRRR Plan with the four fourplexes to get thirty-year, 5 percent mortgage loans at $168,000, or 70 percent of the full value. For the financing of the seven duplexes, you start with a combination of personal cash, private money, and short-term loans. You then apply the Rental Debt Snowball Plan to help pay off the debt on all the duplexes as soon as possible. These duplexes are your income floor.

When the dust settles, your down payments and equity paydown have cost you about $828,000 total. This cash/equity requirement is about the same as the example of the seven free-and-clear houses I referenced way back in Chapter 4 ($120,000 x 7 = $840,000). I make this point because someone who had the financial resources to do the single-family house income floor plan could also do this one. Here is what the portfolio balances look like in this case:

PORTFOLIO BALANCES — 7 DUPLEXES AND 4 FOURPLEXES				
Property	Full Value	Purchase Cost	Cash Invested	Debt
Duplex #1	$120,000	$100,000	$100,000	$0
Duplex #2	$120,000	$100,000	$100,000	$0
Duplex #3	$120,000	$100,000	$100,000	$0
Duplex #4	$120,000	$100,000	$100,000	$0
Duplex #5	$120,000	$100,000	$100,000	$0
Duplex #6	$120,000	$100,000	$100,000	$0
Duplex #7	$120,000	$100,000	$100,000	$0
Fourplex #1	$240,000	$200,000	$32,000	$168,000
Fourplex #2	$240,000	$200,000	$32,000	$168,000
Fourplex #3	$240,000	$200,000	$32,000	$168,000
Fourplex #4	$240,000	$200,000	$32,000	$168,000
Total:	$1,800,000	$1,500,000	$828,000	$672,000

This is a relatively safe balance sheet with a total debt of less than 40 percent of your portfolio value. But *how* you split up that debt is crucial. You could have spread the $672,000 of debt equally over all eleven properties. But this would be riskier because your inability to make mortgage payments in a disaster scenario could mean losing *all* your properties. Instead, you borrowed more against the four fourplexes and paid off the debt on the duplex part of the portfolio. This gives you one group of properties that's highly leveraged and another group that's free and clear of debt and producing strong income. You may even choose to separate the duplexes and fourplexes into two or more of their own LLCs (limited liability corporations) to keep your assets in different risk buckets.

But the other important early retirement question is: Does this balanced portfolio produce enough cash flow to serve you well as an income floor? Let's take a look.

TOTAL INCOME — 7 DUPLEXES AND 4 FOURPLEXES

Property	Net Operating Income/ Year	Mortgage Payment/ Year	Net Income After Finance/ Year	Depreciation Expense/ Year	Taxable Income/ Year
Duplex #1	$7,800	$0	$7,800	-$2,667	$5,133
Duplex #2	$7,800	$0	$7,800	-$2,667	$5,133
Duplex #3	$7,800	$0	$7,800	-$2,667	$5,133
Duplex #4	$7,800	$0	$7,800	-$2,667	$5,133
Duplex #5	$7,800	$0	$7,800	-$2,667	$5,133
Duplex #6	$7,800	$0	$7,800	-$2,667	$5,133
Duplex #7	$7,800	$0	$7,800	-$2,667	$5,133
Fourplex #1	$15,600	-$10,824	$4,776	-$5,333	-$557
Fourplex #2	$15,600	-$10,824	$4,776	-$5,333	-$557
Fourplex #3	$15,600	-$10,824	$4,776	-$5,333	-$557
Fourplex #4	$15,600	-$10,824	$4,776	-$5,333	-$557
Total/ Year	$117,000	-$43,296	$73,704	-$40,000	$33,704/ Year

With $828,000 equity invested, this portfolio produces $73,704/year in net income after financing. That's more than the $58,800/year in net income for the seven free-and-clear single-family houses. But even better, the *taxable* income for this leveraged portfolio is only $33,704, as long as you still have a depreciation expense. This means you only pay income taxes on the smaller portion. By purchasing rentals with better cash flow characteristics and using some relatively safe leverage, you've increased your take-home income dramatically using a similar amount of savings. And importantly, there is built-in growth with loan amortization to give you upside protection.

But there are always trade-offs. Let's look at the pluses and minuses of this leveraged apartment scenario as an income floor + upside investment.

PLUSES/MINUSES — LEVERAGED APARTMENT PORTFOLIO AS INCOME FLOOR + UPSIDE INVESTMENT	
Plus	**Minus**
More income ($73,704 vs. $58,800)	More tenants and units to manage or worry about (30 vs. 7)
Greater depreciation to shelter more income	Lower-price rentals ($600) may be more difficult to manage and keep tenants than houses at twice the rent ($1,200)
Built-in growth with principal paydown	More buildings to repair and replace over time
Possibly greater appreciation growth because of greater asset values and debt leverage	Debt adds risk in a depression-like economic cycle (less flexibility to lower rents on fourplexes)

As you can see from the pluses and minuses, there is no clear winner between this portfolio and the other with debt-free houses that produce less income. The better choice depends on which characteristics are more important to you.

And based on the early retiree profiles I included with this book, real-life early retirees are also split between these types of portfolio choices during an early retirement. Some wanted no debt, and others were comfortable with a high percentage of debt compared to their overall portfolio value. Some only wanted a few properties, and others wanted many more. Feel free to find variations that you like best. Your job is to adapt basic templates like I've given you here to your circumstances and local market realities.

And while long-term rentals may form the core of your early retirement withdrawal strategy, don't put all your eggs in one basket over the long run. Diversification can be the final piece of the puzzle to ensure a long, successful early retirement.

Diversify Your Withdrawal Strategies

I am obviously a fan of building your early retirement income around a *core* of real estate. But other non–real estate income sources have their benefits as well. Todd Tresidder and his excellent book *How Much Money*

Do I Need to Retire? influenced a lot of my thinking on a successful early retirement withdrawal plan.[30] In that book, Todd says this about income diversification:

> You should be no more willing to bet your entire retirement on an insurance company's ability to pay an annuity than you would rely on the government to honor its promises for Social Security. It's okay to make each one a piece of your retirement equation, but each income source has risks which must be managed. Never leave yourself exposed to a single default that can wipe out your financial security.

So a wise approach is to diversify your income sources. This can start by owning properties and other real estate investments (like private loans) in various, uncorrelated locations. But in addition to your core of real estate investments, you could add other non-real estate sources over time. With a variety of income sources built on a foundation of quality real estate, you'll give yourself the best chance of long-term success. Here are some reliable income sources that you could use to diversify your early retirement withdrawal plan:

- Social Security pension (full benefits at age 67 for those born after 1960[31])
- Pension from corporation, military, or government (if applicable)
- Stock dividends
- Annuities (a contract with an insurance company to pay you income for life)
- Interest from bank certificate of deposits
- Bond interest
- Retirement account withdrawals

Retirement account withdrawals aren't really an asset class by themselves. You could actually own many of these other assets within your retirement account. But because these accounts are such a critical piece of most people's retirement income puzzle, the entire next two chapters will go into detail on the role of retirement accounts for early retirees, both as a source for your income floor and an upside investment.

---

30 Todd Tresidder. *How Much Money Do I Need to Retire?* FinanialMentor.com, 2013.

31 "If you were born in 1960, your full retirement age is 67." U.S. Social Security Administration. Last accessed March 12, 2018. www.ssa.gov/planners/retire/1960.html.

DAVE BOROUGHES
Location: Newport, Rhode Island
Chad's Favorite Quote from Dave:
"I'd rather live modestly and vacation four or five times a year than to not be able to do anything but come up with money to pay for my McMansion."

WEALTH-BUILDING STATISTICS
- **Profession/Career:** Retail store manager, real estate investing on the side
- **Income During Wealth-Building Phase:** $150,000 to $199,000/year
- **How Big a Role Did Real Estate Play in Wealth-Building?** Primary role
- **Primary Real Estate Strategy(ies):** Long-term buy and hold, fix-and-flip

FINANCIAL INDEPENDENCE STATISTICS
- **Age at Financial Independence:** 36 to 40
- **Annual Expenses in Retirement:** $75,000 to $100,000
- **Ideal Number of Rentals in Retirement:** 11 to 20
- **Primary Source of Retirement Income:** Rental income
- **Secondary Source of Retirement Income:** Dividends from public stocks, Social Security income
- **Ideal Debt Level of Real Estate Portfolio:** Less than 25% loan to value

———— Q&A ————

Q: Can you explain in more detail how you built your current wealth?
Long-term buy and holds, with some fix-and-flips along the way. I held a regular salaried career job with a major corporation to be able to continually take out more mortgages. Once I was married, my wife began taking out mortgages in her name (she had a good-paying career

job as well) and we just grew and grew our long-term rental property portfolio. I retired from my day job five years ago at age 38 and do real estate investment full-time. We have our portfolio of properties that provides the cash flow to live life, and I do fix-and-flips on the side (I've been successful with every flip, each time producing more and more profit). I also obtained my real estate salesperson license to gain access to new MLS listings and save thousands on commissions.

Q: What were the biggest obstacles and setbacks during your wealth-building stage? How did you overcome or push through them?
Our debt-to-income ratio began to hinder our ability to obtain more mortgages. Even though all my properties cash flowed, and I had a steady income from a major company and a great credit score, with all the write-offs from all the properties, the banks didn't like how I looked on paper. I had to think creatively. I got a HELOC on my primary residence in order to come up with enough of a down payment for a larger investment on an apartment building. I then renovated and refinanced the multi-unit property. I've also used a 1031 exchange once to purchase a replacement investment property and save some tax money while maintaining the same cash flow and putting some cash in my pocket.

Q: What's your No. 1 best tip for those looking to build wealth with real estate investing?
You have to make sure the numbers work, especially today. Twenty years ago, the numbers worked on anything. Nowadays, not so much. You need a long-term plan. Always be thinking of how you can obtain the next deal. And only start investing in real estate in a market you are very familiar with.

Q: Can you explain in more detail your post–financial independence income? How do you plan on living off of this income?
My real estate portfolio throws off enough cash flow for me to live. I'm not driving a Porsche just yet, but it won't be far off. My flipping business helps me accumulate large amounts of cash for investments, which also pay dividends and provide a cushion to fall back on if needed.

Q: What concerns do you have for the future related to retirement income? How will you address them?

I don't have any concerns. I continue to live modestly within my means. I'd rather live modestly and vacation four or five times a year than to not be able to do anything but come up with money to pay for my McMansion.

Q: Do you plan to start selling your real estate holdings? If so, when and how?

I don't have any plans to sell anything. Maybe I'll hire a property manager when I get older and don't want to deal with the headaches anymore. If I get in a bind, I can always sell a property, but I don't have any plans to at this point. I have heard of people who sell to their kids (and hold the note) to let them become involved in the business, while still keeping the real estate empire in the family for the next generation. This sounds appealing.

Q: What's your No. 1 best tip for those looking to live off of investment income after retirement/financial independence?

Plan, plan, plan. Have streams of income from more than just real estate. Invest in long-term mutual funds in Fortune 500 companies, buy into bonds, even hold some money in CDs. Diversify, as they all say!

CHAPTER 21

THE ROLE OF RETIREMENT ACCOUNTS FOR EARLY RETIREES

Retirement accounts are one of the most important tools for anyone who wants to reach financial independence. Because of their tax advantages, retirement accounts allow you to grow and compound your wealth much faster than normal. Along with real estate investing, retirement accounts are one of the few ways to build wealth in a tax-efficient way.

The table below shows an example of the improved results investing inside a retirement account like a traditional IRA or 401(k). In one scenario, a couple puts $10,000/year into a pre-tax, traditional IRA account. In the second scenario, another couple puts $10,000/year into a regular taxable investment account. The second couple with the taxable account has a tax rate of 30 percent on all earnings (combined federal and state taxes). In both cases, their investment earnings are 10 percent a year, and they will continue making contributions and growing their investments for thirty years. Here's what the results look like.

TAX-FREE VS. TAXABLE GROWTH				
Year	Contributions ($10,000/Year)	IRA Balance	Non-IRA Balance	Difference
Year 5	$50,000	$61,051	$57,507	$3,544
Year 10	$100,000	$159,374	$138,164	$21,210
Year 15	$150,000	$317,725	$251,290	$66,435
Year 20	$200,000	$572,750	$409,955	$162,795
Year 25	$250,000	$983,471	$632,490	$350,981
Year 30	$300,000	$1,644,940	$944,608	$700,332

The difference in the final result is incredible. The first couple with the IRA account has a balance of more than $1.6 million, and the couple with the taxable non-IRA account has less than $945,000. That's a difference of more than $700,000 with the same contributions and the same investment returns! Here's what that looks like in graph form.

Tax-Free vs. Taxable Growth

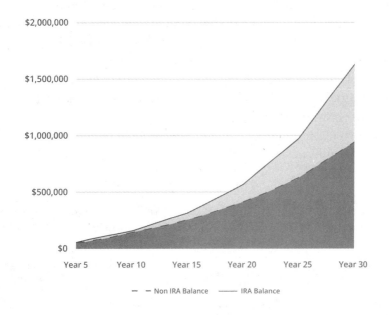

For this reason, from a young age you should always max out your contributions to retirement accounts, if possible. But the role of retirement accounts is a little trickier for someone who plans to retire earlier.

Early Retirees and Retirement Accounts

Most retirement accounts have early withdrawal penalties before age 59.5. There are exceptions to the penalty that I'll discuss later in the chapter. For someone retiring early at age 45, you have fifteen years (age 45 to 59.5) until you can begin withdrawing from your retirement accounts penalty-free. That is why I spent so much time thus far on real estate wealth-building plans you can use *outside* of your retirement account. You will need to depend heavily on these non-retirement-account investments to pay for your lifestyle as an early retiree.

But that doesn't make retirement accounts unimportant. Even if you retire early, you'll *still* reach traditional retirement at some point. Ideally, that means you'll contribute money *inside* a retirement account and you'll save *outside* your retirement account. The high savings rate we discussed in Part 3 comes in handy here. But if savings are very limited, you may have to make a tough choice between the two. You'll ultimately have to make that call based on your goals and timeline for early retirement.

Those of you already at age 59.5 may choose to use retirement accounts right now as part of your retirement withdrawal plan. In this chapter I am going to focus more on the situation of earlier-age retirees. If you are approaching age 60 right now, there are many books and internet sites you can find for traditional retirement withdrawal strategies. In particular, I recommend you read a blog post titled "Our Retirement Investment Drawdown Strategy," from my blogging colleague Fritz Gilbert at theretirementmanifesto.com.[32] His post goes into detail about which accounts he plans to tap first in order to optimize retirement account wealth after age 60.

For current early retirees or those planning to retire early, my own situation may be informative.

The Pre-60 and Post-60 Plans

My general approach to early retirement investing has been to create two parallel plans. The first plan is to build wealth to live on *before* my wife and I

---

32 Fritz Gilbert. "Our Retirement Investment Drawdown Strategy," theretirementmanifesto.com. Last accessed April 3, 2018 at www.theretirementmanifesto.com/our-retirement-investment-draw-down-strategy/.

turn 60 years old. The second plan is to build wealth to live on *after* we turn 60 years old.

I use 60 years old because age 59.5 doesn't roll off the tongue as easily! As I mentioned before, at 59.5 you can begin withdrawing retirement account savings without penalty. Therefore, I look at these retirement accounts as something to put under lock and key until later in life. We won't touch them so that they can safely compound and grow. At this point in our lives, retirement accounts are essentially pure upside investments that provide extra cushion in our later years. If we get to the point where we have less flexibility to work or if something should happen to our real estate investments, these accounts will be there as a backup plan.

Our pre-60 plan (I'm 38, and my wife is 40 years old as I write this) is all about real estate investing *outside* of retirement accounts. Most of the real estate wealth-building plans you've read about thus far apply to this pre-60 plan. Our post-60 retirement plan is mostly *inside* retirement accounts, and it's a mix of self-directed real estate investments (mainly private notes, tax liens, and limited real estate partnerships) and low-cost stock index funds.

We plan to live off rent, interest, and occasional work income in the pre-60 plan. If we ever find ourselves short of money before 60, we could sell or refinance properties to access equity. Knowing we have retirement accounts would make us less worried about reducing the principal of our wealth in that case.

But if all goes well, we should still have most of our pre-60 real estate investments to combine with our retirement account investments after age 60. They'll also be worth more if we picked the locations well in the first place. But the future is uncertain and things may not go well. Separating the wealth-building plans into pre- and post-60 gives us peace of mind. We're not putting all our eggs in one basket for our old age.

But questions about retirement accounts for early retirees still remain. Like, which retirement accounts should you contribute to as an early retiree? And what types of investments should you focus on in these retirement accounts? I'll give you some general guidelines on those topics in the sections that follow.

Types of Retirement Accounts

In terms of tax benefits, there are two major types of retirement accounts: pre-tax and post-tax.

Pre-Tax Accounts:

This is the most common type, and it includes the 401(k), traditional IRA, 403(b), and 457(b). These accounts have the following characteristics:
- Contributions are made pre-tax (they reduce your taxable income)
- Money grows tax-free
- Withdrawals are taxed at your ordinary income tax rate

Here's a simple illustration, courtesy of my blogging friend and fellow early retiree at the madfientist.com. Contributions are tax free (dark color), growth is tax free (dark color), withdrawals are taxed (light color).

Post-Tax Accounts:

This type of account includes a Roth IRA and Roth 401(k), which have the following characteristics:
- Contributions are made post-tax (i.e., you pay taxes up front)
- Account grows tax-free
- Withdrawals are tax-free

Again, here's an illustration. Contributions are taxed (light color), growth is tax free (dark color), withdrawals are tax free (light color).

Both types have their benefits compared to investing in a taxable or non-retirement account. But based on the characteristics of these retirement account types, here are a couple of generalizations about which one to invest in.

If you have a large income subject to high tax rates *and* you plan to retire early, you should probably max out *pre-tax* accounts like a 401(k) or traditional IRA. The compound growth on the up-front tax savings makes an enormous positive difference in your wealth over the long run. Plus, as I'll explain in the next chapter, there are ways to legally move money in pre-tax accounts to a post-tax Roth IRA using a Roth IRA conversion at a later date.

If you have a lower income or large deductions (as some real estate investors do) that put you in lower tax brackets, you should probably make contributions to a post-tax Roth or Roth 401(k). This may also occur in years where you temporarily have lower income, say, when you're between jobs or during a mini-retirement.

Keep in mind that everyone's situation is different. Think about these options, then be sure to run your decisions by your tax professional before actually executing your strategy. But once you have money in these accounts, the next challenge is figuring out how to invest it.

The Best Investments Inside a Retirement Account

As you can tell from this book, I am a big fan of real estate investments—both inside and outside your retirement account. But there is nothing wrong with using your retirement account for a non-real estate, well-diversified investment like low-cost index funds. Real estate investors I respect, like Paula Pant, who is featured in an early retiree profile in Chapter 8, do exactly that. And it's the approach Warren Buffett recommends for most passive investors.[33] If you prefer not to invest in real estate inside your retirement account, no problem. And if you want to learn more about low-cost index-fund investing, I recommend the book *The Simple Path to Wealth* by J. L. Collins (jlcollinsnh.com).

I actually plan to continue increasing my holdings of low-cost index funds over time to about 50 percent of my retirement portfolio. But I have also had success in my retirement account investing in what I know: real estate. I'll explain more about how that works in case you're interested.

To directly invest in real estate or related investments, you must first place your retirement funds with a custodian who allows you to *self-direct* your investments. I personally use the company American IRA, LLC, out of Asheville, North Carolina, but you can Google "self-directed IRA real estate" to find a long list of self-directed custodians. These special custodians allow you to open self-directed IRA, Roth IRA, Solo 401(k), and Health Savings

---

33 Dan Burrows. "Warren Buffett: Why Index Funds Trump Hedge Funds," January 8, 2018. www.kiplinger.com/article/investing/T030-C008-S001-warren-buffett-why-index-funds-trump-hedge-funds.html.

Accounts, depending on your preference.

Once you have a self-directed custodian, you will then be able to choose your own investments. But the first thing to know about self-directed retirement investing is that the IRS has *strict* rules about prohibited transactions. If you break the rules, the penalties are *severe*. So start by reading the IRS's regulations by visiting its website or Googling "retirement account prohibited transaction rules."

But know, in general, that the prohibited transaction rules say you can't self-deal. This means you can't use your retirement account money to benefit yourself, your family members of lineal descent (father, mother, son, daughter, etc.), or your close business associates. For example, you can't lend money to your son. And you can't buy or sell a property between you (or your company) and your retirement account. You need to think about your retirement account investments as a *completely* separate operation.

As long as you follow all the rules, you can then invest in pretty much anything except exotic assets like collectibles, art, and insurance annuities. Real estate is fair game. But the veteran self-directed retirement account investors I've studied over the years (my go-to sources besides BiggerPockets resources are Dyches Boddiford at assets101.com and John Schaub at johnschaub.com) recommend only certain types of real estate investments for your retirement account. These include:

- Private mortgage notes
- Limited partnerships
- Property tax liens
- Option contracts to buy real estate

You'll notice this does not include directly owning rentals, fix-and-flip properties, or more active types of real estate transactions. While it's possible to invest in those, my approach as an early retiree is to stick to the more passive investments that don't require your direct involvement. This avoids potential IRS issues of improperly contributing your labor to increase the value of your account (like painting a house owned by your IRA to "save" money). And it also keeps you in the role of a passive, long-term investor so that you can put most of your day-to-day time into your job or your non-retirement account investments.

Of all the available retirement investments in real estate, I like private mortgage notes the best. This means you become the lender for other property owners instead of owning the property yourself. A private mortgage note gives you the security and control of real estate investments along with the benefit of more passive interest income. And because your retirement account earns this interest, it can grow tax-free and compound quickly over time.

Owning actual real estate properties in a retirement account is less ideal because some of the big benefits like leverage, long-term capital gains treatment, depreciation, etc., don't typically help you in a retirement account. Plus, those strategies involve more moving parts, accounting headaches, active involvement, and potential risks that you probably want to avoid.

If you want to learn all the details about mortgage note investing, BiggerPockets has the book *Real Estate Note Investing* by long-time expert Dave Van Horn.[34] You can also see my article on BiggerPockets.com called "The Beginner's Guide to Building Wealth with Private Notes."[35] But, in general, private mortgage note investing means lending money to other real estate investors who are buying properties to flip or rent. You can use your skills as a real estate investor to evaluate the property and the person behind the loan. And you can decide whether you want to:

A. Make loans directly to borrowers you trust.

B. Invest in a fund or partnership that lends to multiple borrowers.

C. Invest through newer but interesting real estate crowdfunding platforms that allow you to make smaller loan amounts to a larger number of borrowers.

Many of the private partnerships and crowdfunding platforms require you to be an accredited investor. According to Regulation D of the U.S. Securities and Exchange Law,[36] this means you must have a net worth of more than $1 million (excluding your personal residence) or that you have earned more than $200,000 per year for the last two years (or $300,000 as a married couple). If you don't fit that criteria, which many of you won't, you'll just need to find partnerships or platforms that don't have that requirement. Or you can just stick to more direct forms of note investing.

Now that you understand more about the role of retirement accounts for an early retiree, there is one more related topic to cover. Most of you will want to optimize your retirement accounts during early retirement to maximize

---

34 You can purchase the book at www.biggerpockets.com/noteinvesting.

35 Chad Carson. "The Beginner's Guide to Building Wealth with Private Notes," BiggerPockets. Last updated December 1, 2017. www.biggerpockets.com/renewsblog/private-note-wealth-building-plan/.

36 Securities Act of 1933, 17 CFR. § 230.501 (1933).

their effectiveness later in life. And some of you may even need to access your retirement account funds early (before age 59.5). We'll look at both of those topics in the next chapter.

─────── **PROFILE OF A REAL ESTATE EARLY RETIREE** ───────

FELISA SAVAGE

Location: Jacksonville, Florida

Chad's Favorite Quote from Felisa:

"Have a combination of resources: rentals, Roth IRA, IRA, taxable accounts, business/side gigs. It gives you a lot more flexibility."

WEALTH-BUILDING STATISTICS

- **Profession/Career:** Health care sales
- **Income During Wealth-Building Phase:** $75,000 to $99,000/year
- **How Big a Role Did Real Estate Play in Wealth-Building?** Equally as important as other investment vehicles
- **Primary Real Estate Strategy(ies):** Long-term buy and hold

FINANCIAL INDEPENDENCE STATISTICS

- **Age at Financial Independence:** 41 to 45
- **Annual Expenses in Retirement:** $50,000 to $75,000
- **Ideal Number of Rentals in Retirement:** 2 to 5
- **Primary Source of Retirement Income:** Rental Income
- **Secondary Source of Retirement Income:** Dividends from public stocks/equities, periodic sale of stocks/equities
- **Ideal Debt Level of Real Estate Portfolio:** Between 26% to 50% loan to value

─────── **Q&A** ───────

Q: Can you explain in more detail how you built your current wealth?
The majority of my real estate wealth was built on the long-term buy and hold strategy of buying single-family three bedroom, two baths, within ten miles of my house. When my husband and I first started, we

bought a house, lived in it for one to two years, then bought another house and made the first one a rental. This allowed us to get owner-occupied financing and fix the house up as we lived there. Once we had kids, we stopped moving but would put a second mortgage on a rental house and take the equity as the down payment on the first house.

At our highest point, we had twenty properties. We also did a few flips along the way but learned that we weren't especially handy, and after we accounted for all the time spent fixing, we didn't make that much money. We did a few 1031 exchanges as well but found the timing requirement hard to control.

Q: What were the biggest obstacles and setbacks during your wealth-building stage? How did you overcome or push through them?
We had a lot of success and failure during our wealth-building stage. The biggest, by far, was 2008, which was a horrible time for us. We were doing everything just to hold on. Our biggest downfall was private lending/notes. I would not recommend this to anyone!

We were hard-money lenders in 2006 to 2008, and even though the notes were secured by the property, when the market crashed, people would just hand us the keys back. They didn't really care about their credit. Then you had a property that was halfway through a repair job. We found that most people hadn't pulled proper permits, hadn't paid property taxes, and had poor workmanship. We then either had to put more money into the property to fix it, sell it for a loss, or let it default for taxes.

We also had some blanket lines of credit, and when the crunch came, the banks called the notes due, even though we could still pay. They didn't care and just wanted their money back. We lost four houses due to this. (Side note: We watched the bank hold on to these properties, which were vacant for about two years, and they ended up selling them for way less than what we were paying. But for them it was all about the control of the asset.)

Q: What were the long-term effects of these challenges on your life?
We kept holding on, sinking all of our available cash into keeping things afloat. We thought we could just ride it out. We didn't make it.

In 2010 we had to file for a Chapter 11 business reorganization bankruptcy. It had to be a Chapter 11 because we had more than a million in assets (less any liabilities) and all the debt was tied to the real estate business. We didn't have fancy boats, cars, or credit card debts—it was all real estate. We thought this would allow us to reorganize the debt and get us back on our feet, but looking back it still wasn't worth it. All they really did was reset all the loans back to thirty years at a fixed rate of 5.25 percent. So the payments came down, but it wasn't a great rate and didn't reduce the amount owed. We had to pay $68,000 in lawyer fees and owed the same amount in the end.

If you don't have money, it is easy to walk away, but if you have any type of assets, it will drain every penny. It ruined our credit, but along with that it just became a paper nightmare. I am still dealing with banks seven years later, even though the bankruptcy was discharged as completed in 2011. They still don't have their computer systems correct. We also held on too long thinking we could ride it out. It would have been much better to financially walk away, but instead we dumped all of our cash into keeping things afloat. It was our word, our reputation, our credit, and our pride. But in the end, it didn't matter. It was the most embarrassing day of my life when we had to file; before this I never even had a bounced check or a credit card balance.

It also was too much of a financial strain and caused our divorce. I will forever think about the effects this had on my children. I can't change the past, but it had a profound effect on my life. We had to split up the number of houses, but we are still tied together financially because we can't refinance each other out (too many mortgages under our names and bankruptcy). I'm now at twelve houses, but they all have significant equity and cash flow after prices and rents went up. I don't ever want to be over-leveraged again. I love the cash flow, diversification, and tax benefits of real estate, but it is definitely not a passive investment.

Q: What's your No. 1 best tip for those looking to build wealth with real estate investing?
My best tips would be to follow the One Percent Rule (make the rent

greater or equal to the mortgage so, at worst, you break even), make sure the house is within thirty minutes of your own house, don't over-leverage yourself, and have an exit strategy.

Q: Can you explain in more detail your post–financial independence income? How do you plan on living off of this income?

My FI income is a combination of rental income, cash flow from index funds, and proceeds from selling the real estate. After 2011, I started saving about half of my W2 salary and investing it in the stock market. I have also spent the last few years using the rental income to fix up some of the properties so I could increase the rent.

Q: What concerns do you have for the future related to retirement income? How will you address them?

I worry about sequence of returns risk, so I am trying to build up my cash cushion and prepare for the long term. I'm not calling for a stock market or real estate crash, but both seem to be at the peak right now, and I want to be able to weather the storm.

Q: Do you plan to start selling your real estate holdings? If so, when and how?

This is a big challenge to me, and the one thing that most real estate investors don't talk about. No one talks about how or when they will sell, only how they will buy. I want to travel more, and I don't want to get calls about the AC or late payments. I also want to minimize the tax recapture. Real estate is great for tax treatment when you are buying, but it hurts when you are selling. I sold two last year, and it killed me in taxes. I ended up losing my Roth IRA contribution, child tax credit, etc., because it pushed me into a higher tax bracket.

My plan is to sell one or two properties a year for the next ten years. I need to do this slowly so I don't get the tax hit. I may live off of the proceeds or maybe pay off another mortgage. (I know, not a good use of leverage, but at this stage of my life, I would really like to have zero debt and strong cash flow.) I may try to skip a year here or there so I can do some Roth IRA conversions, but it is really hard to plan. My best plan is that as a tenant moves out, I will just fix up that place and put it on the market.

My fear is that I will have a few move out in the same year, and I will have to re-rent instead of sell or take the tax hit. I have looked into selling as rentals, but they don't sell as high that way because everyone wants a deal. I have thought about leaving the rentals to my kids, but they really don't want them. And, tax-wise, the only real benefit comes if I die. And I plan on living for a long time!

Q: What's your No. 1 best tip for those looking to live off of investment income after retirement/financial independence?
Have a combination of resources: rentals, Roth, IRA, taxable accounts, business/side gigs. It gives you a lot more flexibility.

CHAPTER 22
RETIREMENT ACCOUNT OPTIMIZATION AND EARLY WITHDRAWALS

As you saw in the previous chapter, most retirement accounts have early withdrawal penalties before age 59.5. As a result, for most early retirees, a retirement account is best used as a long-term investment vehicle that you can access a decade or two in the future. This means you want to optimize and grow your account as much as possible while you are waiting. To help you do that, let me first introduce an important retirement account rule called required minimum distributions.

Required Minimum Distributions

One of the catches of pretax retirement accounts like a 401(k), 403(b), and traditional IRA is the required minimum distribution (RMD), which begins at age 70.5. An RMD means you must distribute or take out a certain amount of money from your account each year (and pay ordinary income taxes on it). The minimum withdrawal amount depends on your age and other factors. You can find the formula on the IRS website or use the good RMD calculator at schwab.com.[37]

If you have a small IRA or 401(k) account balance and draw on it starting at age 59.5, this may not be a problem. But many early retirees could have large balances after years of contributions and compounding. So, RMDs could push

---

37 "RMD Calculator." Charles Schwab & Co, Inc. Last accessed on 3/13/2018. www.schwab.com/public/schwab/investing/retirement_and_planning/understanding_iras/ira_calculators/rmd.

you into higher, expensive tax brackets after age 70.5 as you're forced to take out large withdrawals. And those higher tax bills reduce the amount of money you can depend on for later years of retirement or for passing on to your heirs.

Unlike pretax retirement accounts, however, Roth IRAs do not have required minimum distributions. And Roth IRA withdrawals are tax-free for both you and your heirs once you die. Even better, *contributions* to a Roth IRA can be taken out *anytime* (even before age 59.5, as long as you follow the five-year waiting rules I'll explain later). This makes Roth IRAs the ideal retirement account once you're at a traditional retirement age.

A helpful strategy in early retirement is to prepare for traditional retirement by converting the money in pretax accounts to a Roth IRA account. This can reduce the sting of RMDs, optimize your taxes during a traditional retirement, and make more funds available for an early withdrawal if needed.

The Power of a Roth IRA Conversion in Early Retirement

I hope it's clear that you'd rather have most of your funds in your Roth IRA during the traditional retirement years. But the trick is getting the funds from the pretax accounts to the Roth IRA account. It's legal and simple to roll over funds from a pretax account to a Roth IRA.[38] This is called a Roth IRA conversion. But the funds are taxed in the year you make the conversion, so you have to be strategic about *when* you do the conversion.

If you're still working and earning a lot of money, doing a Roth IRA conversion puts you in higher tax brackets. It doesn't really make sense to expose the converted funds to high taxes right then. But if you have a temporary down income year, like between jobs or during a mini-retirement/sabbatical, that would be a perfect time to convert some of the money to a Roth while you're at temporarily lower tax brackets. And for *permanent early retirees* who only produce enough income to meet their core needs (i.e., an income floor) and who often get tax shelter from rental property depreciation, the lower tax bracket situation could last for years! This makes the Roth IRA conversion a very powerful long-term tool.

By strategically doing Roth IRA conversions over a number of years, it's possible to move most or all of your money into a Roth IRA account by the time you reach traditional retirement age. And depending on the amount of additional income you generate, you could pay lower or even no tax on the conversions.

---

38 For step-by-step guidance on a Roth IRA conversion, see Jeff Rose's excellent guide "The Ultimate Roth IRA Conversion Guide" at www.goodfinancialcents.com/roth-ira-conversion-tax-rules/.

And as icing on an already very tasty cake, the converted funds can be withdrawn before age 59.5 tax- and penalty-free after waiting five years![39] Withdrawing Roth IRA funds early isn't optimal because it's better to let these valuable funds continue to grow and compound tax-free. But in a pinch, this early withdrawal of converted funds could help.

To make this Roth conversion strategy more real, let's look at an example using the situation of an early retiree at age 45.

Roth Conversion Case Study: 45-Year-Old Early Retirees

A married couple, Craig and Stephanie, choose to retire early from their jobs at age 45. This will give them more time to spend with their 12-year-old daughter. They also look forward to pursuing fun part-time work in their spare time, like buying and fixing up a house or two per year.

For fifteen years, they worked extra hard to build wealth. They have a $500,000 balance between their two 401(k) plans, and they own five single-family rentals free and clear of debt. The rentals produce $42,000 in net rental income (before taxes). But the rentals produce *taxable* rental income of only $25,635 after subtracting $16,365 of depreciation expense (just a paper loss). This means the depreciation shelters $16,365 of income and keeps it free from tax (until the depreciation runs out, usually after 27.5 years).

As I mentioned before, Craig and Stephanie also buy one or two fixer-upper properties per year that become a short-term rental property. After a couple of years doing this, they'll begin selling one short-term rental house per year and generate an extra $30,000/year of long-term capital gain income. For fellow tax nerds, I assume this $30,000 includes unrecaptured section 1250 depreciation (but check with your tax professional on this route!).

The couple's *total combined income* on their tax return between rental and capital gains is $55,635 ($25,635 + $30,000). But they'll also have a standard deduction (as of 2018) of $24,000. This means their *taxable income* is only $31,635. This puts them well below the top of the 12 percent tax bracket for 2018, which is $77,400 for a married couple filing taxes jointly (see table below). Their tax bracket placement is important for at least two reasons:

1. They pay 0 percent tax on most[40] of the $30,000 capital gains as long as total taxable income is in the lowest two tax brackets.

---

39 Roth IRAs, 5 U.S.C. § 552 (1996).

40 I say most because tax law gets tricky when selling depreciable property like rentals. Something called a gain from unrecaptured section 1250 depreciation will likely require a tax of 25 percent on a small portion of the $30,000 gain.

2. They have $45,765 of space ($77,400 – $31,635) to do a Roth conversion at a lower 12 percent tax rate.

2018 FEDERAL TAX BRACKETS (TAXABLE INCOME)			
Tax Rate	Single Filers	Married Filing Jointly or Qualifying Widow(er)	Head of Household
10%	Up to $9,525	Up to $19,050	Up to $13,600
12%	$9,526–$38,700	$19,051–$77,400	$13,601–$51,800
22%	$38,701–$82,500	$77,401–$165,000	$51,801–$82,500
24%	$82,501–$157,500	$165,001–$315,000	$82,501–$157,500
32%	$157,501–$200,000	$315,001–$400,000	$157,501–$200,000
35%	$200,001–$500,000	$400,001–$600,000	$200,001–$500,000
37%	$500,001 or more	$600,001 or more	$500,001 or more

Next, Craig and Stephanie decide to start rolling over funds from their 401(k), pretax accounts to new Roth IRA accounts at the beginning of each year as long as it makes sense. Because their income from rentals and property sales is fairly steady, they plan to roll over $45,500 each year. This means they'll pay 12 percent or $5,460 of federal tax (plus state income tax) each year. They pay this tax out of their personal cash, so they lose out on the use of that money. But the benefit is that the tax amount is less than they would have paid while working a full-time job—and it's likely lower than they would pay at higher tax brackets if they're forced to take out large chunks with required minimum distributions after age 70.5. And in an emergency situation, they will also have access to *all* of these conversion funds *tax- and penalty-free* five years after each conversion is done.

In real life, the taxable income numbers of this example may not stay exactly the same each year. Income will rise and fall, deductions will change (like if the rentals run out of depreciation), and tax brackets will likely change. But with all of that acknowledged, here is what the concept of moving all the money from the 401(k) to Roth accounts could look like. In this simple case, it takes nineteen years because the 401(k) continues growing even as it's being drawn down.

ROTH IRA CONVERSION OVER TIME

Year	401(k)/Roth Growth Rate	401(k) Balance	Roth Conversion	Roth IRA Balance
Year 0	7.0%	$500,000	$45,500	$0
Year 1	7.0%	$486,315	$45,500	$48,685
Year 2	7.0%	$471,671	$45,500	$100,778
Year 3	7.0%	$456,004	$45,500	$156,517
Year 4	7.0%	$439,239	$45,500	$216,159
Year 5	7.0%	$421,301	$45,500	$279,975
Year 6	7.0%	$402,107	$45,500	$348,258
Year 7	7.0%	$381,470	$45,500	$421,321
Year 8	7.0%	$359,595	$45,500	$499,498
Year 9	7.0%	$336,081	$45,500	$583,148
Year 10	7.0%	$310,922	$45,500	$672,654
Year 11	7.0%	$284,001	$45,500	$768,425
Year 12	7.0%	$255,197	$45,500	$870,899
Year 13	7.0%	$224,375	$45,500	$980,547
Year 14	7.0%	$191,397	$45,500	$1,097,871
Year 15	7.0%	$156,109	$45,500	$1,223,406
Year 16	7.0%	$118,352	$45,500	$1,357,730
Year 17	7.0%	$77,952	$45,500	$1,501,456
Year 18	7.0%	$34,723	$45,500	$1,655,243
Year 19	**7.0%**	**$0**	**$34,723**	**$1,808,264**

In the end at age 65, Craig and Stephanie have more than $1.8 million that can be withdrawn tax-free from their Roth IRA! I assumed they did not withdraw any funds with this example, but they also could have begun withdrawing the $45,500 conversions tax- and penalty-free five years after each conversion. Now that they are at traditional retirement age, they can use all of their retirement funds (contributions and growth) and Social Security income to pad their retirement.

This example shows the power of strategically using Roth conversions well before traditional retirement age. But there are also other ways to legally access retirement funds early if needed.

How to Access Retirement Funds Early (If Necessary)

The lawmakers in the federal government decided at some point that age 59.5 was a reasonable age to retire. I guess they didn't read this book. But fortunately, they also created legal ways to pull money out early from tax-advantaged accounts if it's needed. I'll cover a few of the most popular ways here.

Official Exceptions to the Rule

According to the IRS,[41] early distributions from retirement accounts are *not* subject to the 10 percent penalty in the following exceptions:

- **Separation from Service After Age 55:** If you separate from service (that is, leave your job) during or after age 55 (or age 50 for public safety employees of a state, or political subdivision of a state, in a governmental defined benefit plan) you don't have to pay a penalty on withdrawals
- **Medical Expenses:** Amount of unreimbursed medical expenses greater than 7.5 percent of adjusted gross income (10 percent if under age 65)
- **Health Insurance for Unemployed:** Health insurance premiums paid while unemployed
- **Disability:** Total and permanent disability of the participant/IRA owner
- **Inherited IRAs:** If you inherit an IRA, you can take the money out before you get to 59.5
- **Qualified Higher Education Expenses:** For you, your kids, or your grandkids
- **Up to $10,000 for a First Home:** But the IRS defines a "first home" as not having owned one for the past two years. And it can be the first home of your kids or grandkids, too.
- **IRS levy of the retirement plan**
- **Military Reservist Distribution:** If a military reservist gets called to active duty, he or she does not have to pay the 10 percent penalty

---

41 "Retirement Topics — Exceptions to Tax on Early Distributions," IRS.gov. December 29, 2017. www.irs.gov/retirement-plans/plan-participant-employee/retirement-topics-tax-on-early-distributions.

These are very specific situations, but they're all good to keep in mind in case you run into a situation where you need to withdraw early. Another early withdrawal strategy involves a 457(b) account.

457(b) Accounts

This is a special type of tax-advantaged account available to governmental and some nonprofit workers in the United States. It's very similar to 401(k) or 403(b) retirement accounts, except that funds can be taken out without penalty at *any age* after leaving your job with the employer who sponsored the plan. If you have this type of account, you can take funds out before 59.5. Taking them out before tapping cash in other retirement accounts is probably a good idea anyway, because the money in the account is still tied to your former employer. In some cases, it could even be subject to your former employer's creditors!

Health Savings Account (HSA)

An HSA is probably *the* best "retirement" account when used strategically. This government-regulated account is designed to help you pay for medical expenses using *pretax* money, which means you can get a tax deduction right away on any contributions to the HSA. Then the money grows tax-free (like a traditional or Roth IRA), but you can take it out at *any time* for qualified medical expenses. To qualify for an HSA, you must have a high-deductible health plan and have no other health insurance coverage (see IRS Publication 969 for more details[42]). I have personally purchased my HSA-qualified plans on my Affordable Care Act (ACA, aka "Obamacare") state health insurance exchange, but you can often get them through employers as well.

But instead of using an HSA to pay current medical expenses, I like a different approach. You can build up your HSA balance as a long-term investment account for future medical emergencies. And it also acts as a flexible backup retirement account. The strategy works like this:

1. **Make Your Annual Tax-Deductible Contribution:** In 2018, this was a maximum of $3,450 for an individual and $6,900 for a family.[43]
2. **Invest Wisely:** I use a self-directed real estate HSA to buy tax liens and make loans. You can also find administrators who allow you to invest in low-cost stock index funds.

---

42 "Health Savings Accounts and Other Tax-Favored Health Plans," IRS.gov. February 10, 2017. www.irs. gov/pub/irs-pdf/p969.pdf.

43 "Internal Revenue Bulletin: 2017-21," IRS.gov. May 22, 2017. www.irs.gov/irb/2017-21_IR-B#idm139889987038144.

3. **Save Medical Receipts:** While you don't apply for reimbursements now so that your tax-sheltered money can grow, you can save receipts and receive reimbursements anytime in the future when you need them (tax-free!).

4. **Take Withdrawals as Needed:** Anytime in the future when you need money, you can take tax-free withdrawals up to the amount of current medical expenses and past medical expenses (with receipts saved as mentioned in #3). You can also use HSA funds for long-term-care insurance premiums, health care continuation coverage (such as coverage under COBRA), health care coverage while receiving unemployment compensation, or Medicare and other health care coverage if you are 65 or older (other than premiums for a Medicare supplemental policy, such as Medigap). As you can see there are many valuable and permissible uses to take money out tax-free.

5. **Withdraw Like an IRA After Age 65:** Any leftover funds in an HSA are treated like a traditional IRA after age 65. This means you can withdraw them for any reason and pay ordinary income taxes.

Because of these flexible benefits, the HSA has been the first account I make deductible contributions to each year. The only exception to this approach might be if you get matching contributions from your employer with your 401(k) or 403(b), which I don't as a self-employed entrepreneur.

72(t) Substantially Equal Periodic Payments (SEPP)

The SEPP rule is an exception that allows you to withdraw retirement funds well before age 59.5. It works by "annuitizing" your account balance, which means you take out an equal amount each year so that it will all be gone by a certain time in the future. Your life expectancy determines how much you can withdraw, although you have three different options you can choose among[44] (I recommend working with a tax professional to help you with this).

Once started, you must continue to take these withdrawals for at least five years, or until age 59.5. But by following these rules, all funds withdrawn are penalty-free (but you do pay ordinary income taxes). Although this is not something I have done, there may be situations where you have extra-large

---

[44] "Retirement Plans FAQs regarding Substantially Equal Periodic Payments — Question #7," IRS.gov. December 20, 2017. www.irs.gov/retirement-plans/retirement-plans-faqs-regarding-substantially-equal-periodic-payments#7.

retirement accounts and few nontaxable funds—in which cases, this arrangement makes sense.

Roth Conversion Ladder

I spent a lot of time on the Roth conversion in a previous section. And I briefly mentioned that conversion amounts can be withdrawn penalty- and tax-free after five years. While I don't recommend taking out Roth funds early unless absolutely necessary, you could use this strategy to supplement your pre-59.5 income needs. You could do conversions each year, and then after five years, you'd have funds available to withdraw each and every year, or what we call "a ladder."

Roth IRA Contributions

If you have a Roth IRA and have made contributions at least five years ago, you can withdraw any of the original *contributions* tax-free at any time (earnings cannot be withdrawn without penalty). Again, this is not a wise growth move, because you lose the ability for these dollars to grow and compound tax-free. But it is an option, and many people I know use a Roth IRA like an emergency fund for this reason.

Just Pay the Penalty

If you are financially savvy enough to buy and read this book, you probably haven't thought of the idea of just paying the 10 percent early withdrawal penalty. I normally wouldn't either, but I read an article at madfientist.com that made me reconsider. The math in the article helped me realize it could be reasonable compared to other options.[45]

The tax-deductible contributions and tax-free growth within retirement accounts mean that you could still come out ahead paying a penalty compared to just investing the same funds in a non-retirement account. You may choose to do this, for example, in early retirement when you are in a low-income tax bracket. The 10 percent penalty plus your tax rate may be acceptable to you in order to get the funds. I'd still rather let the money grow until later (or convert it to a Roth IRA), but yet again, it's another option for flexibility in early retirement.

Our journey to the peak of early retirement has taken us through the topics of income floors, upside investing, retirement accounts, and early withdrawals.

---

[45] "How to Access Retirement Funds Early," MadFientist.com. www.madfientist.com/how-to-access-retirement-funds-early/.

But what happens when your original plans don't work out perfectly? In the next chapter, it's time to look at some early retirement backup plans.

############## PROFILE OF A REAL ESTATE EARLY RETIREE ##############

LUCAS HALL
Cozy (https://cozy.co)
Location: Portland, Oregon
Chad's Favorite Quote from Lucas:
"Diversify! Don't just rely on investment properties for your only source of income or wealth."

WEALTH-BUILDING STATISTICS
- **Profession/Career:** Technology consulting/software
- **Income During Wealth-Building Phase:** $75,000 to 99,000/year
- **How Big a Role Did Real Estate Play in Wealth-Building?** Equally important as other vehicles (stocks, bonds, businesses, etc.)
- **Primary Real Estate Strategy(ies):** Long-term rentals

FINANCIAL INDEPENDENCE STATISTICS
- **Age at Financial Independence:** 51 to 60 (goal)
- **Annual Expenses in Retirement:** $100,000 to $150,000
- **Ideal Number of Rentals in Retirement:** 20 to 50
- **Primary Source of Retirement Income:** Rental income
- **Secondary Source of Retirement Income:** Dividends from public equities
- **Ideal Debt Level of Real Estate Portfolio:** Less than 25% loan to value

############## Q&A ##############

Q: Can you explain in more detail how you built your current wealth?
I used a combination of house-hacking (to get started in real estate), long-term buy and hold rentals, a 401(k), and a Roth IRA. Living with roommates (house hacking), is very affordable, and more often than not, your roommate's rent will cover most or all of your mortgage. After

living with roommates loses appeal, you can leverage the equity you have in your first home to buy and move into another. From there, you can rinse and repeat, or save up to buy other investment properties. But even as great as it is to build wealth with real estate, I still don't think it's wise to put all your eggs in one basket. Try to set aside 7 to 10 percent of your income into a savings account until you have 3 to 6 months' worth of expenses saved. If you're working a full-time corporate job and they offer a 401(k) match program, I suggest you invest 3 to 5 percent of your paycheck to max out the match they give you. Diversification is still a smart move. If your employer doesn't offer an investment match, you're better off investing in a Roth IRA through Fidelity, Vanguard, or Personal Capital that you can manage on your own. Roth IRAs are a much better investment tool than Traditional IRAs because you pay the taxes at the time of the deposit, rather than at withdraw.

Q: What were the biggest obstacles and setbacks during your wealth-building stage? How did you overcome or push through them?
The constraints on conventional financing were a huge setback. After 2008, getting low-interest money was not impossible, but it was difficult through traditional lenders. I was able to leverage my equity in my existing properties to get the money I needed to meet the tighter constraints of government-regulated loans. I haven't dabbled in hard money yet, but I'm sure there will be an appropriate day for that in the future.

Q: What's your No. 1 best tip for those looking to build wealth with real estate investing?
Diversify! Don't just rely on investment properties for your only source of income or wealth. Use Roth IRAs and salary-based income to provide the foundation for wealth generation while you build a rental portfolio, until you have enough equity to be a real estate investor full-time.

Q: Can you explain in more detail your post–financial independence income? How do you plan on living off of this income?

1. **Rental income:** After my current investment properties are paid off, I will have $15,000–$20,000 in monthly rental income that I can live off of. That income only goes up with each additional rental property that I purchase before retirement.
2. **Stocks/mutual funds:** I've worked a full-time career job most of my life. I've squirreled away 8–10 percent of my income every year. Once that sum reaches $1–$2 million, and I'm able to withdraw from it, the interest earned will be a nice complement to my rental income. If all my rentals disappeared, I could ideally live off of the interest and leave the rest to my estate.

Q: What concerns do you have for the future related to retirement income? How will you address them?
The devaluation of U.S. currency. I always plan to invest in something that humans need: shelter. No matter the state of the economy, people will always need housing.

Q: Do you plan to start selling your real estate holdings? If so, when and how?
I don't know yet. I'm always thinking about it, but it has to make sense. If it does make sense or helps me accomplish my goals faster, I will sell any property.

Q: What's your No. 1 best tip for those looking to live off of investment income after retirement/financial independence?
Multifamily or high-rent single-family homes are less stress and more revenue.

CHAPTER 23
EARLY RETIREMENT BACKUP PLANS

If plan A doesn't work, the alphabet has 25 more letters—204 if you're in Japan.

—CLAIRE COOK, *SEVEN YEAR SWITCH*

This entire book has been about planning and strategy. But how likely is it that your application of these strategies will go *exactly* as planned? Not likely! So for every early retirement plan A, there must always be a plan B, C, D, and E. In *Can I Retire Yet?* Darrow Kirkpatrick calls his backup plans "lifeboat strategies."[46] Lifeboats are the small boats kept in reserve on a big ship *just in case* the worst happens and the ship starts to sink. They are like insurance policies because they give you peace of mind that you can survive a sinking ship.

So I'm going to borrow Darrow's concept and suggest some financial backup plans for your real estate early retirement. The backup plans will be ways to decrease your expenses or increase your income. You may never need to use these, but just by preparing you'll increase your feeling of security during early and traditional retirement.

But before we start, keep one important piece of information in mind. By using any of these income or expense backup plans, you essentially reduce the amount of savings you need in retirement. For example, let's say you assume

---

[46] Kirkpatrick, *Can I Retire Yet?* Chapter 5.

a 6 percent cash rate of return, as I discussed in an earlier chapter. Reduced expenses or extra income of $1,000/month ($12,000/year) avoids needing to save an additional $200,000 for early retirement investments ($12,000 / .06 = $200,000).

If you've arrived at retirement short of funds or if you just want to retire earlier and not wait, these backup plans might become part of your *primary plan*. They can become your tools for escape to a better life. I find it liberating that you can use your creativity and entrepreneurial spirit to dictate your early retirement instead of just mindlessly saving and following formulas. Look at the strategies that follow as opportunities to increase your control and security, no matter what your financial situation may be.

Expense Backup Plans

Reducing expenses is an area you have the most control over. I'll also give you income backup plans in the next section, but they generally take a little longer to get started. Here are a few ideas that may be helpful in a challenging financial or early retirement situation.

Live Frugally (and Happily)

For some people, "living frugally" are bad words. It means cutting discretionary expenses like eating out, travel, new clothes, and luxury items. Yes, I know these things are nice to have. But if you have either a temporary or permanent financial challenge, these non-necessities can be cut quickest (and reinstated quickest, once things get better).

To test this situation out, I recommend that you identify which items are essential (like housing, insurance, medical care, basic food items, utilities, etc.) and which items are discretionary (that is, optional) in your budget. Then do an experiment of cutting out *all* the discretionary spending for one month. Just do it and see how you feel.

This exercise is exactly what one of my favorite Stoic philosophers, Seneca, recommended more than 2,000 years ago in the "Moral Letters to Lucilius/Letter 18." Here are his exact words:

> Set aside a certain number of days, during which you shall be content with the scantiest and cheapest fare, with coarse and rough dress, saying to yourself the while: "Is this the condition that I feared?" ... Let the pallet be a real one, and the coarse cloak; let the bread be hard and grimy. Endure all this for three or four days at a time, sometimes for

more, so that it may be a test of yourself instead of a mere hobby. Then, I assure you, my dear Lucilius, you will leap for joy when filled with a pennyworth of food, and you will understand that a man's peace of mind does not depend upon Fortune; for, even when angry she grants enough for our needs.

You may find that you agree with Seneca's sentiment: "Is this the condition that I feared?" By practicing "poverty," you may actually realize that the worst-case scenario is not that bad. As a result, this reduces your anxiety and increases your sense of security. And if you're lucky, you might also find that a simpler life with fewer hassles can also be much happier. It's one of the reasons I love camping so much. I walk into the woods with a backpack that has all I need for a few days, and I walk out with peace of mind that I can be happy with very little.

Location Arbitrage

OK, perhaps I lost some of you with the F-word in the previous section. You didn't retire early in order to chop your discretionary expenses and be ultra-frugal so fast. Here's another possibility that can allow you to live as good or better while spending less. It's called location arbitrage.

There are probably places within your own country and around the world that are much cheaper than where you live right now. And this is especially true if you live in a big city or on the East or West Coasts of the United States and Canada. Location arbitrage means changing locations to a place that has a lower cost of living. By doing so, you can live a much better lifestyle for the same amount of money.

I have experienced this firsthand by living with my family in Cuenca, Ecuador, for more than a year. We already lived in a low-cost-of-living part of the country in South Carolina, but we lived even better for less in Ecuador. It's a relatively safe and stable country with good (and inexpensive) health care and the most delicious fruits I've ever eaten. And it's only a four- to five-hour plane ride from major U.S. airports.

There are many other similar locations around the world where expats have figured out this same concept long ago. Just begin exploring travel blogs and expat online forums, and drop your preconceived notions about "good" and "bad" international locations. For example, I have friends living wonderfully and affordably in the amazing city of Medellín, Colombia, in South America. Yet, a couple of decades ago, it was known for drug wars and cocaine cartels. The world is changing fast, so make sure your impressions don't get stuck in the past.

Another benefit of international location arbitrage for those in early retirement is health care. An international move alone can save you thousands of dollars a year in health insurance and health care expenses. As many are finding out, health care systems around the world deliver care similar to that in the United States for much lower expense. For many of you, this can mean the difference between retiring early or not.

But even within the United States or Canada, the same concept applies. Small cities, college towns, and rural destinations are much cheaper for housing and other core expenses. And when you are free from the need to work, you have the flexibility to live anywhere. Just start exploring housing costs on zillow.com in the locations you already like, and you'll probably be amazed at the wide range of rents and prices. Location arbitrage, whether domestically or internationally, may turn out to be the most fun backup plan you could have imagined!

Downsize or Get Creative with Housing

Your home equity is sort of like deadweight to your investment portfolio. If you have enough wealth and income elsewhere, it may not matter. But if you're struggling to meet your early retirement needs, this is an obvious place to optimize. And this will work especially well if you own a home in a high-cost area or if you just own an expensive home.

Downsizing can mean selling a four-bedroom, three-bath mini-mansion and buying a smaller townhouse, condo, or simple single-family house. For example, if you own a $750,000 home free and clear of debt, you could sell (likely tax-free, depending on your basis) and buy a $250,000 townhome. You'd then have $500,000 to invest. At a 6 percent income return, you could generate an extra $2,500/month for your early retirement by making that move. Aside from the financial benefit, these simplification moves may give you increased peace of mind. Because you likely own a smaller, newer home with less maintenance, you can focus on other things that matter more.

And don't rule out more extreme (yet potentially fun) housing transitions. What if you sell your big home and travel in a luxurious RV? With $30,000 to $50,000, you could buy a very comfortable home and move it to wherever the most beautiful weather and scenery might be. You could also look for engaging (and free) housing-job opportunities like campsite hosts at state or national parks. You could find yourself living free (and getting paid!) in some of the most beautiful places in the world. And finally, you could use location arbitrage domestically or internationally as I mentioned before. Not only can luxurious housing be found for much less, but you can also choose locations where property taxes and state income taxes are low or nonexistent.

In a financial challenge, your options are usually to decrease expenses or increase income. We've looked at the big ways to optimize those expenses. Let's now turn to backup plans that increase your income.

Income Backup Plans

My idea of an entrepreneur isn't just someone who starts a business. It's simply someone who is resourceful and confident in their ability to create income and survive financially. So thinking of yourself as an entrepreneur in early retirement is a fabulous (and increasingly essential) skill for survival in the dynamic, modern economic world. It gives you an ever-present backup plan beyond the wealth you've built in the previous stages. I'll give you some specific entrepreneurial ideas below, but use your own creativity and resourcefulness to find ways to increase income.

Buy and Sell Properties

If you've learned to buy rental properties to build wealth, there's no reason you can't buy and sell properties for the rest of your life. It only takes one house per year to make a substantial difference in early retirement. If you earn a net of $30,000/year from one sale, that's $500,000 you don't need to save! This is because $30,000 ÷ 6% = $500,000 (I assumed a 6 percent rate of income on your savings).

You could do a fix-and-flip business where you find a fixer-upper at a discount and resell it for a profit. This gets you cash faster and requires less long-term financing. But if possible, I prefer more tax-advantaged strategies like short-term holds (for long-term capital gains treatment) or even live-in flips, where you can make profits tax-free after two years of living in the residence.

If you are really in a pinch or if you have plenty of assets elsewhere (like in your retirement account), you could also consider selling off some of your core rental portfolio and living off the profits and principal. As you know from the income floor chapter, I'm not a fan of eating into investment principal. But especially if you are later in life with other income sources, the extra cash flow and increased simplicity may be a wise move. Just be sure to discuss this strategy with your CPA or tax attorney before selling, because you will likely have large depreciation recapture and capital gains taxes when you sell.

Refinance a Rental

If you find that you need extra short-term cash in early retirement, it could make more sense to refinance a rental property instead of selling it. As I mentioned in the previous section, tax bills will likely be enormous if you've held that rental for a long time. But refinance proceeds are completely tax-free. You can use 100 percent of the loan proceeds instead of setting aside some of the cash for taxes.

And as long as you refinance carefully with good debt (fixed interest rate, long-term, strong positive cash flow), you can let your tenants slowly repay the mortgage over time so that you're rebuilding equity. Just be sure to ask your tax professional about the deductibility of interest expenses in this situation. Using the proceeds of the loan for personal benefit and not an investment purpose could make it not a deductible business expense.

Seller Finance to Amortize Your Equity

Another alternative to selling and cashing out your rental equity is selling with an installment sale (that is, seller financing). I have bought properties this way from many landlords. They were typically ready to transition to a more passive role with the property while still receiving an income stream. Instead of paying income taxes and putting the money in the bank, these passive landlords keep their equity secured by a property they know and understand while receiving a reasonable interest rate.

And if you as the seller have a large capital gain, this can also avoid the trap of increasing your tax bracket and paying extra taxes in the year of the sale. Because the installment sale spreads your sale out over many years, you get to spread your tax liability over many years as well (potentially keeping you in lower tax brackets). But do keep in mind that you still have to pay depreciation recapture taxes at the initial time of sale, so you'll need cash funds to cover those taxes.

This seller financing arrangement is very similar to an insurance annuity in which you *annuitize* your equity in the property. An annuity, in this case, is the opposite of a mortgage loan. Instead of receiving a loan and paying it back, you *invest* your principal up front (finance the sale) and receive all of the principal plus interest back over time. As I'll discuss with simple insurance annuities next, annuitizing your equity is a solid way to increase your income and security in the later years of retirement, especially if you are short on assets.

Buy a Single Premium Immediate Annuity

This gets into non–real estate and uncharted waters for me, but I would be remiss not to mention an essential retirement income tool for many: an annuity. Because there are a dizzying number and types of annuities out there, I'm specifically talking about the type called a single premium immediate annuity (SPIA). Jim Dahle at whitecoatinvestor.com calls this "the good annuity," because it's low-cost and free of the complex terms of many other annuities.

An annuity is essentially a contract with an insurance company. And an SPIA is a type of contract in which you give the insurance company a lump sum of money (like $100,000) up front, and the company pays you an income stream for life. When you die, the payments stop. But as long as you're living, the payments keep coming in.

So, in essence an SPIA is a form of longevity insurance that covers the risk of outliving your other money. It's also a way to annuitize your savings and turn them into a passive income stream for life. SPIA payments usually give you a larger income stream than the equivalent interest or dividends in a traditional (non–real estate) portfolio. Although you could get comparable or better income from real estate, annuities are much more passive. It's a way to diversify your income streams away from a single source of real estate.

But do keep in mind that the annuity payments are only as good as the company that guarantees them. Most states have state guaranty associations (kind of like the FDIC for bank accounts) that will cover up to a certain amount if your insurance company goes out of business. You can get an exact SPIA quote and a list of state guarantee associations at immediateannuities.com.

Get a Reverse Mortgage

Like annuities, reverse mortgages are a controversial financial product because they can also be complex, laden with fees, and oversold by commissioned salespeople. But with the right product and for those with a large amount of equity in their home who don't want to downsize, it can be an income backup plan during early or traditional retirement.

With a reverse mortgage, you essentially borrow money without having to make payments while you're alive and still in the house. The loan doesn't have to be paid back until you die, sell the property, move out of the home, or default (for instance, not paying your taxes and insurance). You or your heirs will never owe more than the value of your house.

The main point is that you can pull money from your home equity without increasing your expenses in retirement. It's yet another tool to increase your income. The downside is that you and your heirs lose control of the home to some extent, because after you die or move, the lender can take the property and sell it to recover its principal.

Does it make you more confident to have backup plans for your early retirement? I know it does for me. Feel free to brainstorm and add your own. The more you have, the better. Now let's move on to the next chapter about how to have *true* security in early retirement. And here's a sneak peek: It doesn't always come from money in the bank or a certain number of properties.

———— PROFILE OF A REAL ESTATE EARLY RETIREE ————

MATT B.
Location: San Diego, California
Chad's Favorite Quote from Matt:
"I like deals that are 'forever' holds. ... If I never sell, I never pay the capital gain!"

WEALTH-BUILDING STATISTICS
- **Profession/Career:** Stock fund manager
- **Income During Wealth-Building Phase:** $200,000+/year
- **How Big a Role Did Real Estate Play in Wealth-Building?** Primary role
- **Primary Real Estate Strategy(ies):** Long-term buy and hold, limited partnership with multifamily apartments

FINANCIAL INDEPENDENCE STATISTICS
- **Age at Financial Independence:** 36 to 40
- **Annual Expenses in Retirement:** $100,000 to $150,000
- **Ideal Number of Rentals in Retirement:** 50+
- **Primary Source of Retirement Income:** Rental income
- **Secondary Source of Retirement Income:** Angel investing
- **Ideal Debt Level of Real Estate Portfolio:** Between 51% to 75% loan to value

---

Q&A

Q: Can you explain in more detail how you built your current wealth?
I earned my initial wealth as a stock fund manager investing in "deep value with pending catalyst" and "special situation" micro-cap stocks, mostly. I quit stocks in March 2007, bought a few minority stakes in private companies, flipped houses for a while, and fortuitously found multifamily limited partnerships (LPs) in 2011. I have roughly half my net worth in about 25 different LP deals—mostly value-add, work-force apartment complexes going for a rent of about $1,000/month in Denver, Phoenix, Portland, Salt Lake, Houston, San Antonio, and San Diego. All the deals I'm in are structured as long-term holds, although I occasionally participate in for-sale development deals too in San Diego. All of the above happened somewhat organically. It's only over the last few years that I've developed a conscious program dedicated to multifamily exposure. As I see liquidity, I will continue to add to my multifamily LP portfolio.

Q: What were the biggest obstacles and setbacks during your wealth-building stage? How did you overcome or push through them?
I lacked discipline and a conscious plan on both the spending and investment front. I did not live with a personal budget and bought too much house, car, expensive travel, etc. Probably 40 percent of my net worth is tied up in a handful of private company and angel deals that I totally regret. In hindsight, those were big obstacles and setbacks— especially because, had I put those monies into multifamily deals, my net worth would be double what it is now, and my multifamily portfolio would be probably three times its current size.

Q: What's your No. 1 best tip for those looking to build wealth with real estate investing?
Dollar cost average into direct investment limited partnership (LP) deals with an excellent asset manager (GP) who:
1. Specializes in well-located value-add workforce multifamily in growing areas.
2. Invests at least 10 percent of its own capital in their deals.

3. A firm with (a) decades of direct experience and track record, (b) a large dedicated staff, and (c) a large portfolio for economies of scale.
4. Has long-term relationships with A-grade institutional (private equity firms, endowments, etc.) co-investors.
5. Makes acquisitions using conservative LTCs of 60–70 percent.
6. Focuses on "forever" hold deals to avoid taxes. Depreciation offsets income, and if you never sell, you never pay capital gains tax. In tune with the BRRRR strategy, try to hold all LP interests "forever" and reinvest all refinancing capital returns into news deals.

Q: Can you explain in more detail your post–financial independence income? How do you plan on living off of this income?
My after-tax multifamily income more than covers my expenses and will continually grow as I engage the portfolio and as the value-add phase of the deals complete (value-add phase where about 50 percent of income goes into internal and external improvements is typically five to six years). As I see liquidity from my private company investments, I will redeploy into multifamily LPs.

Q: What concerns do you have for the future related to retirement income? How will you address them?
I have enough cushion to feel solid. I've discussed a hypothetical 2008–2009 stress test scenario with my asset manager who models a 20–25 percent drop in cash on cash distributions from my portfolio, which I could sustain. My monthly spending is approximately $13,000, so I could easily make substantial cuts if needed.

Q: Do you plan to start selling your real estate holdings? If so, when and how?
My favorite holding period is forever, and so I mainly do limited partnership investments in "long-term hold" deals. If I hold forever, I can enjoy the depreciation offset while avoiding the ever-growing capital gains amount that would be triggered by a sale. Instead of selling, I just wait to get my equity refinanced out—then I own the asset for free and roll that equity into another LP deal. Mine is basically a BRR-

RR strategy, except I use LP exposure. Now occasionally, but rarely in the deals I choose, a GP does sell and there's a capital gain event. But ideally, rather than doing an outright sale, it can be 1031 exchange. Selling makes very little sense to me. Even if I was worried about a bad cycle, I know that well-placed, properly leveraged workforce housing in growing MSAs can ride through a disaster like 2008–2009 and stay healthy and cash flow positive. In this scenario, rent prices and vacancy rates are far less volatile than asset values. And if you never sell, asset value is relatively meaningless.

CHAPTER 24
HOW TO HAVE TRUE SECURITY IN EARLY RETIREMENT

The greatest stock market you can invest in is yourself. Finding this truth is better than finding a gold mine.

—BYRON KATIE, *LOVING WHAT IS*

When we began this book, I told you my motivation for wanting to retire early and achieve financial independence. I wanted freedom, autonomy, and control over my life. But that was only a partial truth. When I dig deep, I realize there's another, more primal motivation: *fear*. And attached to that fear is a deep need for security. Maybe you've felt that at some point, too.

For a long time, I saw money in the bank, wealth-building, and all the real estate investing plans I've shared as my primary form of security. If I could just acquire more assets and build more income streams, my security blanket of wealth would protect me. Then I would be less anxious and could relax. And there's no doubt that, to some extent, that idea is true. The more wealth you have, the less financially vulnerable you become. But this is not the whole story.

I've also met people with millions of dollars in assets who feel less secure than someone who has much less money. That multimillionaire feels anxious and afraid on a daily basis, while the person with $25,000 in the bank feels confident and carefree. Obviously, there is something more to security than just money in the bank. The gem of a little book titled *Spiritual Economics* by Eric Butterworth[47] provides a clue to the true meaning of "security" by going back to the Latin root of the word. The original meaning had two parts:

- *Se*—without
- *Cura*—care, concern, anxiety

So, the word "secure" originally meant "to be without care." It's an inner phenomenon, not a particular number of investment properties. You can have all the money in the world, but if you are constantly anxious and concerned, you don't have security. And if you have little money, but you have confidence, skills, and hope, you do have security. My ideal would be to have enough money while *also* feeling a sense of inner security. This concept reminds me of a beautiful quote by French poet Victor Hugo:

Be like the bird
That, pausing in flight
While on boughs too slight,
Feels them give way
Beneath her, and yet sings,
Knowing she hath wings.

The image of this small, confident, joyful bird is perfect. It's how I think we should ultimately approach financial independence and wealth-building. This book has been all about helping you build and use actual, tangible real estate assets. These physical assets and the knowledge and skills you obtain in the process are like your wings. But ultimately, you need to have the inner security to use those wings when life pulls a branch out from under you (and it will).

So this chapter is all about developing the inner security of that little bird on a falling branch. Because no matter how well you plan, life and real estate investing will never work out exactly the way you want. You can't buy complete security in the real estate markets. You've got to earn it inside your mind and heart. I'll help you build that true security by investing in your greatest asset (you!) and maintaining flexibility.

47 Eric Butterworth. *Spiritual Economics: The Principles and Process of True Prosperity*. Missouri: Unity School of Christianity, 1998.

Invest in Your Greatest Asset (You!)

It's no exaggeration to say that you are your greatest asset. It's true on a practical level because every financial and life decision starts and ends with you. And until you are dead or incapacitated (morbid, I know), you'll continue playing that important role.

But even if you didn't have to make decisions or worry about your wealth, what's the point of financial independence if you lack the peace of mind, good health, and personal relationships to enjoy them? Remember the beginning of this book—money and wealth are just tools to do what matters. And what matters is your life.

So if you are your greatest asset, what does it mean to invest in yourself? How can you allow yourself to grow and compound just like your wealth does? The specifics will obviously be very personal and unique to you, but I'll share a few of my own strategies to help you start.

I try to focus on consistently investing time and energy in three areas of my personal life: 1) physical health, 2) my mind, 3) my relationships. Just as we do with bank accounts, we can either add value to these areas of our life or drain them. And also as with bank accounts, when we take out too much without replenishing the reserves, we acquire an overdraft. When your health, mind, or relationships fail, your wealth and other projects lose much of their importance.

Investments in Physical Health

You probably already know the basics of a physically healthy life. They aren't complicated. Regular movement, good nutrition, and good recovery (like sleep and downtime) are my personal foundations of good health. Prioritizing these three pillars makes everything else you do in life more effective, including jobs, wealth-building, and relationships.

If you're looking for additional reading to improve in this area, a great starting point is the book *Eat Move Sleep* by Tom Rath.[48] It's a practical book written by someone who has, in part, used healthy living habits to help battle a rare disease for more than twenty years. The book assembles some of the best well-researched ideas on food, movement, and sleeping into easy-to-digest, conversational content.

---

48 Tom Rath. *Eat Move Sleep: How Small Choices Lead to Big Changes*. California: Missionday, 2013.

Investments in Your Mind

Your mind is as important as your physical health. Most people know not to put toxic or unhealthy food into their bodies, but it's much harder to guard unhealthy content from entering your mind. A practical habit to put healthier "food" into your mind is what you're doing right now: reading for self-improvement! Regularly feeding your mind with helpful information, fascinating stories, and inspiring ideas enriches your life.

And while you get into the habit of feeding your mind helpful content, also eliminate the junk. Most mental junk food comes from mindless wandering on social media or TV. If you need those activities to decompress, try healthier alternative activities, like taking a walk, working in the yard, or making art. And try to avoid hanging around people who don't have the values and behaviors you want to emulate. If the people you hang around constantly bombard you with negativity, complaining, gossip, and other toxic behaviors, it's bound to affect your mind.

I also like to work on *practices* that improve my ability to control my mind. The Stoic philosophers of ancient Rome are one of my favorite sources of guidance in this practice. The central Stoic philosophy is that you can control some things in life and other things you can't. So, practicing Stoicism is to focus and put energy only on the things you *can* control. The Serenity Prayer is a modern-day application of this philosophy, and it's used as a part of the twelve-step program of Alcoholics Anonymous:

> God grant me the serenity to accept the things I cannot change,
> Courage to change the things I can,
> And wisdom to know the difference.

You can practice this philosophy throughout the day in every situation of your life. For example, instead of instantly raising your voice at your kids when they do something wrong, you can try to pause and consider the best response. You can't directly control your kids in that moment, but you can control how you respond to them. Easier said than done, I know! But like exercising a muscle, you can get better by regularly practicing it every day. This, of course, helps you in your personal life, but it also pays great dividends as you deal with stressful situations in your real estate investing and other professional pursuits.

Investments in Relationships

Finally, you invest in yourself by investing in personal and business relationships. We are social creatures, and our close relationships make an enormous difference in our happiness and in our sense of internal security. This is another one I probably don't have to remind you of. But if you're like me, it takes deliberate effort to make your important relationships a priority.

In part three of the book *The 7 Habits of Highly Effective People,*[49] author Stephen Covey introduces a concept that's been very helpful to me called "emotional bank accounts." The metaphor essentially reminds you to make deposits of kindness, helpfulness, and love toward the people in your personal life and business life. We all have conflict and problems with other people, but when we regularly make those deposits and sincerely give our best to others, we build *trust*. And that trust is better than any amount of money in the bank because trust is the glue that holds together our personal lives, our businesses, and even our society at large.

I was reminded how important trust is in real estate investing during the 2008–2010 economic recession and real estate collapse. My business partner and I had grown our portfolio significantly in 2007 (too much, as it turns out). So in 2008 and the years after, we had to adjust quickly to survive. While we hustled and did all we could, it was trusting relationships with contractors, tenants, and private money lenders that ultimately saw us through. I can think of a few specific examples where our close, trusting relationship with a private lender helped us obtain loans that avoided bigger problems.

There are no shortcuts to trusting relationships. You must invest your time and energy, and you must be sincere. Techniques that manipulate people may work in the short run, but the true intentions behind them will shine through eventually. From a practical standpoint, you just have to prioritize and build time for the important people in your life and business.

Personally, the mini-retirements I've taken throughout my adult life have been one manifestation of this idea. These extended breaks from the grind of work and wealth-building give me time to grow personally and to grow closer to my family and friends. And in business, I do my best to build a small but closer network of mutually beneficial relationships. Then I spend time with these people as often as I can.

A whole book (or books) could be written on investing in yourself! But

---

[49] Stephen R. Covey. *The 7 Habits of Highly Effective People: Powerful Lessons in Personal Change.* New York, NY: Simon & Schuster, 2004.

this has been a brief overview to help you see how important it is to have true inner confidence and security. Now, let's continue our exploration of true security by looking at the importance of staying flexible.

Be Flexible in Early Retirement

The future is *impossible* to predict with certainty. So rather than trying to predict it exactly, a more reasonable approach is to stay prepared and flexible. This is particularly important in early retirement when you're living off of your income from years of investments. As I already told you, my business partner and I faced some challenges in the 2008–2010 recession like many other people in the real estate business. Up to that point in our brief careers, we had been able to sell properties fairly easily. Credit was cheap and easy to get, so buyers were easy to find. But when the credit markets collapsed, all of that changed overnight. We were faced with the prospects of *keeping* many of the properties we had intended to resell.

This time period required a major pivot in strategy for real estate investors. If we had been rigid and inflexible, we would have likely failed financially. But when our normal method of flipping houses didn't work well, we pivoted and began seller financing and renting houses instead. And we cut our expenses both personally and in business so that we could survive off less income. Because of this flexible approach (and the trust built with our core business relationships), we were able to ride through the economic storm until the seas calmed.

I'm certain you'll face your own unique challenges during your early retirement journey. But your challenges won't look exactly like ours. The only way to keep moving forward is to stay flexible. Here are a few additional ideas for how to do that.

- **Diversify:** Vary your investments. For example, don't buy properties all in one neighborhood or one market. And diversify your overall portfolio between real estate investments and non-real estate investments over the long run. We didn't do this before, but it is part of our flexibility plan for the future.
- **Reduce Debt:** A common theme with businesses and people who struggled or failed during the 2008–2010 recession was excessive debt or leverage. This is why I've emphasized that at least a part of your portfolio should be free and clear of debt.
- **Flexible Mind-set:** Remember, everything starts and ends with you. So, avoid a fixed mind-set in which change and setbacks are seen as

permanent failures. Instead, have a growth mind-set that accepts and prepares for challenges. To learn more about a growth mind-set, read the excellent book *Mindset: The New Psychology of Success* by Carol S. Dweck.[50]

A Life Without Absolute Security

This entire chapter has been about security. As with the bird that sings while the branch falls beneath her, the goal has been to acquire inner, true security. And we have looked at steps, both inside our own head and in very practical ways, to build this feeling.

But speaking for myself, I doubt if there will ever be a state in which I'll feel absolutely secure. And I also think that's OK. After all, nothing has ever been guaranteed in life. It's only in modern times that we've even created this idea that we could ensure or build wealth to eliminate every risk.

From the time we are born to the time we die, risks of all kinds are a constant reality. There is no way to avoid the ultimate end that we're all destined for: death. In some ways, realizing this and accepting it makes us feel more alive. So do the best you can to mitigate risk and build security for yourself and your loved ones. But at some point, it's time to get back to the original premise of this book: doing what matters while you still can. Don't let a need for absolute security get in the way of actually living.

It's now time to wrap up. We've covered a *lot* of ground, from the base of the mountain to the peak of an early retirement. Now in the last two chapters I want to give you a step-by-step plan that will allow you to start working toward your own real estate early retirement.

---

50 Carol S. Dweck, PhD. *Mindset: The New Psychology of Success*. New York: Ballantine Books, 2016.

PROFILE OF A REAL ESTATE EARLY RETIREE

DOUG AND TRACI BURKE
Mountain Sky Rentals (http://tdcbinvestments.com/)
Location: Asheville, North Carolina
Chad's Favorite Quote from Doug and Traci:
"Educate yourself, find a mentor, and just do it!"

WEALTH-BUILDING STATISTICS
- **Profession/Career:** Health care
- **Income During Wealth Building Phase:** $150,000 to $199,999/ year
- **How Big a Role Did Real Estate Play in Wealth-Building?** Primary vehicle
- **Primary Real Estate Strategy(ies):** Long-term rentals

FINANCIAL INDEPENDENCE STATISTICS
- **Age at Financial Independence:** 51 to 60 (still working but close to goal)
- **Annual Expenses in Retirement:** $75,000 to $100,000
- **Ideal Number of Rentals in Retirement:** 50+
- **Primary Source of Retirement Income:** Rental income
- **Secondary Source of Retirement Income:** Social Security income
- **Ideal Debt Level of Real Estate Portfolio:** Less than 25% loan to value

Q&A

Q: Can you explain in more detail how you built your current wealth?
Ten years ago, we just thought we would buy property as a means of making some money. We didn't really have a big picture. Then we thought we would buy one property a year for ten years as a retirement strategy. After educating ourselves, we surpassed that goal pretty quickly. We also started seeing a bigger picture of what we could accomplish through real estate investing. Ten years later we now own close to forty units and are on track to double that in the

next two years through several small multi-unit construction projects we are currently working on. Most of what we have purchased has been long-term holds.

Q: What were the biggest obstacles and setbacks during your wealth-building stage? How did you overcome or push through them?
Our mind-set and the fact that we were high-income earners proved to be our biggest obstacles. We have worked very hard to renew our minds to have a positive and abundance mentality. It has been very challenging to replace the high income we earned with passive income. And for many years, we funded our own projects with our own money and failed to put the effort into pursuing private funding.

Q: What's your No. 1 best tip for those looking to build wealth with real estate investing?
Educate yourself, find a mentor, and just do it!

Q: Can you explain in more detail your post–financial independence income? How do you plan on living off of this income?
Cash flow from well-located, long-term-hold single-family homes and small multi-unit apartment buildings close to the city center in Asheville. Our goal has always been to hold just enough properties to cover all of our ongoing living expenses (replace the earned income with the passive). This will provide us with freedom to do the things we love to do.

Q: What concerns do you have for the future related to retirement income? How will you address them?
Doug and I really have no concerns for the future regarding our retirement income. We believe wholeheartedly in our plan and the ongoing need/demand for rental units. Also, we have other streams of income that you could call our "backup" plan. They are not passive income streams but a means to earn dollars if there happen to be dips in the rental market from time to time.

Q: Do you plan to start selling your real estate holdings? If so, when and how?
At some point, utilizing seller financing to continue bringing in passive income.

Q: What's your No. 1 best tip for those looking to live off of investment income after retirement/financial independence?
Have a plan, then put it into action.

PART 7

YOUR TURN TO CLIMB

How to Get Started with Real Estate Early Retirement

CHAPTER 25
THE 5-STEP REAL ESTATE EARLY RETIREMENT PLAN

Vision is not enough; it must be combined with venture. It is not enough to stare up the steps; we must step up the stairs.

—VACLAV HAVEL, TWENTIETH-CENTURY
CZECH WRITER AND PRESIDENT

You've made it to the final section of the book, and what a journey it's been! You began at the bottom of the mountain as you got clear on your destination of financial independence. You then learned how to improve your savings rate, the foundation of building wealth. Next you applied those savings to either starter or core real estate wealth-building plans in order to grow your wealth. And finally, you learned what life is like at the peak of the mountain and beyond when you can live off of investment income.

At this point, you may feel overwhelmed by the size of the real estate investing climb before you. If that's true, don't worry. It's normal to feel that way. Lofty goals are beyond your comfort zone, and that means you may be a little uncomfortable. The key is to turn your focus back to the present.

So, for the last part of the book, I want to challenge you to apply what you've learned and get started. Specifically, I want to help you create a customized plan. This will help you get moving and take the next small steps right in front of you.

Line Up Your Dominos

Speaking of next small steps, did you realize that a domino can knock over another domino about 1.5 times its size? Which means if you strategically lined up a series of dominos starting with a tiny two-inch-tall one, the twenty-third domino could be as tall as the Eiffel Tower in Paris. And the thirty-first domino would be taller than the highest point on earth, Mount Everest. Think about it: All of those huge dominos could begin to topple over because of a gentle push of a tiny, two-inch domino![51] Lining up the dominos is your real estate early retirement plan, and that initial, gentle push is you taking action on those next steps in real estate investing.

To help you line up those dominos and take those all-important next steps with your real estate early retirement journey, I've prepared a 5-Step Real Estate Early Retirement Plan. Don't think of this as a long, in-depth plan you'd prepare in an MBA class. Instead, think of this as a fun way to break a big project (early retirement) into smaller, manageable steps (your first dominos). The goal is simply to get you headed in the right direction. Feel free to return to this plan and to other parts of the book as you continue to make progress.

To get the most out of this plan, I recommend that you pull out a pen and paper (yes, those old-fashioned things that don't distract you with pop-up notifications). The idea is for you to answer questions and put your ideas on paper. The brainstorming you do by writing it all down is the primary benefit of the plan.

At the same time, I recommend giving yourself a limited amount of time to answer each question. Don't try to be perfect or precise for now. Give yourself two to three minutes and write down the first answers that come to mind. Then keep moving forward.

So, please go get that paper and pen. I'll wait for you!

Step #1: Get Clear on Your Why (What Matters?)

What motivated you to read this book or think about early retirement in the first place? What matters to you? If money were not an issue, what would you spend more of your time doing? Perhaps you want to have more free time with family, travel the world, restart an old hobby, or begin a new meaningful job or business. Whatever it is, just write it down.

---

51 I learned this amazing fact and the idea of "the domino effect" from the awesome book *The One Thing*. Gary Keller and Jay Papasan. *The One Thing*. Austin, TX: Bard Press, 2013.

Now, think about what's *not* perfect right now. What do you not enjoy about your current life situation? What could be different? Perhaps you don't like the hours of your job, the commute to work, or the lack of energy you have at the end of the week. Or maybe you just don't enjoy working for money, and you'd rather give more of your time to causes or people without a monetary benefit. Whatever isn't perfect now, just write it down.

It's OK to have more than one answer for the questions above. The point is to dig deep and identify your true motivation. This may take more than one session of reflection. But once you have it, be sure to refer back to your answers often. If you can stay clear on your deep motivations (i.e., your why), it will give you the energy and enthusiasm you need to build and follow through on a real estate early retirement plan that you can be proud of.

Step #2: Calculate Your Financial Independence Number and Wealth Goals

How much money do you need to cover your personal expenses right now? How much will you need in the future, say, fifteen years from now? This is your financial independence number. And yes, I know that there is uncertainty when estimating the future. Predicting certain expenses, like in my case, health insurance, is difficult. But pick a number anyway so that you can do some rough estimating. You don't have to have a perfect number right now to start making progress.

Next, estimate how much wealth you need to cover those future expenses. There are two ways to make that calculation. First, you can figure out how many free-and-clear rental properties you would need to cover your personal expenses. Calculate the annual net operating income (the after-expense rental income if you had no debt payment) of a typical rental in your target area. Then divide your total expenses by this number. That will tell you about how many rentals you need to own free and clear of debt to cover your expenses.

Or if you want to take a more flexible approach, just calculate how much general wealth you need to accumulate to pay for these future living expenses. With a heavy real estate portfolio, I typically use an income yield of 6 percent because I can find conservative deals that produce that. But you're welcome to be more conservative with a lower number like 4 percent or more aggressive with a number like 8 percent. Then just divide your annual expenses by that percentage to get a rough estimate of wealth needed. For example, if your expenses are $100,000 per year, $100,000 ÷ .06 = $1,666,667.

In either case, you now have a rough target for the number of properties or the net worth goal of your wealth-building plan. That's the peak of your financial mountain. Of course, the target could change over time. But having this clarity will help guide and motivate you as you begin climbing.

Step #3: Determine Your Wealth Stage

Now that you have a free-and-clear property and/or net worth goal from the previous step, let's look at how close you are to your goal by determining your wealth stage. In Part 3, I explained these wealth stages:

1. **Survival:** Focus on paying the bills and staying out of crisis mode.
2. **Stability:** Out of crisis mode. Now pay off personal debts and create an emergency fund.
3. **Saver:** Increase your savings rate and start stashing away cash savings.
4. **Growth:** Begin investing your savings and growing them by purchasing assets.
5. **Withdrawal:** Have large enough net worth, now need income, safety, and low-hassle investments.

Where do you see yourself in these wealth stages right now? Be honest with yourself. Wherever you are, that's OK. The point is to be aware of your financial situation so that you can take the appropriate next steps.

Step #4: Pick Your Real Estate Wealth-Building or Retirement Income Plan

Now that you're clear on your wealth stage, let's pick a real estate wealth-building or income plan that's a good place for you to *start*. If you are in survival stage, I don't recommend trying to invest yet. Instead, focus on increasing your income, decreasing your expenses, and building a solid financial base. You can definitely begin learning real estate and even trying to make money with it as a part-time or full-time job (this is what I did by finding deals for other investors). But it's better not to invest in real estate until you're out of financial crisis mode.

If you're in the Stability, Saver, or Growth stages, and you're just getting started with real estate investing, consider picking one of the starter wealth-building plans from Part 4:

- The House Hacking Plan
- The Live-In-Then-Rent Plan

- The Live-In Flip Plan
- The BRRRR Plan

If you're in the Growth Stage and already have a good financial base, consider picking one of the primary real estate wealth-building plans:
- The Rental Debt Snowball Plan
- The Buy and Hold Plan
- The Trade-Up Plan

Remember that these plans aren't always used alone. They are like tools in a toolbox, and it's your job to look at your situation and decide which tool (or tools) should be used right now. It may be that you use them in sequence, like starting with the House Hacking Plan and progressing to the Long-Term Buy and Hold Plan. Or you may apply them simultaneously, like using the Long-Term Buy and Hold Plan on some properties and the Rental Debt Snowball Plan on others.

And if you find yourself in the Withdrawal stage, then review Part 6 about withdrawing an endless supply of income. Ask yourself how you will transition your wealth into stable, low-risk, income-producing assets for the rest of your life. Do you need more free-and-clear houses? Do you need to improve the quality of your properties? Or do you need to diversify your portfolio more between real estate and non-real estate investments?

Whatever stage you find yourself, the key is to pick *something*. Based on the wealth-building plan you choose, the final step of getting started will become much clearer.

Step #5: Get Started!

A plan without subsequent action is like trying to steer a parked vehicle. It can't be done. You've got to get started taking action on your plan as soon as possible. Ironically, once you take the first steps beyond just reading a book, your real education actually begins!

I recommend that you start small and make a move that doesn't feel overwhelming. If you've never bought real estate before, finding that first deal should be your one and only goal. If you already own properties, take the first step of your wealth-building plan. For the Rental Debt Snowball Plan, that may mean setting up your cash flow and savings to be applied to one mortgage each month. If it's the Trade-Up Plan, that may mean preparing your property to sell and finding the next one to buy. Or if you are near the peak of the mountain, you may begin selling a few properties and paying off debt in order to clean up your portfolio.

As you get ready to take those first steps, remember this quote from a true mountain climber, W. H. Murray.[52]

Whatever you can do, or dream you can, begin it.
Boldness has genius, power, and magic in it.
Begin it now!

Strategy, Tactics, and Additional Resources

The lessons and recommended steps in this book have purposefully been all about strategy. Like a guide to help you up the mountain, my primary purpose has been to give you direction, clarity, and inspiration. I wanted to show you a good map of the journey and then help you find yourself on that map. But, obviously, there is more to climbing the mountain of early retirement than just strategy.

To succeed, you also need *tactics* and details that can help with your day-to-day progress during the journey. Unfortunately, including all the critical tactics of real estate financing, deal analysis, contracts, acquisitions, and property management would have filled another six books! So, my expectation is that this book will get you started and that you will become a lifelong student of tactics who continues to learn along the way.

As part of that continued education, I highly recommend you join the free community of BiggerPockets, the publisher of this book. It's the largest and most comprehensive resource of information on real estate investing on the web. In particular, I recommend getting engaged in the online forums at www.biggerpockets.com/forums, where you can ask questions and learn from others on any topic related to real estate investing. And while you're there, look me up and ask a question under my username: ClemsonInvestor.

You can also find tactical information on almost any topic in the growing library of books published by BiggerPockets at biggerpockets.com/store. There are very specific, tactical books like *Real Estate Note Investing, Set for Life, The Book on Tax Strategies for the Savvy Real Estate Investor, The Book on Flipping Houses, The Book on Estimating Rehab Costs, The Book on Rental*

---

[52] W. H. Murray. *The Scottish Himalayan Expedition*. London: Dent, 1951.

Property Investing, *The Book on Managing Rental Properties*, *How to Sell Your Home*, and *Finding and Funding Great Deals*. I recommend any of these if the topic is something you want to learn.

Finally, I'd love for you to continue to receive tactical advice directly from me. My articles on the BiggerPockets blog are at www.biggerpockets.com/renewsblog/author/chadcarson. And you can also ask me questions and get my free weekly real estate investing newsletter at my personal site coachcarson.com.

So we're going to stay in touch, right? But before we end the book, I'd like to wrap up with some important final advice in the last chapter.

———— PROFILE OF A REAL ESTATE EARLY RETIREE ————

DOUGLAS ORR

Greensburg Alpha Investments
Location: Greensburg, Indiana
Chad's Favorite Quote from Douglas:

"Do your homework. With all the information available on the subject of real estate, there's no reason to not be successful. Then, jump in!"

WEALTH-BUILDING STATISTICS
- **Profession/Career:** Auto manufacturing
- **Income During Wealth-Building Phase:** $75,000 to $99,999/year
- **How Big a Role Did Real Estate Play in Wealth-Building?** Primary role
- **Primary Real Estate Strategy(ies):** Long-term buy and hold

FINANCIAL INDEPENDENCE STATISTICS
- **Age at Financial Independence:** 26 to 30
- **Annual Expenses in Retirement:** $30,000 to $50,000
- **Ideal Number of Rentals in Retirement:** 50+
- **Primary Source of Retirement Income:** Rental income
- **Secondary Source of Retirement Income:** Social Security income (in future), annuities
- **Ideal Debt Level of Real Estate Portfolio:** 76%+

Q&A

Q: Can you explain in more detail how you built your current wealth?
I borrowed $20,000 from my 401(k) and used that money as a down payment for two multi-units. I then continued to reinvest the profits into purchasing more rental units. My strategy is long-term buy and hold. For the most part, I've used conventional financing. This year I've started buying seller-financed deals.

Q: What were the biggest obstacles and setbacks during your wealth-building stage? How did you overcome or push through them?
The biggest obstacle for me has been coming up with more money to invest. I refinanced properties that were value adds and used the money for a purchase and some capital expenses.

Q: What's your No. 1 best tip for those looking to build wealth with real estate investing?
Do your homework. With all the information available on the subject of real estate, there's no reason to not be successful. Then, jump in!

Q: Can you explain in more detail your post–financial independence income? How do you plan on living off of this income?
I plan on living off of my residual, passive income from my rental units. My company will be big enough to put the right people in place so I can step away from my business and not deal with the day-to-day.

Q: What concerns do you have for the future related to retirement income? How will you address that?
My concerns are properly creating a self-sustaining business. I intend to set it up so my family will have income for generations.

Q: Do you plan to start selling your real estate holdings? If so, when and how?
No.

Q: What's your No. 1 best tip for those looking to live off of investment income after retirement/financial independence?

Estimate high on what you think it will take to retire on your investments.

CHAPTER 26
FINAL THOUGHTS

We must all suffer one of two things: the pain of discipline or the pain of regret.

—JIM ROHN

I hope the lessons and examples I've shared with you in this book will serve you well on your early retirement journey. I didn't get the privilege of delivering this content to you in person, but please know that I thought about you each step of the way while I was writing this book. Because, as I told you in the beginning, this book is about more than real estate investing. It's about life. And in this case, it's about *your* life and the wonderful potential you have ahead of you!

One of the topics that was always on my mind as I wrote was how I could help you make real, tangible progress. Because the truth is, most people pick up a book like this and do *nothing.* And as someone who has lived the benefits of the information I've just shared with you, that makes me sad. So I wanted to briefly talk about the sting of regret and the joy of freedom.

The Sting of Regret and the Joy of Freedom

> *That you are here—that life exists ...*
>
> *That the powerful play goes on, and you may contribute a verse.*
>
> —WALT WHITMAN, *O ME! O LIFE!*

Have you ever done that exercise where you imagined what it would be like when you're on your deathbed? I know, it's sort of a morbid thought. But it's also a very insightful thing to do because the important question to ask is this:

Now that you are on your deathbed, what do you wish you had done more of in life?

Go ahead and take out a pen. Write down the first answers that come to mind. Did you write down that you wish you'd worked more? Did you write down that you wish you had 100 properties instead of fifty? Or did you write about people, experiences, growth, and contribution? Did you write about what really matters?

Whatever you wrote down, the good news is that you're not dead! There's still life ahead of you. And you can avoid the sadness of still having a song in you when you die. The dreams you have are still possible. And you don't have to regret letting down the people you care about most because you were too busy working for money your whole life.

Helping you avoid that ultimate regret is what this book has been all about. Real estate investing is an amazing tool. When applied well, it can give you personal freedom and choices in life. It can put money in its place so that you control money instead of it controlling you. And at its best, climbing the real estate and financial mountain allows you to do what matters.

I don't know what matters in your life, but I imagine that it's exciting and it's important! It probably involves people you love. Or it involves dreams or ambitions that you rarely talk about for fear of feeling silly. But by setting the goal to achieve financial independence using real estate investing, you're creating space for those important dreams. And by removing money as a central part of the life equation, you will now have the time and the energy to contribute more of yourself to what really matters. If this book has helped you even a little bit in that journey, I will call it a success.

Remember the Purpose of Plans

Man plans; God laughs.

—OLD YIDDISH PROVERB

This book has been about giving you a plan to climb the financial mountain using real estate investing. But as proverbs have told us since the beginning of time, even our best plans are bound to be imperfect. They are doomed to break against the harsh reality of life.

Does that mean that plans are useless? Should you just throw up your hands in defeat? Not at all! You just have to remember the purpose of plans and books like this. They are here to give you *direction* and *confidence*. But like a sailboat on the ocean, you have to continually stay alert at the helm. You are the captain of your ship, and you have to keep steering with your eyes open!

This book is meant to help you internalize the fundamental lessons of successful real estate investing and early retirement. It's meant to get you started and unstuck from analysis paralysis. And it's meant to be a reference that you can return to over and over again when you need help. But the ideas in this book won't drive themselves! You will need to keep learning, adjusting, and surrounding yourself with a team of able people who can help you follow through. Let this book be the beginning!

Commit to the Process

My final message is to commit to and fall in love with *the process*. Early retirement is the peak of the mountain. It's the destination and result at the center of everything in this book. But you can't *do* early retirement. You can't helicopter yourself to the peak of the mountain. You just have to climb—step-by-step—and follow the process.

The basic process is this:

1. **Get clear on your destination:** What does an ideal life look like? How much does this life cost? And how much wealth do you need to build to pay for that ideal life?
2. **Save money:** You'll never become an investor until you have money to invest. Increase your savings gap.
3. **Do your first deal:** The first savings and the first deal are always the hardest. Use a starter strategy to buy a property and gain momentum.

4. **Build wealth:** This is the slow and steady climb to the top. You can't run up the mountain. You've got to consistently and persistently invest your time, energy, and money into plans that work.

And don't forget to enjoy the journey. Life isn't lived on the peak of the mountain. It's lived while you climb and at the many plateaus along the way. Rest, enjoy the scenery, take a mini-retirement, and remember why you started climbing in the first place.

It's been an honor to share this journey toward early retirement with you. I wish you much success in your real estate investing. And I hope you'll let me know the impact you've made on the world as you begin doing more of what matters! If the ideas in this book have helped you, I'd love to hear from you. Please send your successes, challenges, and inspirations to book@coachcarson.com. To *your* real estate early retirement, and a life full of doing what matters!

Acknowledgements

First, I must thank my wife, Kari, and my daughters, Serena and Ali, for their *infinite* patience, love, and support as I wrote this book. As with most ambitious projects, the scope and commitment to writing this book expanded beyond my initial expectations. Kari, without our partnership, neither this book nor any of my other work would be possible. I love you.

To my business partner, Tommy Crumpton, this book is really about *our* journey and the lessons we learned during the last fifteen-plus years of real estate investing. I couldn't ask for a better business partner, friend, and go-to three-point shooter in pickup basketball.

Dr. Louis Stone, your friendship and mentorship are more valuable than every piece of real estate combined. The core philosophies of this book were hashed out with you in our many long walks and rides around the neighborhoods of Oconee and Pickens counties. Thank you for encouraging me to take the path less traveled. It has made all the difference.

To my parents, Nancy and Tom Carson, thank you for your never-ending support and your shining example as entrepreneurs, parents, and people of character. Like Warren Buffett said about his parents, I won the ovarian lottery. Dad, you were my original real estate and business mentor. I will always be grateful for the lessons you've taught, most especially by your example.

To my brother, Andrew Carson, I hope you don't mind, but much of the time I was writing this book for you! Your friendship and wise counsel are invaluable to me. Thank you for your support and feedback as I wrote the book.

Thank you to the more than 840 people from my coachcarson.com newsletter, the BiggerPockets.com forums, and ChooseFI Facebook Group who completed my real estate early retirement survey. Your collective stories informed and validated many ideas in this book. And thank you to the 25 people/couples who let me interview, profile, and learn from them for this book. Your wisdom and stories expanded my mind. This awesome group of people includes Kat Horn, Sam Dogen, Craig and Jane Horton, Lisa Phillips, Mauricio Rubio, Graham Stephan, Joe Olson, Paula Pant, Seth Williams, Drew N., Tony Crumpton, Mindy and Carl Jensen, Brandon Turner, Greg and Holly Johnson, Richard Carey, Felisa Savage, Doug and Traci Burke,

Elizabeth Colegrove, Liz Schaper, Lucas Hall, Eric Bowlin, Ricky Cameron, Dave Boroughes, Matt B., and Douglas Orr.

I consider myself a student of real estate investing. And I've had many amazing teachers and mentors over the years—both in person and through books. Some that I'd like to acknowledge in particular include Steve Mudge, John Schaub, Jack Miller (deceased), Dyches Boddiford, Greg Pinneo, William Poorvu, Gary Keller, Ron Legrand, Robyn Thompson, Pete Fortunato, Bruce Norris, Mike Cantu, and Vena Jones-Cox. My longtime friends, especially Karla Kuhn, at Upstate Carolina Real Estate Investors Association (CREIA) and Metrolina Real Estate Investors Association (REIA); JC Underwood and Lou Gimbutis in particular are generous, amazing educators and great people. My CPA Brandon Smith of Smith and Shin, CPAs, LLC, has always been there to educate (and correct!) me along the way. To my longtime mastermind buddies and good friends Anthony Petz and Joe Breslin, you've both taught me so much about real estate and life.

Going from *living* the real estate early retirement journey to *organizing and writing* about it was more challenging than I thought it would be. I'm indebted to a few particular thinkers, writers, and practitioners who expanded my mind around the topic of early retirement. Vicki Robin and Joe Dominguez (deceased) and their book *Your Money or Your Life* deeply influenced my thinking about financial independence and the concept of enough. Jeff Brown (bawldguy.com) has forgotten more than I know about using real estate to retire, and his ideas have been extremely helpful. Long conversations about life and real estate with Erion Shehaj (investingarchitect.com) were a source of enlightenment and "aha" moments. Darrow Kirkpatrick and his book *Can I Retire Yet?* helped me immensely in explaining a sound early retirement. Todd Tresidder and his *How Much Money Do I Need to Retire?* validated some core ideas of this book and expanded my mind on many others. Tim Ferriss's *The 4-Hour Workweek* was my original inspiration back in 2007 to value time and flexibility as much as money. It jump-started my fascination with an unorthodox path to mini-retirements, travel, and doing what matters.

I feel fortunate to be part of an online community of bloggers, content creators, and readers who discuss and encourage others to pursue financial independence and early retirement (aka FIRE). Before and during the writing of this book, I was inspired by *many* people in this community, including, but not limited to, people I admire, like Brandon (madfientist.com), Chris Mamula (caniretireyet.com), Carl Jensen (1500days.com), Tanja Hester (ournextlife.com), Pete Adeney (mrmoneymustache.com), J. L. Collins (jlcollinsnh.com),

Brad Barrett and Jonathan Mendonsa (choosefi.com),, Liz and Nate Thames (frugalwoods.com), Physician on Fire (physicianonfire.com), Craig Stephens (retirebeforedad.com), Gwen (fierymillennials.com), Drew (guyonfire.us), Jillian Johnsrud (montanamoneyadventures.com), JD Roth (getrichslowly.org), Michael and Ellen Robinson (uncommondream.com), J Money (budgetsaresexy.com), Jeremy (gocurrycracker.com), and John (esimoney.com and rockstarfinance.com).

A few close friends and family (who fortunately for me are highly intelligent and generous people) read early drafts of the book and gave excellent recommendations that shaped the final outcome. I'll always be grateful to Joe Gibson (for this and much more over the years), Chris Mamula, Drew from guyonfire.us, Richard Carey, Erion Shehaj, Tom Carson, and Nancy Carson. And Kari Carson, my wife, has always been my first reader and editor extraordinaire.

To the BiggerPockets team, I'm honored to be a writer for such a first-class organization. Like the mission of BiggerPockets, my aim with this book was to transform the way people invest and even more the way people live their lives. Brandon Turner, thank you for encouraging me to write the book and for your example as an enthusiastic educator. Joshua Dorkin, thank you for creating such an incredible resource at BiggerPockets and for giving me the opportunity to contribute. Katie Askew, your guidance and encouragement throughout the writing process has been invaluable. Jarrod Jemison, thank you for taking the random images in my head and turning them into something people can use! Scott Trench, your friendship and personal example are inspiring. Mindy Jensen, thank you for your friendship and encouragement. Even bigger thanks go to the editorial team there: Taylor Hugo, Janice K. Bryant, Wendy Dunning, and Katelin Hill.

Last, but not least, I'd like to acknowledge the readers of my blog and newsletter at coachcarson.com. Each week I get the privilege of sharing my thoughts on real estate, financial independence, and life with you. Your stories, feedback, and loyalty have been the fuel and mission that kept me inspired while writing the book. Thank you!

To doing what matters!

Chad Carson, Cuenca, Ecuador, 2018

APPENDIX:
REAL ESTATE EARLY
RETIREMENT SURVEY RESULTS

Based on 848 Responses

What is your age?

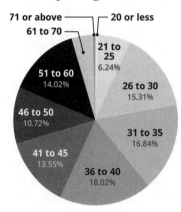

What is your country of residence?

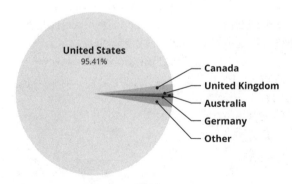

Do you currently have enough wealth/income to cover your personal living expenses without working (other than managing rentals/investments)?

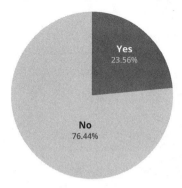

What amount of annual personal expenses do you need to cover in order to consider yourself financially independent?

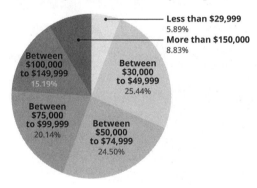

If you have a net worth goal for financial independence, what is it?

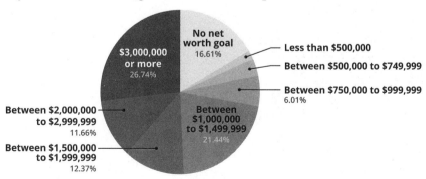

If you consider yourself already financially independent, at what age did you first achieve this?

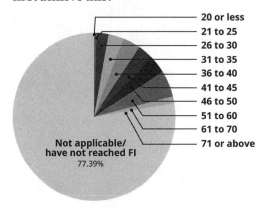

- 20 or less
- 21 to 25
- 26 to 30
- 31 to 35
- 36 to 40
- 41 to 45
- 46 to 50
- 51 to 60
- 61 to 70
- 71 or above

Not applicable/ have not reached FI
77.39%

If you have not achieved financial independence, at what age do you plan to reach it?

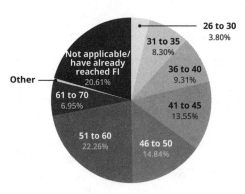

- 26 to 30 3.80%
- 31 to 35 8.30%
- 36 to 40 9.31%
- 41 to 45 13.55%
- 46 to 50 14.84%

51 to 60 22.26%

61 to 70 6.95%

Other

Not applicable/ have already reached FI 20.61%

How big of a role did or does real estate investing play in your wealth-building plans?

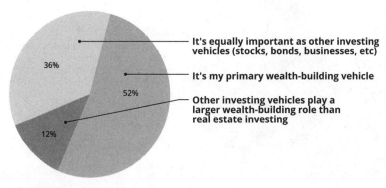

It's equally important as other investing vehicles (stocks, bonds, businesses, etc)

It's my primary wealth-building vehicle

Other investing vehicles play a larger wealth-building role than real estate investing

36%

52%

12%

How much total annual income did/do you make on average during the wealth-building stage (before any deductions, including a spouse/partner)?

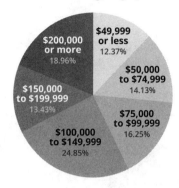

If rental income is part of your retirement/FI plan, what is the ideal number of rental units for you? (*note*—a duplex includes 2 units)

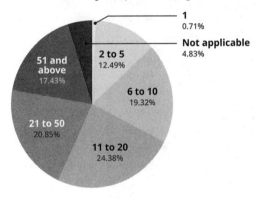

If you plan to own rental properties during retirement/FI, how much debt is appropriate for you at that time?

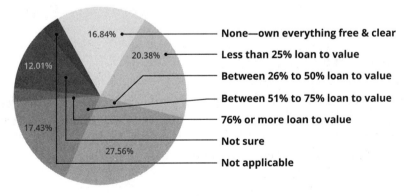

More from
BiggerPockets Publishing

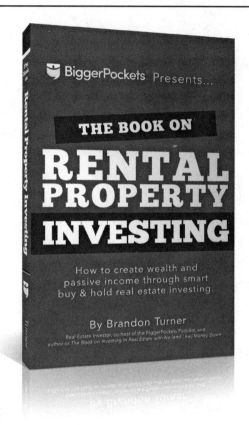

The Book on Rental Property Investing

With nearly 400 pages of in-depth advice and strategies for building wealth through rental properties, *The Book on Rental Property Investing* by BiggerPockets podcast cohost Brandon Turner will teach you how to build an achievable plan, find incredible deals, pay for your rentals, and much more! If you ever thought of using rental properties to build wealth or obtain financial freedom, this book is for you.

If you enjoyed this book, we hope you'll take a moment to check out some of the other great material BiggerPockets offers. BiggerPockets is the real estate investing social network, marketplace, and information hub, designed to help make you a smarter real estate investor through podcasts, books, blog posts, videos, forums, and more. Sign up today—it's free! **Visit www.BiggerPockets.com.**

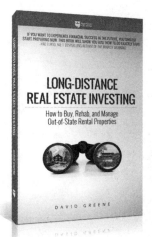

Long-Distance Real Estate Investing

Don't let your location dictate your financial freedom: Live where you want, and invest anywhere it makes sense! The rules, technology, and markets have changed: No longer are you forced to invest only in your backyard. In *Long-Distance Real Estate Investing*, learn an in-depth strategy to build profitable rental portfolios through buying, managing, and flipping out-of-state properties from real estate investor and agent David Greene.

The Book on Investing in Real Estate with No (and Low) Money Down

Lack of money holding you back from real estate success? It doesn't have to! In this groundbreaking book from Brandon Turner, author of *The Book on Rental Property Investing*, you'll discover numerous strategies investors can use to buy real estate using other people's money. You'll learn the top strategies that savvy investors are using to buy, rent, flip, or wholesale properties at scale!

More from
BiggerPockets Publishing

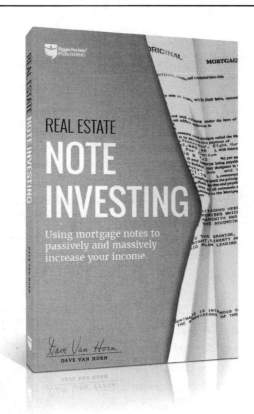

Real Estate Note Investing

Are you a wholesaler, a rehabber, a landlord, or even a turnkey investor? *Real Estate Note Investing* will help you turn your focus to the "other side" of real estate investing, allowing you to make money without tenants, toilets, and termites! Investing in notes is the easiest strategy to make passive income. Learn the ins and outs of notes as investor Dave Van Horn shows you how to get started—and find huge success—in the powerful world of real estate notes!

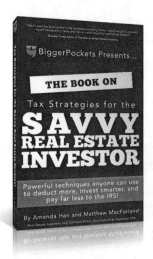

The Book on Tax Strategies for the Savvy Real Estate Investor

Taxes! Boring and irritating, right? Perhaps. But if you want to succeed in real estate, your tax strategy will play a huge role in how fast you grow. A great tax strategy can save you thousands of dollars a year. A bad strategy could land you in legal trouble. That's why BiggerPockets is excited to offer *The Book on Tax Strategies for the Savvy Real Estate Investor*! You'll find ways to deduct more, invest smarter, and pay far less to the IRS!

Set for Life: Dominate Life, Money, and the American Dream

Looking for a plan to achieve financial freedom in just five to ten years? *Set for Life* is a detailed fiscal plan targeted at the median-income earner starting with few or no assets. It will walk you through three stages of finance, guiding you to your first $25,000 in tangible net worth, then to your first $100,000, and then to financial freedom. *Set for Life* will teach you how to build a lifestyle, career, and investment portfolio capable of supporting financial freedom to let you live the life of your dreams.

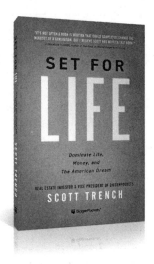

Learn More from
BIGGERPOCKETS

and Become Successful in
Your Real Estate Business Today!

Facebook
/BiggerPockets

Instagram
@BiggerPockets

Twitter
@BiggerPockets

LinkedIn
/company/Bigger
Pockets

Website
BiggerPockets.com